Supporting Neurodiverse College Student Success

Supporting Neurodiverse College Student Success

A Guide for Librarians, Student Support Services, and Academic Learning Environments

Elizabeth M. H. Coghill
Jeffrey G. Coghill

ROWMAN & LITTLEFIELD
Lanham • Boulder • New York • London

Published by Rowman & Littlefield
An imprint of The Rowman & Littlefield Publishing Group, Inc.
4501 Forbes Boulevard, Suite 200, Lanham, Maryland 20706
www.rowman.com

6 Tinworth Street, London, SE11 5AL, United Kingdom

British Library Cataloguing in Publication Information Available

Library of Congress Cataloging-in-Publication Data

Names: Coghill, Elizabeth M. H., 1964– author. | Coghill, Jeff, author.
Title: Supporting neurodiverse college student success : a guide for librarians, student
    support services, and academic learning environments / Elizabeth M. H. Coghill,
    Jeffrey G. Coghill.
Description: Lanham : Rowman & Littlefield, [2021] | Includes bibliographical
    references and index. | Summary: "The growing population of neurodiverse college
    students prompts new approaches to support their success and change traditional
    student services and collegiate experiences. Chapters cover tutoring, learning supports,
    academic coaching and advising, career services, residential living, and classroom
    experiences that impact and assist these students."—Provided by publisher.
Identifiers: LCCN 2020031153 (print) | LCCN 2020031154 (ebook) | ISBN
    9781538137369 (cloth) | ISBN 9781538137376 (paperback) | ISBN 9781538137383
    (epub)
Subjects: LCSH: College students with disabilities—Services for. | College student
    orientation. | Inclusive education. | Motivation in education.
Classification: LCC LC4818.38 .C64 2021 (print) | LCC LC4818.38 (ebook) | DDC
    371.9/0474—dc23
LC record available at https://lccn.loc.gov/2020031153
LC ebook record available at https://lccn.loc.gov/2020031154

∞™ The paper used in this publication meets the minimum requirements of
American National Standard for Information Sciences—Permanence of Paper
for Printed Library Materials, ANSI/NISO Z39.48-1992.

To Nathan and students like him,
may your experiences be heard through this work.

Neurodivergent students struggle to achieve in today's higher education campus environment. Lack of knowledge, unwelcoming spaces, deficient support services, and the impact of busy faculty and staff continue to affect student success. Our quick responses to students to "study more" and inadequate assistance and understanding of neurodiverse learners negatively impacts their collegiate achievement. Biased perceptions regarding their inclusion in the academy despite admission and enrollment on our campuses continue to impact failure rates.

Our imperfect efforts to understand, assist, and care about the success of students with learning differences impacts the students and their families emotionally, intellectually, and financially. Struggling to cope with neurotypical-designed classrooms, challenged to establish meaningful relationships and fully engage on campus, our sons and daughters struggle to succeed academically and socially.

The impetus for this book is the real-life experience of the coeditors, Elizabeth and Jeffrey Coghill, as parents of a neurodiverse son. Sending him off to college without the knowledge of his ADHD and slow processing challenges set failure in motion despite our efforts to advocate on his behalf. His story is not yet complete, and we continue to try to understand and grasp the influence neurodiversity will have on his future opportunities for employment, relationships, and degree attainment.

Not a week goes by as a learning center administrator that I don't encounter students and families like my own—parents advocating for someone on campus to understand their child and to find ways to help them succeed. The hopes and dreams of all our students matter. Their futures depend on our ability to create welcoming campuses where students can thrive, learn, and develop. It is our hope that this book begins your journey toward awareness, understanding, and action on your campus.

Contents

Figures

Preface

As neurodiverse students academically succeed with the help of support services in the K–12 school system, higher numbers are enrolling on post-secondary campuses. Without the same support systems, students are challenged to academically and socially thrive in the post-secondary environment. It is important that we open a campus dialogue to better understand their needs, address post-secondary challenges, and unite as faculty, staff, and administration to establish a welcoming environment for all students. It is incumbent on us, members of the academic academy, to bring these students to campus with the hope that they will succeed and graduate. We know that even for neurotypical students, this is a huge task. The goal of *Supporting Neurodiverse College Student Success: A Guide for Librarians, Student Support Services, and Academic Learning Environments* is to offer suggestions to faculty and staff and provide insights into effective programming and supports utilized by campuses across the United States.

In chapter 1, we will introduce the terms *neurodiverse*, *neurodivergent*, and *neurotypical*. This chapter will lay the critical groundwork that creates the theoretical and practical framework for this book. In chapter 2, "Self Advocacy," we highlight the need to educate students to advocate for themselves on campus. They must be the ones who inform faculty and staff about their needs. And we, as college administrators, must let them tell us about their need for accommodation. Chapter 3, "Academic Advising," focuses on finding campus champions who will give advice and guide a student through their educational journey. Creating welcoming spaces that address the needs of neurodiverse students is presented in chapter 4, "Welcoming Spaces for Learning." Chapter 5, "Classroom Supports," identifies how classroom activities can enhance student learning and how neurodiverse students can find strategies for success. Chapter 6, "Tutoring," focuses on Universal Design for

Learning (UDL) as a backdrop for reimagining tutoring services to help all students learn and thrive.

In chapter 7, "Learning Supports," we examine how campus networks of support may be implemented to reinforce a student's sense of belonging. In chapter 8, "Academic Mentoring and Coaching Services," authors note the academic and social challenges neurodiverse students face and how to aid those students in becoming successful with time management, organization, problem-solving, and self-advocacy. Chapter 9, "Library Services," demonstrates how libraries could leverage what they do best: providing service to all students regardless of ability. We also examine the unique role a library plays on campus to make technology work for the student. In chapter 10, "Campus Living/Residence Hall Services," there is an exploration of how space and the role of resident assistants help establish community in the residential setting. "Campus Health and Wellness," chapter 11, illustrates how all campus culture, both on campus and off campus, creates good health, well-being, and sustainability. Through chapter 12, "Disability Support Services," we note how support for neurodiverse students goes beyond the boundaries of the physical campus. We encourage college personnel to recognize that support services not only assist with academics but also help propel students into the wider world beyond the campus confines. Finally, in chapter 13, "Epilogue," we summarize the book and present a mission call for all campus stakeholders to unite in order to make a difference in the collegiate success of all students: neurodivergent and neurotypical.

Supporting Neurodiverse College Student Success is a labor of love. It was born out of frustration. How can we make the college experience for neurodiverse learners meaningful and fruitful? It recognizes that not all students who attend our college or university campuses are the same. They are not all cut from the same cloth. They bring a myriad of learning differences to campus. Some of these differences are to be expected. Some of these differences are not expected. The impetus for this book is to educate college personnel on the challenges that come with working with a neurodiverse population. Authors provide concrete programmatic examples that campuses have instituted to work with neurodiverse students. Two features—"Campus Essentials for High Impact" and "Campus Spotlights"—are incorporated to introduce recommendations and showcase best practices from campuses across the United States.

Acknowledgments

We'd like to thank our contributors for each chapter of this book. Their willingness to participate in this process and to contribute their time, expertise, and practical knowledge is greatly appreciated. For many, this involvement was the first time they had shared their best practices in this format. Although we have never met many of the contributors, we joined together with a common purpose to further our understanding of neurodiverse students in higher education and make our campuses more inclusive and improve educational environments for all students to learn and thrive.

I'd like to acknowledge the work that Dr. Sarah Williams has contributed to the academic success of neurodiverse students in higher education. Her mentorship has assisted in the development of Universal Design for Learning tools in our campus learning center and directed my journey toward a greater understanding of the needs of neurodiverse students on our campus. Her mentorship, faith, and encouragement made a difference and are greatly appreciated. Thanks for the sisterhood and support!

Thank you to the staff of the Pirate Academic Success Center at East Carolina University. Your willingness to explore new approaches and always put students first inspires me every day. Your dedication to student success is commendable and you are making a difference for the students of East Carolina University! Thank you to Amber Arnold, Monique Barrett, Abby Benzinger, Sarah Cooley, Thomas Kirkman, Julie Smith, Bryan Williamson, and the amazing student staff of the Pirate Academic Success Center.

Elizabeth Coghill

I would like to acknowledge the Information and Research Services librarians at Laupus Library, East Carolina University—Mary Roby, Corey Harmon, Amanda Haberstroh, Jana Schellinger, and Jamie Bloss—for their willingness to become involved in an undertaking that was new to many of them. Thank you.

Jeff Coghill

Chapter One

An Introduction to Neurodiversity

Elizabeth M. H. Coghill

Neurodiverse students are a growing population on today's college campuses, and their increasing numbers and learning needs impact traditional support services and classroom experiences. As the number of college students with learning differences continues to grow, their effect on post-secondary learning environments challenge higher education leadership to identify and implement new approaches intended to increase social connections and campus belonging, eliminate learning and accommodation obstacles, and support academic achievement.

Post-secondary educational outcomes indicate that today's campus services have progressed in addressing the needs of marginalized student groups including first-generation students and students of color. There remains, however, a gap in our understanding of neurodiversity and academic support services for neurodiverse student populations (Fleming et al., 2018). It is estimated that 11% of college students enrolling on post-secondary campuses are neurodivergent: students who have a learning disability or learning difference (Fleming et al., 2018). Studies indicate that these students experience difficulty with academic performance and have lower retention and persistence rates in comparison to their neurotypical peers (Fleming et al., 2018).

Neurodiverse students do not graduate from college at the same rate as their peers without learning differences (Newman et al., 2009). Newman and Madaus (2015) report college completion rates for LD (learning difference) and ADHD (attention deficit hyperactivity disorder) students are 40%, compared to 51% for students without learning disabilities. The achievement gap can be attributed to academic barriers neurodiverse students experience on the college campus. Lightfoot and colleagues (2018) identify six academic barriers that will be explored in this book: (1) experiences with faculty and staff, (2) connections to accommodations, (3) intrinsic factors, (4) timing of

1

disability disclosure, (5) stigma of learning disability, and (6) social connection and belonging.

As neurodiverse students enroll in post-secondary education, the environments within which these students learn can either support or impede their ability to succeed. Simply put, a welcoming campus for neurodiverse students is established when educators recognize that all students process and learn differently, and therefore we must adapt our approaches and services in order to reach and support all students enrolled on our campuses. Welcoming learning environments support key institutional outcomes such as retention, persistence, and graduation rates and can lower the need for disability accommodations. For neurodiverse students, it increases academic engagement, builds self-efficacy, expands learner options beyond the traditional classroom, and positively impacts their ability to make greater campus connections.

DEFINING NEURODIVERSITY

The basic premise of neurodiversity is that there is no "normal" baseline for brain processes, but that all individual brains vary and therefore are diverse (Armstrong, 2012). Neurodiversity recognizes that all learning differences are natural variations on the human species (Austin & Pisano, 2017; Shmulsky & Gobbo, 2019). Neurodiversity emphasizes the differences in brain functioning and recognizes that these differences have strengths and challenges that deserve to be recognized and supported (Shmulsky & Gobbo, 2019). Although neurodiversity applies to diverse human neurology, in the larger context it embraces all types of diversity groups on campus including religion, nationality, sexual orientation, and race (Robertson & Ne'eman, 2008).

When neurological differences are viewed through the lens of neurodiversity, our viewpoint changes from a medical perspective to a cultural perspective or social justice movement (Shmulsky & Gobbo, 2019). In this context, it can be argued that neurodiverse students comprise a new rising identity group on campus. Neurodivergent students come to the campus with distinctive combinations of strengths and challenges that comprise their academic experiences. When higher education leaders regard neurodiverse students in the context of a rising identity group, their marginalization experiences in the post-secondary environment allows leaders to understand them through the lens of other minority groups on campus.

DISABILITY LANGUAGE CHOICE

For the higher education professional, the language surrounding students and disabilities can be confusing, and language preferences often contradict each other. The language choices we make, however, matter to the staff, students, families, and stakeholders we work with. For example, heightened awareness regarding respectful disability language is vital as we explore the needs of neurodiverse students. Portland State University's National Youth Leadership Network provides the following general guidelines:

- Refer to a person's disability only when it is related to the context of the discussion.
- Refrain from referring to people in generalized terms such as "the girl in the wheelchair."
- Refer to accommodations as *accessible* instead of *handicapped* or *disabled*.
- Use the term *disability* rather than antiquated terms like *handicapped*, *differently abled*, *crippled*, or *special needs*.
- Avoid hero language. Having a disability doesn't make the person extraordinarily special or brave.
- Find out what the person prefers in language choice.
- Do not categorize people without disabilities as *normal*. This implies those with a disability are *abnormal*.
- Treat others with respect. Look beyond the disability, and address them by their name.

It is generally accepted to use either *identity-first* or *people-first* language in discussions regarding disabilities. The debate between using *identity first* versus *people first* is a foundation for dialogue shared by higher education practitioners. According to Eric Moore, coauthor of *UDL Navigators in Higher Education: A Field Guide*:

> Language matters, and people often have strong feelings and response to language surrounding human disability. Some people in the disability community prefer what is known as *identity first language*. That is, they prefer to be called *autistic people* or *deaf people*, or *disabled students*, for example. This is often the preference of disabled people. On the other hand, there are also proponents of *people first* language who prefer *people with autism* or *people who are deaf* or *students with disabilities*, for example. (Black & Moore, 2019, p. 73)

For the purpose of this book, the authors will collectively use *people-first* language. Often accepted by higher education journals and publishers, the use of *people first* will be utilized in the context of the book chapters and discussions with the understanding that this choice respects and acknowledges the proponents of *identity-first* language and does not include any intentional offense to others whose language preference differs.

ACCESSIBILITY

As our understanding of neurodiverse students increases, it is important to note the definition of *accessibility* on the post-secondary campus. Section 504 of the Rehabilitation Act of 1973 is an early disability rights legislation that dictates the provision of accommodations or assistance services to disabled individuals within organizations that receive federal funding (www.BestColleges.com). In higher education, Section 504 as well as legislation such as the Americans with Disabilities Act, Individuals with Disabilities Education, and the Assistive Technology Act encompass academic adjustments or accommodations to increase accessibility for individuals with a documented disability, including neurodivergent students. Simply defined, *accessible* refers to opportunities provided to a person with a disability to obtain the same knowledge and experience the same interactions and services in an equitable manner as a person without a disability.

DISABILITY INCLUSION

The Centers for Disease Control and Prevention defines *disability inclusion* as the involvement of people with disabilities in activities and fostering the ability for them to have similar experiences as others who do not have a disability. In the college context, disability inclusion would allow for all students to be provided the opportunity to engage and learn in similar ways.

DEFINING UNIVERSAL DESIGN FOR LEARNING (UDL)

Universal Design for Learning (UDL) plays an important role in supporting the academic achievement of neurodiverse students. UDL is defined by the CAST organization as "an educational approach based on the learning sciences with three primary principles—multiple means of representation of information, multiple means of student action and expression, and multiple means of student engagement" (CAST, 2019).

Applying UDL principles in the higher education classroom ensures students have course concepts presented in varied ways to provide choices regarding resources and materials that help them learn best. This can be accomplished without asking a student to disclose their learning differences. If we adopt the understanding that every student learns a bit differently from another, this inclusive perspective and dialogue allows educators to address the needs of all collegiate learners. Universal Design for Learning applies to spaces beyond the college classroom. Applying UDL principles in offices across campus encompasses the expansion of information delivery methods, includes the redesign of campus websites, and integrates new ways of sharing information with students, faculty, administrators, and stakeholders.

THE ROLE OF EXECUTIVE FUNCTIONING

Executive functioning skills are essential components of student academic success in college and include time management, planning and organization, multitasking, and working independently. For some neurodiverse learners, executive functioning skills are challenging to master and apply in the college environment. Welcoming post-secondary environments incorporate academic coaching, support networks, and effective classroom experiences that foster executive function skill-building.

ESTABLISHING A CAMPUS CLIMATE FOR SUCCESS

Post-secondary campus environments that encourage collaboration and communication and foster opportunities for expression allow higher education leaders to make services inclusive and open learning opportunities to a wider group of students. The foundation of establishing a welcoming learning environment is the belief that all students belong on campus. Welcoming environments that address the needs of all types of learners encourage neurodivergent students to establish campus belonging.

The work of Strayhorn (2012) underscores the importance of belonging for marginalized students. If a student does not feel as though they belong, they will struggle to succeed. This is especially true for rising identity groups like those with learning differences. Collegiate academic success is in "part a function of complicated, inextricably intertwined institutional factors and conditions" (Kuh, 2005, p.1) that culminate in degree achievement. Wondering if they fit in the post-secondary classroom, neurodiverse students are challenged to academically achieve.

Strayhorn's (2012) research helps higher education stakeholders identify ways to support specific student populations, including first-generation students; students of color; Latino students; Native American students; graduate students; science, technology, engineering, and math (STEM) students of color; and lesbian, gay, bisexual, and transgender (LGBT) students. Using a comprehensive definition of *sense of belonging* and *engagement*, Strayhorn (2012) highlights the importance of student perceptions of connection and inclusion in the academic culture. Strayhorn (2012) frames sense of belonging for college students as a basic psychological necessity that impacts motivation and alters student behaviors. Strayhorn (2012) defines *sense of belonging* as the "perceived social support on campus, a feeling or sensation of connectedness, the experience of mattering or feeling cared about, accepted, respected, valued by, and important to the group (e.g., campus community) or others on campus (e.g., faculty, peers)" (p. 112).

The sense of belonging process occurs as students transition to higher education and is reinforced throughout their college experience. Through research on the sense of belonging and engagement of marginalized student groups, Strayhorn (2012) finds sense of belonging rises in significance for students with strong cultural identifications, increases in importance during times of transition, supports a student's feelings of mattering, and produces positive academic outcomes such as persistence and graduation. Placing purposeful attention on the impact cultural identity transition plays in a student's perception of belonging, we find that marginalized students experience challenges in establishing campus connections. Extending Strayhorn's framework explains the feelings of disconnection and alienation frequently expressed by neurodivergent students.

GUIDING PRINCIPLES OF THE BOOK

"Each student brings his or her own story to our community (campus) and each has a unique mix of strengths, gifts and challenges that are part of their undergraduate journey" (Hemesath, 2019, p. 1). As higher education stakeholders, we must dedicate efforts to creating welcoming campus environments for all learners and work to create inclusive environments where students can thrive. This book is intended to further our discourse surrounding the rising identity group of neurodiverse students in post-secondary institutions of learning. By centering on specific areas and services found on college campuses, our intent is to educate faculty, staff, and administrators on the unique strengths neurodivergent students bring to higher education and to the challenges they face on our campuses.

REFERENCES

Armstrong, T. (2012). *Neurodiversity in the classroom: Strength-based strategies to help students with special needs succeed in school and life.* ASCD.

Austin, R. D., & Pisano, G. P. (2017). Neurodiversity as a competitive advantage. *Harvard Business Review, 95*(3), 96–103.

Best Colleges (2020). *Overview of college resources for students with disabilities.* https://www.bestcolleges.com/resources/students-with-disabilities

Black, J., & Moore, E. J. (2019). *UDL navigators in higher education: A field guide.* CAST Inc.

CAST. (2019). *About UDL.* http://udloncampus.cast.org/page/udl_about#.XGRE-2jNKiUk

Centers for Disease Control and Prevention. https://www.cdc.gov/ncbddd/disability-andhealth/disability-inclusion.html

Fleming, A. R., Edwin, M., Hayes, J. A., Locke, B. D., & Lockard, A. J. (2018). Treatment-seeking college students with disabilities: Presenting concerns, protective factors, and academic distress. *Rehabilitation Psychology, 63*(1), 55.

Hemesath, M. (2019, January 11). Neurodiversity goes to college. *Quad 136.* https://blogs.csbsju.edu/mhemesath/2019/01/11/neurodiversity-goes-to-college

Kuh, G. D. (2005). *Assessing conditions to enhance educational effectiveness: The inventory for student engagement and success* (1st ed.). Jossey-Bass.

Lightfoot, A., Janemi, R., & Rudman, D. L. (2018). Perspectives of North American postsecondary students with learning disabilities: A scoping review. *Journal of Postsecondary Education and Disability, 31*(1), 57–74.

National Youth Leadership Network. (n.d.). *Respectful disability language.* http://www.aucd.org/docs/add/sa_summits/Language%20Doc.pdf

Newman, L., & Madaus, J. (2015). Reported accommodations and supports provided to secondary and postsecondary students with disabilities: National perspective. *Career Development and Transition for Exceptional Individuals, 38*(3), 173–181.

Newman, L., Wagner, M., Cameto, R., & Knokey, A.-M. (2009). *The post-high school outcomes of youth with disabilities up to 4 years after high school. A report from the National Longitudinal Transition Study-2 (NLTS2).* SRI International.

Robertson, S. M., & Ne'eman, A. D. (2008). Autistic acceptance, the college campus, and technology: Growth of neurodiversity in society and academia. *Disability Studies Quarterly, 28*(4).

Shmulsky, S., & Gobbo, K. (2019). Autism support in a community college setting: Ideas from intersectionality. *Community College Journal of Research and Practice, 43*(9), 648–652.

Strayhorn, T. L. (2018). *College students' sense of belonging: A key to educational success for all students.* Routledge.

Chapter Two

Self-Advocacy

John B. Caldora II and Elizabeth M. H. Coghill

The higher education system requires students to possess self-advocacy skills to successfully transition to campus life, persist through degree programs, and graduate from the institution. For neurodiverse students, it is imperative that self-advocacy skills are developed and employed for academic success to be achieved. McCarthy (2007) underscores the importance of advocacy proficiency for students and summarizes the process as an advocacy journey in which students develop essential skills to ensure equal access and achieve educational goals.

For neurodiverse students, the transition to the rigor of higher education expectations and campus life is daunting. They come to campus ill-prepared and unaware of the need for self-direction (McCarthy, 2007, p. 12). The role of parents and teachers in high school accommodations and lack of student involvement in these processes creates barriers to their success on the post-secondary campus. Although parents play a vital role to ensure K–12 success and act as passionate advocates for their students, in many cases, parents fail to involve their student in the educational advocacy process. Lack of participation in this process results in a lack of the self-advocacy skills needed to navigate post-secondary accommodations and support disclosure (Bublitz et al., 2015). Vaccaro and colleagues (2015) note that many beginning students transitioning to higher education are ill-equipped to self-advocate and will struggle academically as a result.

Historically, ensuring equal access and use of support services has fallen on the shoulders of faculty and disability support offices. Once accommodations are determined, campus disability support offices are responsible for determining and providing reasonable accommodations in order to support student disability needs. Accommodations are made on a case-by-case basis.

Once reasonable accommodations are determined, it is the role of the faculty member to execute the accommodations. Relying on disability support offices and faculty members, neurodiverse students experience gaps in academic success services needed to achieve success on campus. This chapter explores the causes of gaps in the accommodations and use of academic support services and the self-advocacy skills necessary for neurodiverse student success.

STIGMA AND SUCCESS

Neurodiverse students experience barriers to their academic success, including awareness and resources beyond disability support offices, unwillingness to disclose learning differences, and perceived stigmas on campus. Cortiella and Horowitz (2014) found that only 24% of students who received support in high school went on to disclose their learning differences in post-secondary schools. When neurodiverse students do not disclose, they lack the connection to academic support services that are essential to achieving academic success. Too often academic advisors, faculty, and other staff lack the understanding of neurodiversity and student disclosure patterns, resulting in gaps in receiving effective support services.

As neurodiverse students transition to post-secondary campuses, many choose to not disclose their learning differences. Attempting to leave behind their challenges and separate from their past educational support needs, these students decide not to disclose in a desire to appear "normal" (Squires et al., 2018). According to the National Center for Learning Disabilities, 94% of neurodiverse students receive supports in high school in comparison to only 17% receiving college accommodations (Gose, 2016). In a study of ADHD students, Squires et al. (2018) found that students do not disclose because of perceived stigma and expressed feelings of embarrassment, fear of being singled out, and a desire for independence. Smith and Applegate (2018) highlight internalized stigma as a reaction to societal attitudes regarding neurodiversity and metal health. Defining *internalized stigma* as the internalization of public stigma into a person's identity, they note the negative effect public stigma stereotypes have on individuals with a disability.

Frequently, neurodiverse students transition to college ill-equipped to disclose their disability and utilize accommodations effectively. Students must disclose and identify themselves to disability support offices in order to receive services. Students who choose not to disclose attempt post-secondary education without the accommodations they need. The 2002 National Center for Education Statistics report notes that 9% of undergraduate students registered with campus disability support services, while only 4% self-identified as having a disability (White et al., 2019). Too often neurodiverse students only disclose after failure and recognition that support systems are needed. This is one explanation of why neurodiverse students are unsuccessful on post-secondary campuses. According to Landmark College's research and training blog, only 24% of students with learning differences will ever disclose at their college (Lalor, 2019). Learning self-advocacy skills is essential in supporting the connection to accommodations and support services on campus.

SELF-ADVOCACY ON THE COLLEGE CAMPUS

Vaccaro et al. (2015) define *self-advocacy* as the "ability to communicate one's needs and wants and to make decisions about the supports necessary to achieve them" (p. 673). They emphasize the relationship between self-advocacy and successfully transitioning to a new student role and the realization of academic goals. Key steps in the advocacy journey for neurodiverse students are: (1) understanding their disability and identity (knowledge of self), (2) disclosure and accommodations (knowledge of rights), and (3) self-determination (Sarrett, 2018; Squires et al., 2018; Vaccaro et al., 2015). There is a connection between neurodiverse identity, understanding, acceptance, and the ability to access and use accommodations (Sarrett, 2018). Mastery of self-advocacy skills enables students to formulate and communicate their identities as neurodiverse learners and empowers them to request the support they need to succeed.

SELF-IDENTITY AND STUDENT ROLE

The college experience is filled with the opportunity for self-acceptance and identity development. College students with disabilities or learning differences are not an exception. For neurodiverse students, the steps toward a positive self-identity are essential to the development of a successful student role on campus. Sarrett (2018) highlights the important development of a positive disability identity for neurodiverse students. Similarly, Gobbo and Shmulsky (2016) note that the definition of self is a foundation for wellness and key to developing maturity.

Vaccaro et al. (2015) underscore the connection between self-identity in post-secondary environments and the "student role." In a study on college students with learning differences, Vaccaro et al. (2015) note that mastering the student role involves "feeling like a college student by blending in with peers, being viewed as a legitimate student, and gaining recognition for academic success" (p. 679). In a similar study, Squires et al. (2018) report that identity development is closely aligned with independence as neurodiverse students build success strategies in tandem with collegiate accommodations. Moving beyond disability support services that many neurodiverse students regard as making them less "legitimate" as college students, neurodiverse college students must develop the skills needed to navigate academic success barriers and develop positive self-identities that transcend post-secondary environments.

SELF-ADVOCACY AND AUTONOMY

The objective of self-advocacy is to demonstrate that neurodiverse students can make decisions about themselves and challenge those who do not agree in order to gain autonomy (Test et al., 2005). Student self-advocacy also challenges perceived overprotection of professionals, parents, and caregivers. Self-advocacy is a crucial adult developmental skill and instrumental to self-determination. Self-determined students show better post-school outcomes, financial ability, and overall life skills (Test et al., 2005).

Challenging the overprotectiveness of professionals is a critical step, although it seems to be a counterintuitive development in self-advocacy. Students must begin the process of growth by challenging those who support them. They do this in order to gain the confidence needed to challenge ideas in the classroom and authority outside the educational environment. Of course, such challenge does not mean that the student necessarily gets their way. The objective is to encourage the student to think critically about their rights and responsibilities within a wider world. When a student is challenging a supportive structure, it is important to provide the necessary context as to why that support exists. The student should also be cautioned about the drawbacks of opting out of the support they are challenging and any dangers that may pose.

For example, a student with a single-room accommodation (which gives a single room at the cost of a double) in a residence hall may decide that they want to give up their accommodation and live with a roommate. It would be important to explore this decision with the student. Do they want a roommate because they believe this will be a guaranteed friend or because they are ready to prepare for independent living, which may require a roommate for financial reasons? One only needs to point to the multitude of roommate conflicts handled by residence life professionals on an annual basis to disprove that. Perhaps the student wants to prepare to live with a roommate following graduation? It would be important to go over the various pros and cons of this decision and explain to the student that a single-room accommodation might not be easily regained due to the fluid occupancy of a residence hall and develop a plan for addressing the challenges that living with a roommate presents. Ultimately, the decision, right or wrong, is the student's, so long as that decision falls within the protocols and rules of the institution.

This is just one example; such challenges can take many forms. In almost all cases, due to FERPA, conversations about students should take place with students, regardless of whether the student is neurotypical or neurodiverse. Even if an office has secured a waiver to speak with a parent, the student must remain a critical part of the conversation. Such conversations between parents, students, and staff should be focused on gathering information and encouraging the parent's support of the student in a way that allows the student the support they need, but also the freedom to make missteps if necessary.

Hengen and Weaver (2018) note students who actively participated in their accommodation meetings in primary and secondary school scored significantly higher in a survey of self-advocacy skills. While the study is mostly applied to K–12 education, there are still some implications for higher education. It is even more important at the college level that self-advocacy be encouraged and that students actively make decisions for themselves about seeking accommodations. Students may elect to not pursue accommodations. A study by Squires et al. (2018) examined why students did not seek accommodations. They found four common themes: a desire for independence, a desire to challenge and overcome disability, a function of their identity development, and trying to avoid the stigma of disability accommodations.

SELF-ADVOCACY AS A FRAMEWORK

The Framework of Self-Advocacy for Students with Disabilities, developed by Test and colleagues (2005), provides an outline of critical skills in self-awareness, communication, and group advocacy that can be beneficial for neurodiverse students. They attribute the origin of self-advocacy to three primary events: the concepts of the civil rights movements from the 1950s–1960s, the end of mental institutionalization in the 1970s, and the self-help movement in the 1980s. Each movement supported attributes of self-autonomy and self-actualization. In order to advocate effectively for these movements, individuals needed to develop strategies to advocate for themselves and their group. The framework is composed of four primary areas—knowledge of self, knowledge of rights, communication, and leadership—and will be outlined in this chapter (Test et al., 2005).

Knowledge of Self

Test et al. (2005) see the role of the educational institution as providing education in self-advocacy to students with disabilities, which gives them the ability to move beyond the structured support offered in the United States. The foundation of knowledge of self includes: "strengths, preferences, goals, dreams, interests, learning style, support needs, accommodation needs, characteristics of one's disability, and responsibilities" (Test et al., 2005, p. 49).

Accomplished through modeling skills and providing opportunities to practice self-advocacy techniques, students need to be taught advocacy skills and an understanding of their accommodations. Test et al. (2005) advocate that students, especially by the time they enter high school, should have the opportunity to sit in and ask questions during discussions of their accommodations with parents, clinicians, and teachers. This process allows students to emerge as the primary voice in advocating for accommodations when they enter post-secondary campuses.

Knowledge of Rights

Knowledge of rights—student understanding of how the wider world interacts with their disability—includes "personal rights, community rights, human service rights, consumer rights, educational rights, steps to redress violations, steps to advocate for change, and knowledge of resources" (Test et al., 2005, p. 49). Knowledge of self and rights provide a foundation of self-advocacy through which a student can begin to communicate and to advocate for themselves and others.

Knowledge of rights extends to defining the student role and encompasses many of the areas handled by student affairs and academic affairs professionals. These include a code of conduct, an understanding of Title IX, the ADA, academic procedures and rights, as well as knowledge of how to properly file grievances and appeal injustices. Knowledge of resources can come not only from lists of the multitude of resources an institution offers but also from targeted referrals through case-management resources. Depending on a student's interest in expanding to group advocacy, such knowledge can also be expanded to knowledge of systems and systemic change. For example, it would help a group advocate to understand the different types of higher education institutions and how advocacy might look different at a community college compared to a large politically run flagship institution.

Communication

Within the college environment, neurodiverse students must learn how to make use of the knowledge of themselves and their rights effectively.

Sometimes, this is learning how to communicate their needs in a way that encourages the support of another person. Neurodiverse students need assertive communication skills, which include "effective and appropriate communications of feelings, needs, and desires and an ability to say no" (Test et al., 2005, p. 50). Subcomponents of communication include "assertiveness, negotiation, articulation, body language, use of assistive technology, listening, persuasion, and compromise" (p. 49).

Self-advocacy transitions decision-making from parent to student and establishes the responsibility to seek accommodations in college to the neurodiverse student. Therefore, in every step of the process, from the first meeting with the disability services office to graduation, discussions regarding the student's accommodations should take place with the student, not with a parent. It is a common maxim in education that a student is not going to learn unless they have the opportunity to fail. The only time decisions should be made for a student is a health and safety emergency. As neurodiverse students move into the less defined world of accommodations in employment, they will need the self-advocacy skills developed in college to receive needed accommodations and support.

Leadership

Although the primary goals are for a neurodiverse student to develop knowledge of self and the ability to effectively communicate, leadership is an optional end goal of the self-advocacy journey. For many neurodiverse students, the development of self-advocacy, knowledge of self, and communication skills guides them to adopting a leadership role for their neurodiverse community (Test et al., 2005). These skills are crucial in helping them navigate and grow in a world designed for others. Through these skills, students can advocate for what they need and learn about their neurodiverse identity. They can also use such knowledge to advocate for the wider group.

UNDERSTANDING THE
NETWORK OF NEURODIVERSITY ADVOCACY

Understanding the larger network of neurodiversity advocacy enables campus leaders to foster self-advocacy skills with the neurodiverse students we serve. Considering neurological differences through the framework of neurodiversity changes the theoretical landscape from a medical-based perspective to a cultural perspective or social justice movement (Gobbo & Shmulsky, 2019).

Through this viewpoint, neurodiversity can be categorized as an emerging culture within society. Finding its origins in the age of the internet, the culture surrounding neurodiversity has developed significantly in the last 15 years.

The first organization devoted to self-advocacy for persons with disabilities was People First. People First is responsible for activism and the emergence of the idea that people with disabilities should be the primary voice for their disability. Even today, this is an uncommon idea. For example, Autism Speaks, the world's largest autism charity, only invited members of the autism spectrum onto their executive board in December 2015 (Autistic Self-Advocacy Network [ASAN], 2015). Self-advocacy has formed the cornerstone of the neurodiversity movement.

The internet and digital access supports the neurodiverse community by providing the ability for individuals and groups to connect with one another. It provides a connection for neurodiverse people to make sense of their individual needs in perspective with the wider world and lessen feelings of isolation. For example, some autistic members prefer communicating on autism message boards about the spectrum, their personal interests, and how autism affects their lives (Jordan, 2010). Neurodiverse individuals, particularly members of the autism spectrum, can find using a computer and text-based conversation more comfortable than interaction via voice or face-to-face conversation. Through a computer, members of the spectrum can focus on the substance of a conversation more easily than through other forms of communication. This can allow verbal and nonverbal members of the spectrum to demonstrate intelligence, eloquence, and empathy that may be lost in a phone or in-person conversation (Jordan, 2010).

The internet catapulted the discernment of autism identity into a new level of thinking. Prior to the wider adoption of use of the World Wide Web, the building of autistic community, which would later expand into the larger neurodiversity movement, occurred at the fringes of conferences for parents and professionals about autism. Using the medium of the internet, autism identity could be discussed more freely and frequently, leading to the development of a larger neurodiverse identity.

OUR LANGUAGE MATTERS

As campus leaders, our language choices regarding neurodiversity, disability, and its impact on advocacy is powerful and worthy of deeper understanding and consideration. Knowing what to say can be confusing. Language preferences differ among neurodiverse advocates, organizations, and students. Neurodiverse groups disagree on identity-first versus person-first language.

The question of language goes much deeper to whether neurodiversity is part of a student's identity.

Perspectives differ on language choice within neurodiverse organizations. Consider the autism community: Many self-advocates regard autism as an inherent part of their identity, something that cannot be separated from them. This would be similar to other groups expressing a racial, gender, or sexual orientation identity and is expressed as "autistic person." On the other side, parents and professionals prefer to emphasize the humanity of children and clients by putting the person first, as expressed by the phrase "person with autism spectrum disorder." Identity-first language is also seen as reclaiming an offensive term.

Self-advocates have personal beliefs and reasons for their language preferences. For example, Lydia Brown (2011), an autistic self-advocate, notes that using identity-first language gives a person's identity value. Jim Sinclair (2012), another self-advocate, focuses primarily on three areas: the autistic identity is inseparable from the individual, the identity is an important part of the individual, and there are positive aspects of the autistic identity.

For higher education leaders, it is important to respect the beliefs and opinions of each individual student we encounter. For example, Stairway to STEM (2018), a nonprofit funded in part by a National Science Foundation grant, developed a robust identity language policy that advocates for allowing neurodiverse content contributors to use their own identity language preference and having other contributors use both in their pieces. In cases where a campus leader is uncertain of what language to use, we suggest "member of the autism spectrum," as this will honor both the individual and their place in a larger identity group. It can be an acceptable compromise when working with a student before knowing their personal preferences, or when speaking more generally.

Another concern regarding language is the use of "functioning labels." Saying that a student is "high functioning" or "low functioning" is arbitrary and inaccurate. Sonya Freeman Loftis (2015), a distinguished author in disability studies and English, notes that a "high-functioning" individual might be verbal and capable of living independently at home, but unable to cross the street by themselves. Conversely, a "low-functioning" individual might be nonverbal but be able to communicate beautifully by writing. Loftis concludes by writing, "In any case, these ambiguous terms are clearly implicated in the pathology paradigm since in many ways 'high functioning' means closer to passing for neurotypical" (2015, p. 9).

Loftis notes other language issues regarding neurodiverse students. For example, disabled people often consider the term *differently abled* patronizing, as it minimizes the challenges of navigating a world designed for the able and neurotypical. Using the term *cognitive difference* serves to address the concerns of the neurodiversity advocacy proponents without utilizing language like *cognitive disability* or *mental disorder*, which is steeped in the medical or pathology paradigm.

Language issues can emerge unintentionally when addressing other issues on a college campus. For example, in April 2017 the Equality and Diversity Unit of Oxford University published a list of racial microaggressions to avoid. Included in this list was that a form of microaggression is to not make eye contact with a person or speak directly to them. Recognizing that some neurodiverse individuals experience difficulty making eye contact with others, Oxford University publicly apologized for failing to take disability into account (British Broadcasting Company, 2017).

CAMPUS CASE STUDIES

In considering whether an institution offers the best opportunity for neurodiverse students to succeed, higher education practitioners must continually search for improvements in their processes and outreach to students. The following case studies, adapted from real-world campus events, are designed to encourage campus leaders to consider environmental changes and adaptations to ensure neurodiverse student success.

Police Interactions

Campus police encounter a freshman student who is a member of the autism spectrum. This student was seen pacing outside a classroom building, flapping his arms and playing with a yo-yo. Occasionally people need to walk around the student, but he is not impeding traffic. Responding police officers ask the student what he is doing. The student responds, mumbling, "Stimming." Officers believe that the student is under the influence of an inhaled substance and, when the student refuses to stay in one place, initiate a violent takedown that results in the student screaming, "No, no, I'm okay, I'm okay," at the officers.

The situation is seen via body camera footage as well as being recorded by students passing by. Within 24 hours the story is picked up by both the student media and local media. Statements from administration are issued promising an investigation without any claim of liability. Student protests occur, and campus operations are disrupted. The student's family sues the university for millions, also demanding a personal apology from the officer and for departments to receive training.

This case could have been avoided had the campus police department trained officers on working with neurodiverse individuals. Given the different ways that neurodiverse individuals see the world, they will present differently. The student engaging in stimming, a behavioral response to stress or excessive sensory input, could have been celebrating doing well after a test, or destressing after a particularly difficult class. Alternatively, the student could have been trying to deal with the overwhelming noises of a campus during class change. In any case, had the officers been trained to identify such behavior, the situation likely could have been avoided, or perhaps the student could have been redirected to an area where he was not blocking traffic.

Campus Employment

A neurodiverse student is hired by the campus's dining vendor to work in a fast food concession in the student center. This student is occasionally prone to bursts of excitement that result in shaking hands. The manager of the concession feels that this is an issue where the student is not "otherwise qualified" to perform the job and therefore terminates the student. He reaches this conclusion based on the fact that such hand issues could result in change being issued incorrectly to a customer.

The student in turn complains to his advisor in the disability resource office. This advisor attempts to reach out to the manager to resolve the issue, but the manager declines to speak with her. She then contacts the equal opportunity office at the institution, who attempt to address the situation with the vendor. The vendor believes that the manager, a long-time employee, handled the situation appropriately. Tensions rise as the vendor's contract is up for renewal and a debate ensues as to whether offering the student an alternative task would have met the standards of an appropriate accommodation.

This case is meant to raise two questions. First, do all managers at an institution and vendors have an understating of the ADA? Specifically, do they understand the areas of reasonable accommodations and if an employee is otherwise qualified to perform the position? Second, are an institution's vendors as dedicated to working with diverse populations as the institution itself? Do they share the institution's values?

Conduct/Threat Assessment

On a small liberal arts campus on the West Coast, a transgender member of the autism spectrum allegedly made a threat to "shoot up the campus with a gun," during a meltdown. This was reportedly the latest in a series of behavioral outbursts and panic attacks that had been taken through a combined behavioral intervention and student conduct process. The student had no means to purchase a firearm. A student conduct hearing found the student responsible for disrupting the campus community and failing to abide by a behavioral contract in which they agreed to refrain from "threats and behaviors that may generate reasonable fear in another person." The student was suspended for the remainder of the current semester and the following semester. Two appeals of the process were denied.

Students rallied around the student and are in strong opposition to the administration's decision, claiming instead that the outbursts are "panic attacks related to the student's neurodiversity." Further complicating matters, the student was disowned by their family after they came out as trans and is homeless. Due to FERPA, the institution's only comments on the protest were that they could not "correct errors in the narrative." The student had no place to go after being suspended and lived on the streets briefly until friends organized an online fundraiser. The student eventually returned after serving their suspension.

There are several points of advocacy to consider in this case. Crossing behavioral intervention and student conduct processes may result in issues where such behavioral expectation agreements, especially when centered on a disability, are not legally enforceable. Did the institution review their processes and agreements with their legal counsel? The question should be raised of how much weight to give a subject's current mental status (in the case study, a neurodiverse student's meltdown) when performing a threat assessment. Finally, from a compassion point of view, it is good to ask if an institution has a plan if it must suspend, or otherwise remove, a homeless student from campus. While such responsibility might be legally limited, from a standpoint of student service and equity, it is worth considering how to smooth the transition, perhaps with a connection to community resources.

Title IX and Neurodiverse Students

A member of the autism spectrum is romantically interested in another student in one of their classes. The student is unsure how to properly express this feeling, as they have mostly just seen how dating works through television. The autistic student therefore attempts to express interest by trying to make reasons to spend time with the student they are interested in. They also have repeatedly asked the student out on dates, to which the other student has demurred and made excuses about not attending. While the subject of the autistic student's interest never says outright that they are not interested in dating the autistic student, they feel like the student is stalking them, especially after he shows up frequently at their place of work, the college library. The student reports the situation to the Title IX office, who proceeds to investigate.

Most institutions mandate that students participate in some form of training about their rights and responsibilities under Title IX. However, neurodiverse students will require additional training and support on the subject. For those with social anxiety and members of the autism spectrum, it can be especially difficult to represent romantic interest in a way that can be reciprocated. This is further complicated by difficulty in reading social cues, such as the soft letdown demonstrated by the subject of interest in this case. Therefore, it is important to advocate for additional training in Title IX and social skills for these students. According to Thierfeld Brown et al. (2018), such training should include the topics of "dating, consent, stalking, good and bad touch, rules for texting and online dating, recognizing signs of assault, and reporting of misconduct and abuse" (p. 5). They recommend such trainings be repetitive and that students have the option for individual consultation with a Title IX educator.

Such trainings can be accomplished in a variety of forms. If an institution has a neurodiverse student group, this could be a guest lecture. It could be covered during disability services meetings. These areas can be further incorporated into trainings given to all students. In the worst circumstances, it could be an educational part of a sanction to deal with a situation that has occurred.

CONCLUSION

Campus professionals must ensure that student advocacy forms the foundation of all their work with neurodiverse students. They must work, in any capacity, to encourage students' skills in self-advocacy, to learn about neurodiversity issues, and to confront inequality on their campuses.

Campus Essentials for High Impact

- *Formally educate students in the Framework for Self-Advocacy.* Support the building of advocacy skills and coach and involve students in the accommodation process.
- *Build the neurodiverse community.* Encourage neurodiverse students to engage with one another and to form groups that can advocate for the neurodiversity movement. Seek to involve neurodiverse campus stakeholders in the process.
- *Review campus processes and procedures.* Conduct a systematic review through a neurodiverse perspective to ensure accessibility and equity for neurodiverse campus members.

- *Educate the campus community.* Seek opportunities to inform campus stakeholders on language choice, and conduct training sessions to ensure a heightened awareness of neurosensitive language use.

REFERENCES

Autistic Self-Advocacy Network (ASAN). (2015). *Statement on autism speaks board appointments.* https://autisticadvocacy.org/2015/12/statement-on-autism-speaks-board-appointments

British Broadcasting Company. (2017). *Oxford university sorry for eye contact racism claim.* https://www.bbc.com/news/uk-england-oxfordshire-39742670

Brown, L. (2011). *Identity-first language.* http://autisticadvocacy.org/identity-first-language

Bublitz, D., Wong, V., Donachie, A., Brooks, P. J., & Gillespie-Lynch, K. (2015). Applying universal design to build supports for college students with autism spectrum disorder. *Progress in Education, 36,* 1–24.

Cortiella, C., & Horowitz, S. H. (2014). *The state of learning disabilities: Facts, trends and emerging issues.* National Center for Learning Disabilities.

Freeman Loftis, S. (2015). *Imagining autism: Fiction and stereotypes on the spectrum.* Indiana University Press.

Gobbo, K., & Shmulsky, S. (2016). Autistic identity development and postsecondary education. *Disability Studies Quarterly, 36*(3).

Gobbo, K., & Shmulsky, S. (2019). Should neurodiversity culture influence how instructors teach? *Academic Exchange Quarterly, 23*(4), 12–17.

Gose, B. (2016). How one college helps students with learning disabilities find their way. *Chronicle of Higher Education.*

Hengen, S., & Weaver, A. (2018). Post-secondary students with disabilities: Increasing self-advocacy through educational plan participation. *The School Psychologist, 72*(2), 7–18.

Jordan, J. (2010). Evolution of autism support and understanding via the world wide web. *Intellectual and Developmental Disabilities, 48,* 220–227.

Lalor, A. (2019, March 8). Universally available support services: A predictor of college completion for students with LD. *Landmark College.* https://www.landmark.edu/research-training/blog/universally-available-support-services-a-predictor-of-college-completion-fo

McCarthy, D. (2007). Teaching self–advocacy to students with disabilities. *About Campus, 12*(5), 10–16.

Sarrett, J. C. (2018). Autism and accommodations in higher education: Insights from the autism community. *Journal of Autism and Developmental Disorders, 48*(3), 679–693.

Sinclair, J. (2012). Autism network international: The development of a community and its culture. In J. Bascom (Ed.), *Loud hands: Autistic people, speaking* (pp. 22–70). The Autistic Press.

Smith, R. A., & Applegate, A. (2018). Mental health stigma and communication and their intersections with education. *Communication Education, 67*(3), 382–393.

Squires, M. E., Burnell, B. A., McCarty, C., & Schnackenberg, H. (2018). Emerging adults: Perspectives of college students with disabilities. *Journal of Postsecondary Education and Disability, 31*(2), 121–134.

Stairway to STEM. (2018). *Stairway to STEM (STS) identifying language editorial policy.* https://www.stairwaytostem.org/editorial-policy

Test, D. W., Fowler, C. H., Wood, W. M., Brewer, D. M., & Eddy, S. (2005). A conceptual framework of self-advocacy for students with disabilities. *Remedial and Special Education, 26*(1), 43–54. https://doi.org/10.1177/07419325050260010601

Thierfeld Brown, J., Wolf, L. E., & Sullivan, L. (2018) Understand role of Title IX in misconduct involving students with autism. *Student Affairs Today, 20*(12), 1, 4–5.

Vaccaro, A., Daly-Cano, M., & Newman, B. M. (2015). A sense of belonging among college students with disabilities: An emergent theoretical model. *Journal of College Student Development, 56*(7), 670–686.

White, D., Hillier, A., Frye, A., & Makrez, E. (2016). College students' knowledge and attitudes towards students on the autism spectrum. *Journal of Autism and Developmental Disorders, 49*(7), 2699–2705.

Chapter 2: Campus Spotlight

Learning Community, Pirate Academic Success Center, East Carolina University

Elizabeth M. H. Coghill

Our Mission: Build student self-advocacy skills, increase peer engagement,
and empower students to understand
and apply executive functioning and
active learning skills through learning
community participation.

Program Overview: Neurodiverse
learners are supported through four
program components: (1) learning
community participation, (2) freshman
seminar class and cohort classes, (3)
peer-to-peer academic coaching services, and (4) transition assistance for
students and parents.

Source: ECU Pirate Academic Success
Center

Learning Community Participation: Participants receive academic and college life transition coaching, peer academic success coaching, social and
cultural activities, priority tutoring, STARFISH monitoring, enrollment in
common classes including Freshman Seminar, and learning center employment opportunities.

- A special section of Freshman Seminar is offered for neurodiverse students. Freshman Seminar is redesigned to address the challenges facing
  neurodivergent students and build self-advocacy skills.

Source: **PASC 2019**

Freshman Seminar and cohort classes:

- **Canvas utilization** using features to support executive functioning, submission of weekly plans, establishing a semester rhythm and consistency of due dates, and heightened engagement and accountability with peer assistance and Grade Tracker.
- **Integration of scaffolding major/career project** written through a series of smaller assignments that build into components of the larger paper. Due dates and rubrics that lead to project completion.
- **Offering options of expression** through written text or video submission options.
- **Establishing supportive and welcoming environment** through peer engagement activities, DSS statement in syllabus and discussion during class, self-advocacy discussions, and additional methods of communication: GroupMe, text, call, and e-mail.
- **Room redesign and class startup procedures** to support increased peer engagement with collaborative tables, open response/questions to start class, and group work and activities during class.

Source: PACS 2019

Peer academic success coaching:

- **Peer coaching** services for all of freshman year.
- **Integration of assessment software** for session reports allowing immediate staff follow-up.
- **Empowering student choice** through "Success Coach Matching" where a student selects their peer success coach.
- **Inclusion of executive functioning skill-building processes**. These include initiation/task completion, weekly and daily to-do lists, grade tracking. Supporting working memory with strategies for recall and self-testing. Planning/organization by introducing the use of time-management systems. Improved organization of materials using course content graphic organizers and content-specific study skill strategies. Self-monitoring utilizing a grade tracking system for increased grade accountability and reflection exercises for course progress.

> The PASC provided me with the academic resources of tutoring and mentoring, and the tools for success beyond the campus of East Carolina for internships and community service.
>
> The PASC has been an invaluable advantage for my success as a student and my confidence to excel.
>
> —LC student Autumn Scales

Transition assistance for students and parents, "bootcamp":

- **Learning community students**: Participants arrive 3 days prior to school startup to join a bootcamp experience designed to introduce them to the campus environment, learn expectations of campus culture and norms, establish friendships, and build self-advocacy skills. Students work with staff to identify advocacy communication methods and review support services designed to help neurodivergent students succeed.
- **LC Parents:** On the first day of bootcamp, parents/guardians are invited to participate in a session outlining their new role as a college student parent. Parents learn boundaries established by FERPA and are invited to share educational concerns with professional staff. Situational role play provides parents with self-advocacy supports for their students.

Program Outcomes: Higher average GPAs are earned by neurodiverse students enrolled in special sections of Freshman Seminar in comparison to peers enrolled in other seminar sections.

Chapter Three

Academic Advising

Robert Detwiler

Advising has been supported as a critical factor in the college completion process (Mu & Fosnacht, 2019). Special attention to the needs of and challenges posed by neurodiverse students is needed as well as the exploration of practical ways that faculty, advisors, and primary-role advisors and advising administrators can respond with comprehensive supports. According to the 2005 National Survey of Student Engagement, the "quality of academic advising is the single most powerful predictor of satisfaction with the campus environment at 4-year schools" (as cited in Kuh et al., 2006, p. 60), and the quality of advising also has a positive relationship to student grades and self-perceived learning gains (Mu & Fosnacht, 2016; Mu & Fosnacht, 2019), all of which, according to Astin (1993), lead to positive outcomes in the college environment.

The necessity for a chapter devoted to academic advising is pressing given the lack of recent scholarship on the need for supporting students with disabilities in general, and the lack of discussion on academic advising and neurodiverse students. Speaking to the general dearth of recent literature on supporting students with disabilities through the advising function, the National Academic Advising Association's (NACADA) monograph on advising students with disabilities was first issued in 1997 (Ramos & Vallandingham, 1997) and then revised in 2009 (Vance & Bridges, 2009), but very little literature has been offered since then. Only one *NACADA Journal* article since 2009 has focused on students' needs regarding advising through health/wellness issues, a qualitative study of five students with chronic illnesses and the implications for advisors to work with students with chronic illnesses such as Crohn's, sickle cell anemia, and diabetes (Houman & Stapley, 2013). While important, this article on supporting students with persistent medical issues does not directly address neurodiverse students. In addition, while the term *neurodiversity* first appeared in 1998 (Blume, 1998), Vance and Bridges or their colleagues do not mention or discuss the term *neurodiversity* in their 2009 updated monograph.

I wish to offer four notes to readers regarding this chapter. First, this chapter is written mainly with undergraduate students in mind, but the strategies for student success discussed in this chapter will be applicable to both undergraduate and graduate/professional students. Second, the chapter is mainly organized by topic (e.g., career advising, intrusive advising, etc.) with some secondary organization by pathologies (ASD, ADHD, TBIs, etc.). The chapter organization is done intentionally so that advisors and allies can quickly find resources for different interventions and strategies depending on student needs. Third, this chapter combines the approaches of academic advising and academic coaching in its practical suggestions for faculty and primary-role advisors. Finally, this chapter offers information that is reinforced in other chapters in this book with the intention that advisors will understand both their part and others' in the university ecosystem. I argue that advisors need to be well-versed on many areas of college success, including tutoring, academic coaching, and disability services, among others, given that students regard advisors as a bridge for assistance and guidance with many areas of concern and resources.

IMPORTANCE OF ACADEMIC ADVISING AND NEURODIVERSE STUDENTS

In 2003, Charlie Nutt wrote that "the issue of student retention and persistence has continued to grow in importance throughout the history of higher education in our country." Then associate director, now executive director, of NACADA: The Global Community for Academic Advising, Nutt wrote in a recent book endorsement that "at no time in the history of American higher education has student success been more important" (Fox & Martin, 2017). As proof of this increased focus on retention and persistence, NACADA, other professional organizations, researchers, and administrators are continually gearing their conferences and professional development efforts toward a national goal of increasing college completion and degree attainment. Examples abound, including Complete College America's "15 to Finish" campaign (Complete College America, n.d.), Achieving the Dream (Achieving the Dream, n.d.), and the Yes We Must coalition (Yes We Must, n.d.). Despite these interventions, only 41% of neurodiverse students will earn a college degree in comparison to 52% of all students (Gose, 2016).

In higher education, the attention to neurodiverse students is driven by numerous reasons, among them financial, moral, and ethical. The call for public universities to manage and increase their graduation rates is becoming increasingly difficult due to either stagnant or decreasing state support for higher education. Many states like Ohio have mandated that the State Share of Instruction or similarly titled state subsidy be tied to persistence and completion rates. Evidence of stagnant or decreasing support can be found in most states across the country, but perhaps nowhere as striking as in Alaska, where Gov. Mike Dunleavy led the push to have more than 40% of the entire state system's budget cut with the beginning of the new fiscal year in July 2019 (Harris, 2019). According to Policy Matters Ohio (2019), funding for state colleges (adjusted for inflation) has decreased by 18.1% over the 2008 to 2018 timeframe. The management adage is most likely true in all states: doing more with less.

The increased focus on retention and graduation with usually no additional resources (and the threat of taking away existing resources) has not increased outcomes for students with disabilities. According to the authors of a landmark study published by the National Center for Special Education Research, "Of the 63 percent of young adults with disabilities who had ever enrolled in postsecondary education, but no longer were attending, 38 percent had graduated or completed their programs" (Sanford et al., 2011, p. 19).

As growing numbers of neurodiverse students enroll in post-secondary education, it becomes a moral and social justice imperative for advisors to respond by assisting these students to achieve positive educational outcomes. Consider the cost of student loan debt on students who do not graduate. The student loan debt burden is greater than ever on college graduates and even more so for those who do not complete a degree and are often stuck with low-paying jobs to address living needs and the cost of their past education. According to the authors of a landmark study published by the National Center for Special Education Research, out-of-high-school students with disabilities earned an average hourly wage of nearly $4/hour less than the general population, a result that is statistically significant at the $p < 0.001$ level (Sanford et al., 2011). College completion and a successful transition to the workforce can eliminate these significant wage gaps and help neurodiverse students live a better quality of life.

ADVISORS AS A BRIDGE TO RESOURCES

While academic advisors can act as a catch-all for student concerns, advisors are an important bridge between students and resources. As a referral source to appropriate offices and campus services, student advising demands knowledge and understanding of neurodiverse student needs. As such, advisors would be well served to know about local resources for community care, religious support, counseling and free clinics/doctors, and campus resources such as TRiO Student Support Services, Office of Disability Resources/Office of Accessibility, the Counseling Center, and the Career Center. Identify an ally in each office who is sensitive to students with special needs and is willing to learn and expand their knowledge base on neurodiversity, and offer to collaborate with them on programming. Academic advisors cannot know, and should not know, everything about every subject on the campus. But "knowing enough to be effective" can help advisors see the university from the "forest instead of the trees" and can effectively connect students and professionals on campus.

NEURODIVERSITY AND THE ROLE OF COACHING

The most recent edition of the *Diagnostic and Statistical Manual of Mental Disorders* (*DSM-5*) was released in 2013, and one of the most significant decisions in that manual was to eliminate all subsets of Autism Spectrum Disorder (especially Asperger's) and categorize them under ASD with specifiers regarding the intensity presented (mild, moderate, severe) and the levels of support needed (requiring support, requiring substantial support, and requiring very substantial support, respectively). A new category was created called *Social Communication Disorder,* which "includes children who have difficulties communicating socially, but who do not display the repetitive behaviors that are often a hallmark of the autism spectrum" (Pearson, 2013). The publication of the *DSM-5* in 2015 provides additional credence for an updated discussion on the reframing of the utility of academic advising in supporting students with disabilities and neurodiverse students.

Strategies often used by academic coaches can be effective in advising neurodiverse students. These strategies include encouraging students to ask for help, helping them initiate study groups with classmates, and giving suggestions on how to speak up or self-advocate when there are issues with a group. McClellan and Moser (2011) offer a useful conceptual and practice-oriented model for "advising as coaching" that can be used in this context. The authors suggest the combination of advising and coaching best practices to develop relationships with their students. They advocate for advisors to go beyond a prescriptive advising (advising as scheduling) approach to a mutual trusting relationship approach. The relationship approach utilizes coaching strategies to work with the whole student, especially neurodiverse students.

FYE AND GATEWAY COURSE REDESIGN

First-Year Experience (FYE) classes are very common at American colleges, and many first-year "traditional-age" students are required to take them. For neurodiverse students a redesigned FYE class and consideration of redesign in key gateway courses would assist in achieving success. Gateway courses generally function as a "gatekeeper" to future study and degree completion (Koch & Pistilli, n.d.). Gateway courses are often an introductory course in a major, a general education/core course that leads to other cognates in a major, or a foundational class providing necessary conceptual skills and tools for success in capstone courses or graduate study.

Course redesign within gateway courses that incorporates activities and materials that are accessible to all regardless of ability is necessary. Effective approaches include Universal Design for Learning (UDL) principles for accessing materials via the campus learning management system (LMS) and include activities that will support students with neurologically diverse backgrounds and create activities that will allow them to build skills in important soft skills such as self-advocacy, asking for help, creating a study group, and building study skills that are needed to transition from high school to college (Mader & Butrymowicz, 2017).

In the college setting, there is a greater impetus for students to use executive functioning skills in time management, future planning, and following up with instructors and advisors with no prodding or pushing from a parent, teacher, or counselor. FYE courses often address time management, and while this is an important skill for all students, the need is more pressing for neurodiverse students due to the switch from a highly structured high school environment to an unstructured college environment. Advisors can assume that high school environments and parent guidance have not taught all students the skills needed for academic success on campus. Students may not be able to advocate for themselves due to social anxiety, fear of being labeled a failure, fear of authority figures, and so on. Ideally, these skills would have been taught prior to post-secondary enrollment, but we know that is not always the case. Advisors can help fill the skills gap by empowering students to develop skills that are necessary for academic and life success.

The needs of neurodivergent students necessitates the redesign of campus interventions and skills education with the students' differences in mind. Mader and Butrymowicz (2017) illustrate the importance of redesign. They cite an example of a neurodiverse student whose use of a planner for time management was ineffective since his ADHD would cause him to forget about assignments. Similarly, students with a history of traumatic brain injury require a restructuring of traditional interventions, dictated by reduced ability to focus, ability to remember details, and ability to synthesize a large amount of information. One redesign strategy to address this in either the FYE course or an advising session is to have students review some of their syllabi from other classes in the FYE course and use either a paper or electronic method to track all of their assignments, quizzes, tests, group projects, and off-campus experiences (internships, field experience, field trips, volunteering, etc.). Advisors can assist students in marking off time for work, travel to and from school (particularly for commuters), athletic practices and games, and meetings with advisors and other support staff around campus. Constant reminders about workload through iPhone/Android notifications, regularly scheduled alarms, and notes on whiteboards around a dorm room/apartment can also be good strategies for students who have a tendency to be easily distracted and/ or forget information quickly (Mader and Butrymowicz, 2017).

Advisors may be called on to adjust or change methods of information delivery for their neurodiverse students. Milliken (2017) recommends turning difficult skill-building situations and challenges into games to appeal to neurodiverse students. Other suggestions include advisors implementing a reward structure for their advisees. For example, a student gets a prize or a badge for completing a certain number of assignments, achieving a good grade, talking with campus resources, or submitting a planner to the advisor for review each semester.

FOSTERING STUDENT IDENTITY AND ADVOCACY

Self-efficacy is lower for neurodiverse students whose peers see them as "lacking" rather than seeing their disability as a "difference" (Griffin & Pollak, 2009). Advisors can help by having intentional means for students to reflect on their identity through individual and small-group assignments in first-year seminars, in group advising settings, and in individual advising sessions. Students will be able to utilize services more effectively in the collegiate setting when they themselves can move away from deficit language and "embrace it (autism) as part of their identity" (Bumbalough et al., 2018). Such class assignments or advising sessions can take advantage of learning-centered theory (Bumbalough et al., 2018) and multiple intelligence theory (Gardner, 1983; Shearer, 2019) to allow students to reflect on their neurodiverse identity through vision boards, journaling, blogging, creating videos, composing songs about their history, leading a small-group discussion session, or performing a dance or play. One word of caution, however: Advisors should be conscious about their personal intelligence(s) when meeting with students and be able to adapt their advising approach to working with the student's personal preferred means of expression. It can be easy for an advisor to recommend an approach that works for us but may not necessarily be fruitful for your advisee.

Patrick Schwarz writes in *From Disability to Possibility* (2006) about the power of raising self-efficacy through having students act as a teacher or peer tutor. His approach is about raising the self-efficacy of students in the K–12 system, but his method can be utilized in the collegiate setting as well. Ask students with math phobias to help another student out in a lower-level class with their math homework. If a sophomore feels that they are not good with their interpersonal skills, consider inviting them to apply to be an FYE peer mentor, peer advisor, orientation team member, tour guide for admissions, or tutor. Advisors can also recommend organizations and leadership opportunities to their students where the advisor knows that the student has an interest in the topic/group focus and can improve or utilize strengths in a certain skillset (interpersonal relations, data analysis, planning and organizing). Giving students a safe space to succeed (and fail) helps build confidence and self-esteem, and hopefully shed the negative connotations of their disability.

A special note is warranted here about the use of peer advisors in FYE courses and/or in the general advising process. Extra training on cultural diversity, sensitivity, and confidentiality is of high concern and importance when employing undergraduate students in a capacity of assisting peers with a FYE course, class registration, or providing general support. These students should not receive the letter of accommodation if they are a peer mentor in an FYE course or college success transition class, since they are not a co-instructor. Peer educators should, however, be prepared to assist with these special needs if the student decides to self-disclose.

COLLEGE PERSISTENCE ISSUES

The transition from high school to college is a deeply studied field, but the issues faced by students persisting to their second year are much less studied. Promising works such as *Helping Sophomores Succeed* (Hunter et al., 2010) and programs like the Second Year Institute at Case Western Reserve University (n.d.) and the Upper-Class Experience at Siena Heights University are focusing on the developmental needs of second-year students and beyond.

Advisors are encouraged to consider the developmental needs of their neurotypical and neurodivergent students and to have a deeper set of intentional questions and learning outcomes that are geared toward each of the second, third, and fourth years of college. In particular, Hunter et al. (2010) highlight academic engagement among sophomores is less than the first year, and advisors can fill this gap by encouraging students to participate in internships, field experiences, shadowing opportunities, research mentoring, student organizations, discussion groups, research, community events, and meeting faculty in office hours to discuss academic matters beyond their academic performance in a given class. Advisors should have a checklist of typical questions to ask in each of the student's years in college to ensure that they are helping students focus on their needs at the right time. In many cases, neurodiverse students do not advocate for their own needs. Even when students know existing resources, if they lack in advocacy skills, resources can go unused. The need is even more pressing, as they usually do not have the knowledge of what to ask and when—the adage is true that "you don't know what you don't know."

COURSE SCHEDULING

While course scheduling is not the entirety of what should take place in an academic advising program/setting, it is unescapable that advisors play a critical role in the scheduling of classes and help provide a roadmap to college completion. As such, advisors need to be aware of numerous issues with the scheduling function and how the needs of neurodiverse learners need to be taken into account when building a semester schedule.

Advisors should note course-delivery methods for their students. When scheduling classes, your institution should have a clear way to denote the way the courses are delivered (online, hybrid, service learning, accelerated, etc.). This can be in the course section letter code or in the notes on the course schedule. The Registrar's Office normally has the start and end date of the course on the schedule of classes so students and advisors can have conversations regarding whether a course is offered through an accelerated format (e.g., 4, 6, 8 weeks), and notes if off-campus travel is required for a class. If this is not easily discernable on your campus, advisors are encouraged to meet with the appropriate individuals to advocate for easier course denotations that will lead to easier and more efficient scheduling.

This is critically important in serving students with autism, who will have a desire to have everything planned and organized and a set routine. These students will not deal well with significant unknowns. For example, signing up for a course that appears to be fully in person but in reality is a hybrid incorporating significant online instruction and off-site experiences would be very upsetting to any student, but much more so for students who may have intentionally shied away from these courses due to the setting not being inclusive for their needs.

Advisors should be aware of how course delivery affects neurodiverse students. Some of these delivery modes may be beneficial to students but not that great a fit for others. Online courses are offered in either synchronous or asynchronous formats; synchronous requires students to log into the course site at a given day and time, and asynchronous allows students to manage their time as they see fit. Asynchronous online classes will usually not be a good fit for students with ADHD, as this structure will not allow students to have a built-in accountability system with instructors or classmates reminding them of upcoming assignment due dates and tests and exams. Many an online student has forgotten about a due date for the course, as there is a great deal to master in the online environment, and while the best online courses are designed with Quality Matters standards or a similar rubric in mind, there is no standardization for online course experiences. Students with ASD may also struggle with online and hybrid courses if they are not given the opportunity to practice and master content that aligns with their learning preferences, and group work may also be a problem if they are expected to collaborate with other classmates in different locations.

Regarding all course scheduling, it is very helpful for advisors to know, if possible, the instructor's typical rhythms and whether they are predictable or change often. Advisors should seek to understand as much as possible regarding the content and structure of the courses they recommend to students. Does this course require group work or individual assignments? Is the majority of the course graded through projects, tests, essays, presentations, and/or reflections?

After the registration session, advisors should follow up with their student before the end of the add/drop period to see if the student is taking the courses and sections that were recommended and to act, if necessary, to correct a course. Soon after the start of the semester, an additional advising session would be helpful to discuss the expectations in the syllabus, how the student should conduct themselves in class, getting organized with due dates, and setting a follow-up schedule with the advisor to discuss academic performance.

Finally, regarding students with generalized anxiety and/or obsessive-compulsive disorder, Oslund (2014) cautions advisors that these students can focus intensely during the registration process on their past grades, how they are doing this semester, and the potential "what-ifs" that may occur if they pass with a low grade, fail a course, or do not get into their desired graduate program. These students benefit from continual support and conversations to reassure them of the potential pitfalls of forecasting "what-if/worst case scenario" before it actually occurs.

That said, advisors need to set boundaries with their advisees in that they will not be available on a very regular basis to discuss all of the scenarios and hand-wringing that can occur. Encourage students to discuss their situation and concerns with their faculty, the college counseling center, and their physician, and if needed, encourage them to advocate for themselves with their health care team if the strategies being used are not effective.

Degree audits and graduation plans can also be a challenge in that they are heavily detailed and can be a challenge for students who will worry over the details of course rotations, delivery modes, and the sequence of pre- and co-requisites. Advisors should stress to the student that it is acceptable and encouraged to have a backup plan, but to have no more than one or two backup plans since there are some unknowns about how the student will do. The best you can do for a student with anxiety or OCD in this situation is to emphasize the desired outcome rather than what will happen on the way to the outcome; put another way, assure the student that you are a support for them and that you will do everything possible to help them get a degree on time.

CAREER ADVISING

Academic advisors play an important role in major and career selection. Academic advisors should discuss the student's major, why they selected their major, and what they want to do with their major. All stakeholders in the college completion puzzle (legislators, employers, students, families, the college itself, etc.) are very much aware of the investment that is put into higher education. Some question the value of the college experience and whether going to college at all is worth it (Friedman, 2019).

Advisors Assist Students with Career Advising

It bears mentioning the difference between career counseling and career advising, since they are notably different and share similarities at the same time. As Virginia Gordon notes in *Career Advising* (2006), "Career advising may be thought of as a less psychologically intensive approach than career counseling. The emphasis is on information and helping students understand the relationships between their educational choices and general career fields rather than how to cope with intense career-related personal concerns" (pp. 11–12). While academic advisors will act in a different capacity than the career development office, they "can assist students in gathering information and providing advice that leads to informed and realistic academically related career planning" (p. 22).

Advisors can and should engage all students in the major selection process and utilize different models for exploring strengths and weaknesses, including appreciative advising (Bloom et al., 2008) and learning-centered theory (Bumbalough et al., 2018). Advisors should utilize various tools from the career development office to assist them in learning about the student's personality, which can then be used to help guide the student in the selection of a major, minor, concentration, and elective courses that all align with their personal, career, and professional goals. For neurodiverse students who may struggle with organizational skills, time management, focus, and slow processing, these conversations may need to take place over a period of time in a shorter format, allowing them to "chunk" the information and process it more effectively. Advisors need to adapt delivery styles to the student over prescriptive approaches and methods.

Students benefit from their involvement with internships, shadowing, field experiences, student teaching, and clinical experiences. Some majors require field work, such as business, engineering, education, nursing, and other allied health fields. While they are sometimes optional, it is hard to debate the value of these experiences that allow students to apply their learning in the workforce and also learn real-life lessons from those in the trenches. Shadowing is a great idea for students who want to observe those in the field to gather whether a given field of study is their ideal place for the future. Shadowing and observation hours may also be required of a student's graduate school aspirations, especially in allied health fields. For example, the Physical Therapist Centralized Application Service lists whether each graduate program requires observation hours. Many schools require supervised hours to be able to apply to the graduate program, with a few requiring 100 hours before applying (Physical Therapist Centralized Application Service, n.d.).

The involvement of neurodiverse students in their field and applied experiences can be challenging, and advisors can assist them before, during, and after their experiences. It is worth noting that most experiences in the field are supervised by a faculty member. For accredited programs, this is almost a guarantee given that the accrediting agency (CSWE for social work, CAEP for education, etc.) has strict requirements regarding the experiences that students must take in order to be able to sit for a state licensure exam. If known in advance, advisors could have a conversation with the faculty member in charge of the experiences to give them some background information that can assist the faculty supervisor. A regularly scheduled conference with accessibility services, the faculty supervisor, career services, and the student may be beneficial to set expectations and have a regularly scheduled check-in to discuss the student's progress and experience.

PROBATION, SUSPENSION, AND DISMISSAL ISSUES

Neurodiverse students experience higher rates of class withdrawals and academic probation rates than their neurotypical peers. For some neurodivergent

students, if their poor performance leads to a committee review for probation and suspension appeals, it may be a good idea to have someone from
the accessibility/disability services office on the committee to advocate for
students who have signed releases to have the office discuss their situation
with other college personnel as needed. Neurodiverse students should be
held to the same academic standards as all students at their colleges, but it is
worth considering, as with any probation or suspension appeal, evidence for
extenuating circumstances.

If there is no ability to expand the person(s) who consider the appeals, I
recommend a few strategies. First, if you have an advisee who you know has
challenges with a neurodiverse condition, seek their permission to advocate
on their behalf to appropriate college personnel. I do not recommend sharing
sensitive information from the student without their permission, but if they
do consent, that would be helpful in having the review committee at least
consider it.

Second, if the student is afforded the opportunity to appeal the probation,
suspension, or dismissal action, encourage the student to share their condition
and their challenges in their letter (to the extent they feel comfortable). Your
advisee may not feel that they would want to share such information with
upper-level administrators or other personnel on campus. If this is the case,
advise them that any discussions with the committee should be considered
confidential and that they would not share the discussions or results of their
review with any individuals who do not have a legitimate need to know under
FERPA.

Third, as I recommend later in this chapter regarding additional advice for
advisors, be an advocate for neurodiverse students on your campus by sharing
research, news articles, policy guidance, and other resources on serving all
students with disabilities. This can be done in general to the campus community through presentations to an advising council, advising center newsletters,
individual meetings with campus personnel, and lunch meetings. Advocacy
can be done on the individual, group, and community level, and all are recommended for maximum campus impact.

FURTHER DIRECTIONS IN RESEARCH AND PRACTICE

In looking at the connection between academic advising and the needs of neurodiverse students, it has become readily apparent that while this chapter is a
positive step forward, additional work is needed in research and professional
practice. Additional research needed includes, but is not limited to: advisors'
understanding and acceptance of a worldview that sees neurological differ-

ences from a difference lens rather than a deficit lens; faculty and staff advisors' comfort level with understanding the needs of students with all kinds of disabilities; and the experiences of neurodiverse students with the advising function. Griffin and Pollak (2009) note in their study that neurodiverse students either saw themselves from a "difference" or "medical/deficit" perspective, an issue of self-efficacy that can be addressed in the short and long term through advising approaches influenced by positive psychology and appreciative inquiry. Some of these advising approaches include academic coaching (McClellan, 2013; McClellan & Moser, 2011), appreciative advising (Bloom, Hutson, & He, 2008; Bloom & Martin, 2002; Habley & Bloom, 2007), advising informed by self-authorship theory (Schulenberg, 2013), and motivational interviewing (Hughey & Pettay, 2013), among others.

Little collaboration exists between professional organizations that serve college students, faculty, and staff. Some of them that could easily collaborate to create powerful and dynamic programming and training on academic advising needs for neurodiverse students include NACADA, the National Association of Colleges and Employers (NACE), American College Personnel Association (ACPA), National Association of Student Personnel Administrators (NASPA), and the Association on Higher Education and Disability (AHEAD). As a long-standing member of NACADA and other higher education professional organizations, it seems that most of each organization's programming is delivered to fit a narrow need for those individuals who work in disability services (AHEAD), advising (NACADA), career services (NACE), student affairs (ACPA/NASPA), or other areas, but very little intentional programming has been developed and offered to individuals that crosses these professional areas. For example, AHEAD, NACE, and NACADA could collaborate together on a pre-conference session, a webinar series, or journal articles on how colleges can more effectively meet the career development and career advising needs of neurodiverse students. Usually the answers to each of these vexing issues has been done in a vacuum by each professional organization, but the community of practice has not done as well as it should in collaborating to help lift and broaden the knowledge base of faculty, staff, and administrators.

ADVISORS AS ALLIES

Advisors can play a role in educating neurotypical students about their neurodiverse peers. They are not to be stigmatized. Rather, their differences can be celebrated as part of the larger approach to diversity. Griffin and Pollak (2009) note, "Neurodiversity is both a concept and a civil rights movement.

. . . The concept of neurodiversity defines atypical neurological development as a normal human difference that should be tolerated and respected in the same way as other human differences" (p. 25).

Being an ally for emerging diverse identities is important. The need for courageous advisors and college personnel to advocate for neurodiverse students supports the creation of an inclusive and welcoming environment for all. As Mara Sapon-Shevin (2007) argues in *Widening the Circle: The Power of Inclusive Classrooms*, "Inclusion means asking about access. . . . Inclusion means valuing multiple forms of communication. . . . Inclusion is about structuring our classrooms so that typical hierarchies of 'smartness' are broken down and replaced with an understanding that there are many ways to be smart. . . . Most important, inclusion means engaging all members of the school community in explicit discussions of the value of inclusiveness" (pp. 14–16).

How can advisors become allies? Apply the tenets of Universal Design for Learning in the way we think about our neurodiverse students: produce materials in the advising office that are designed for multiple intelligences; consider the student's individual differences in how you conduct the advising meeting, how you contact students (email, phone, videoconferencing, social media platforms, etc.), and how you apply coaching strategies. Apply the strategies discussed in this chapter, and also bring up these issues regarding neurodiversity on your campus in an advising council, faculty senate, or other relevant committees. Get involved with your professional organization (ACPA, NACADA, NACE, etc.), and advocate for the inclusion of students, staff, and faculty with disabilities.

CONCLUSION

I end with a personal note: At the time of this writing, my wife and I have one precious son who is a little more than 3 years old. During the time I was writing this chapter, he was diagnosed with high-functioning autism with symptoms that align with Asperger's. While my wife and I were not very surprised with the diagnosis, it was a pivotal moment in our family's history. I found myself worrying about our son's future with a label and how he would be treated in school, at work, with friends, and how he would perform at school. He is fortunate to have a great preschool, resources, and advocates around him who believe in his future. He is also fortunate to be growing up in this time when students with ASD, ADHD, dyslexia, dysgraphia, and traumatic brain injuries, among others, are becoming less stigmatized and are seen more as those who have differences rather than being someone who is "less than."

That said, while education should be one of America's most inclusive environments for those with differences, we are not yet to a place of true acceptance and inclusion. Receiving a diagnosis and years of treatment can be incredibly frustrating and expensive, and do cause barriers to success in college and in life. However, my sincere hope is that readers of this chapter and book will apply the approaches described, see neurodiverse students as individuals with dignity and worth, and believe that they are worth extra effort to learn how they operate in the world and how we can align our practices to remove all barriers to their success.

My boy is sweet, smart, caring, and empathic. I see the best of humanity in him and hope that he never loses those traits. I trust that anyone reading this would see that in children of your own, family members, and the college students who you serve. We deserve the best from each other, especially those who have differences and challenges. My dream is that academic advisors and the college ecosystem will move from tolerance not just to acceptance but also to a deeper level of understanding. As Jefferson Fish (2014) argues, "It is possible to tolerate or accept someone without understanding him or her, and the same goes for tolerating or accepting a different culture. And the converse is also true." May this be deep in your hearts, as well as in the heart of the lucky and special person who will be my son's future college academic advisor.

Campus Essentials for High Impact

- *Identify an ally in campus service offices.* Find professionals who are sensitive to neurodiverse students and are willing to learn and expand their knowledge base on neurodiversity and offer to collaborate with them on programming.
- *Redesign FYE and gateway courses.* Guide campus discussions of UDL and create activities that support skill-building for neurodiverse students.
- *Be an advocate or ally for neurodiverse students.* Share research, news articles, policy guidance, and other resources on serving students with disabilities.
- *Initiate collaboration in professional organizations.* Assist in fostering a dialogue between organizations on behalf of neurodiverse students.

REFERENCES

Achieving the Dream (n.d.). *Why join ATD?* https://www.achievingthedream.org/why-join-atd

Astin, A. W. (1993). *What matters in college? Four critical years revisited.* San Francisco: Jossey-Bass.

Bloom, J., & Martin, N. A. (2002, August 29). Incorporating appreciative inquiry into academic advising. *The Mentor: An Academic Advising Journal, 4*(3). psu.edu/dus/mentor/020829jb.htm

Bloom, J. L., Hutson, B. L., & He, Y. (2008). *The appreciative advising revolution.* Stipes Publishing.

Blume, H. (1998, September). Neurodiversity: On the neurological underpinnings of geekdom. *The Atlantic.* https://www.theatlantic.com/magazine/archive/1998/09/neurodiversity/305909

Bumbalough, M. N., Johns, S., & Sosanko, A. (2018, December). Proactive approaches for academic advisors supporting students with autism. *Academic Advising Today, 41*(4). https://nacada.ksu.edu/Resources/Academic-Advising-Today/View-Articles/Proactive-Approaches-for-Academic-Advisors-Supporting-Students-with-Autism.aspx.

Case Western Reserve University. (n.d.). *Second year institute: About the program.* https://case.edu/studentlife/activities/leadership-development/second-year-institute

Complete College America. (n.d.). *15 to finish.* https://completecollege.org/strategy/15-to-finish

Fish, J. M. (2014). Tolerance, acceptance, understanding. *Psychology Today.* http://www.psychologytoday.com/blog/looking-in-the-cultural-mirror/201402/tolerance-acceptance-understanding

Fox, J. R., & Martin, H. E. (Eds.). (2017). *Academic advising and the first college year.* University of South Carolina, National Resource Center for the First-Year Experience and Students in Transition; and NACADA: The Global Community for Academic Advising.

Friedman, Z. (2019, June 13). Is college worth it? *Forbes.* https://www.forbes.com/sites/zackfriedman/2019/06/13/is-college-worth-it/#40d3c56b778d

Gardner, H. (1983). *Frames of mind: The theory of multiple intelligences.* Basic Books.

Gordon, V. N. (2006). *Career advising: An academic advisor's guide.* Jossey-Bass.

Gose, B. (2016). How one college helps students with learning disabilities find their way. *Chronicle of Higher Education.*

Griffin, E., & Pollak, D. (2009). Student experiences of neurodiversity in higher education: Insights from the BRAINHE Project. *Dyslexia, 15*, 23–41. DOI: 10.1002/dys

Habley, W. R., & Bloom, J. L. (2007). Giving advice that makes a difference. In G. L. Kramer (Ed.), *Fostering student success in the campus community* (pp. 171–192). Jossey-Bass.

Harris, A. (2019, Aug. 15). Alaska still hasn't saved its universities. *The Atlantic.* https://www.theatlantic.com/education/archive/2019/08/alaskas-higher-education-system-still-trouble/596191

Houman, K. M., & Stapley, J. C. (2013). The college experience for students with chronic illness: Implications for academic advising. *NACADA Journal, 33*(1), 61–70.

Hughey, J., & Pettay, R. (2013). Motivational interviewing: Helping advisors initiate change in student behaviors. In J. K. Drake, P. Jordan, & M. A. Miller (Eds.), *Academic advising approaches: Strategies that teach students to make the most of college* (pp. 67–82). Jossey-Bass.

Hunter, M. S., Tobolowsky, B. F., & Gardner, J. N. (2010). *Helping sophomores succeed: Understanding and improving the second year experience.* Jossey-Bass.

Koch, A. K., & Pistilli, M. D. (n.d.). *Analytics and gateway courses: Understanding and overcoming roadblocks to college completion.* https://www.insidehighered.com/sites/default/server_files/files/Analytics%20and%20Gateway%20Courses%20PPt.pdf

Kuh, G. D., Kinzie, J., Buckley, J. A., Bridges, B. K., & Hayek, J. C. (2006). *What matters to student success: A review of the literature.* National Postsecondary Education Cooperative. https://nces.ed.gov/npec/pdf/Kuh_Team_Report.pdf

Mader, J., & Butrymowicz, S. (2017, November 11). The vast majority of students with disabilities don't get a college degree. *The Hechinger Report.* https://hechingerreport.org/vast-majority-students-disabilities-dont-get-college-degree

McClellan, J. (2013). Advising as coaching. In J. K. Drake, P. Jordan, & M. A. Miller (Eds.), *Academic advising approaches: Strategies that teach students to make the most of college* (pp. 159–179). Jossey-Bass.

McClellan, J., & Moser, C. (2011). A practical approach to advising as coaching. http://www.nacada.ksu.edu/Resources/Clearinghouse/View-Articles/Advising-as-coaching.aspx

Milliken, K. (2017). *PlAyDHD.* Bookbaby.

Mu, L., & Fosnacht, K. (2016, April 8). *Effective advising: How academic advising influences student learning outcomes in different institutional contexts.* Presented at the annual meeting of the American Educational Research Association, Washington, DC. http://nsse.indiana.edu/pdf/presentations/2016/AERA_2016_Mu_Fosnacht_paper.pdf

Mu, L., & Fosnacht, K. (2019). Effective advising: How academic advising influences student learning outcomes in different institutional contexts. *Journal of Higher Education, 42*(4), 1283–1307.

National Survey of Student Engagement. (2005). *Student engagement: Exploring different dimensions of student engagement.* Indiana University Center for Postsecondary Research.

Nutt, C. L. (2003). Student retention and persistence. *Academic Advising Today, 26*(1). https://nacada.ksu.edu/Resources/Academic-Advising-Today/View-Articles/Student-Retention-and-Persistence.aspx

Oslund, C. (2014). *Supporting college and university students with invisible disabilities.* Jessica Kingsley Publishers.

Pearson, C. (2013, May 20). DSM-5 changes: What parents need to know about the first major revision in nearly 20 years. *Huffington Post.* https://www.huffpost.com/entry/dsm5-changes-what-parents-need-to-know_n_3294413

Physical Therapist Centralized Application Service. (n.d.). *2019–20 Physical Therapy Observation Hours.* http://aptaapps.apta.org/ptcas/observationhours.aspx

Policy Matters Ohio. (2019, May 10). *Budget bite: Public higher education.* https://www.policymattersohio.org/research-policy/quality-ohio/education-training/higher-education/budget-bite-public-higher-education

Ramos, B., & Vallandingham, D. (1997). *Advising students with disabilities* (Monograph No. 5). NACADA: The Global Community for Academic Advising.

Sanford, C., Newman, L., Wagner, M., Cameto, R., Knokey, A.-M., & Shaver, D. (2011). *The post–high school outcomes of young adults with disabilities up to 6 years after high school.* Key findings from the National Longitudinal Transition Study-2 (NLTS2) (NCSER 2011-3004). SRI International.

Sapon-Shevin, M. (2007). *Widening the circle: The power of inclusive classrooms.* Beacon Press.

Schulenberg, J. K. (2013). Academic advising informed by self-authorship theory. In J. K. Drake, P. Jordan, & M. A. Miller (Eds.), *Academic advising approaches: Strategies that teach students to make the most of college* (pp. 121–136). Jossey-Bass.

Schwarz, P. (2006). *From disability to possibility: The power of inclusive classrooms.* Heinemann.

Shearer, C. B. (2019). A detailed neuroscientific framework for the multiple intelligences: Describing the neural component for specific skill units within each intelligence. *International Journal of Psychological Studies, 11*(3), 1–26.

Vance, M. L., & Bridges, L. (Eds.). (2009). *Advising students with disabilities: Striving for universal success* (2nd ed.). NACADA: The Global Community for Academic Advising.

Yes We Must (n.d.). *About the Yes We Must Coalition.* https://yeswemustcoalition.org/about

Chapter 3: Campus Spotlight

Beacon College, Leesburg, Florida

Robert Detwiler

Our Mission: Beacon College was founded in 1989 and was America's first college devoted to serving and teaching students with learning differences (Beacon College, n.d.a). The college boasts an 83% 4-year graduation rate, far above the 38% reported in the National Longitudinal Transition Study-2 (Sanford et al., 2011).

Source: Beacon College

Navigator PREP is offered to incoming Beacon College students and any neurodiverse high school student seeking to prepare in advance for the transition between high school and college. Program fees apply, and the program is delivered entirely online over a 3-, 6- or 9-month period.

Parent Inclusion: While most colleges are hesitant to include parents and supporters in its program design and delivery, Beacon College intentionally includes parents in helping their student successfully transition to college. In addition, parent testimonials on Beacon's website attest to the importance the program has had on them in alleviating their anxiety about their child going to college and whether they would be successful.

Navigator PREP focuses on six areas:

1. Assessments
2. Student contacts
3. Notes
4. Parent contacts
5. Webinars
6. Newsletters

NAVIGATOR PREP PROCESS

Assessment: Starts with an assessment questionnaire that "helps identify student strengths and weaknesses across executive functioning, social, emotional regulation, and independent living skill domains" (Beacon College, n.d.b).

Transition Counselor Engagement: Students in the program interact with their transition counselor on a regular basis and have different topics to tackle each month while they are in the program.

Parent Webinar Meetings: Parents have regular webinar meetings with the transition counselor to assist them in building knowledge and self-efficacy with helping their child in the program and in their senior year while getting ready for the college transition.

Transition Summary Notes: Beacon also sends along detailed summary notes after each webinar meeting and records each meeting in case family members or other support individuals are not able to attend a webinar meeting.

Monthly Thematic Newsletters: Sent to students and families addressing topics such as assistive technology and campus safety (Beacon College, n.d.b).

A Navigator PREP video is available at https://www.beaconcollege.edu/admissions/navigator-prep.

REFERENCES

Beacon College. (n.d.a). *About Beacon College.* https://www.beaconcollege.edu/about-beacon-college

Beacon College. (n.d.b). *Navigator PREP Program highlights.* https://www.beacon-college.edu/admissions/navigator-prep/navigator-prep-program-highlights

Sanford, C., Newman, L., Wagner, M., Cameto, R., Knokey, A.-M., & Shaver, D. (2011). *The post–high school outcomes of young adults with disabilities up to 6 years after high school.* Key findings from the National Longitudinal Transition Study-2 (NLTS2) (NCSER 2011-3004). SRI International.

Chapter Four

Welcoming Spaces for Learning

Stacey Blackwell, Amanda Haberstroh, and Anna Sandberg

As institutions of higher education experience an increase in neurodiversity on campus, it is a pedagogical and ethical imperative that we turn our attention to the physical environment in which students learn, live, and prepare for their futures. When considering design, there are multiple levels of inclusion: exclusive neurotypical spaces, ADA-compliant spaces (minimal inclusivity), Universal Design for Learning (UDL) spaces, and neurodiverse spaces. The first is unacceptable in an educational environment that values equity, and the last is difficult to achieve within the constraints most higher education professionals face when designing learning spaces. Although a fully neurodiverse space may not be possible due to budgetary restrictions, unalterable physical elements of the space, and/or other challenges, higher education professionals should aim to incorporate as many neurodiverse design elements as possible into their plans, ideally falling somewhere between a UDL space and a fully neurodiverse space. The context of space, design, and the ways theoretical learning frameworks influence key design elements are important for higher education leaders to explore. Examining space as a mechanism for support and its beneficial impact when integrated into post-secondary learning environments is imperative for the success of all students, especially those identifying as neurodiverse.

UNDERSTANDING THE EFFECTS OF SPACE

As higher education practitioners consider the campus environment, the objective of any design should be to maximize the extent to which a learning space enhances the pedagogy used within it and supports students' diverse needs and ways of engaging in learning activities. Designers and educators should focus on changing the space, not trying to change the learner. This principle is reflected in the Universal Design for Learning approach, which "ensures a model is not based primarily on changing, or 'fixing,' student behavior but creating educational environments that are respondent and accessible to a variety of learning needs and cognitive styles" (Sarrett, 2018, p. 680). As instruction continues to expand to incorporate more of the Universal Design for Learning guidelines, the learning environments where instruction takes place become increasingly important as a facilitator for absorbing the delivered material (Rappolt-Schlichtmann & Daley, 2013; Siegel & Claydon, 2016).

This chapter will address ways designers and higher education administrators should consider neurodiverse learners in their design of learning spaces. Utilizing Universal Design for Learning, the ASPECTSS model, and other frameworks on neurodiverse student needs and preferences, we will discuss the impact of effective (and ineffective) spaces on the students who use them, as well as offer advice on how to translate the theoretical information presented by researchers into practical implementation in learning spaces on campus. We will also discuss potential collaborators in redesign projects. In addition, the chapter focuses on smaller projects, such as individual centers and buildings, to examine how these design principles can translate into discrete projects and therefore be more quickly and easily implemented than an entire campus master plan. It will use learning spaces, such as libraries, classrooms, and learning centers, as an example for implementation as a case study, because these spaces are often multipurpose and involve a vast diversity of needs, involving both pedagogical decisions and social considerations, as well as typical design restrictions, and therefore require careful consideration and intentional decision-making.

IMPACTS ON STUDENT AFFECT

Although UDL and other concepts for the design of physical space provide tangible and specific criteria for creating effective neurodiverse spaces, universities must also aim to address less tangible aspects, particularly the ways redesigned spaces nurture a sense of belonging for all students and adapt to their specific needs and preferences.

The first step is to reduce the stigma surrounding neurodiversity and to address the siloed learning spaces on campus that are designed exclusively for either neurotypical or atypical students. By creating separate spaces for specific student populations, students are often faced with outing themselves to both space gatekeepers and their peers in order to gain access or utilize them. In creating a campus community that accepts neurodiversity in both words and deeds, universities must consider designs that create open and collaborative learning spaces for a diverse student body that best meets their differing needs and preferences, while also reducing the stress of "outing" oneself (Sarrett, 2018). Rather than focusing primarily on the needs of neuro-typical students, newly redesigned spaces should consider boundary-crossing and flexibility as some of the most important elements. By creating learning spaces with multi-functionality that allow students to seamlessly cross boundaries between activities, students can also "transfer and use their skills and knowledge in a variety of contexts" without having to access separate spaces or locations (Kersh, 2015, p. 845). This not only addresses the functionality of the space but also allows students to access "a continuum of experiences and interaction with resources, technologies and people" within one location (Watson, 2013, p. 145). Creating adaptable and flexible spaces may also relate to the ways others use them, including offering varied formats for instruction (Sarrett, 2018) or activities within those spaces to model possible usage to students. While it may not be feasible to create a perfectly accommodating space that meets the idiosyncratic needs for all students at once (Kanakri et al., 2017), it is important to consider whether the current design allows for enough adaptation to meet the needs of most students regardless of ability or needs (Sarrett, 2018).

Creating flexible spaces and modeling possible usage to students further enable them to exercise agency within their learning spaces. Because students are usually aware of their own learning preferences (Griffin & Pollak, 2009), learners should be presented with a variety of spaces, technologies, and services that enable them to make choices regarding their own preferences (Kersh, 2015; Watson, 2013). Additionally, designers and staff should consider ways to keep thresholds of entry low in order for students to browse space usage and services prior to making a commitment to join or utilize services or technologies themselves (Schendel et al., 2013). Strategies for doing so may include a reduction in gatekeeping to enter spaces, the implementation of technology that can be used without extensive prior training or demonstrations, or the ability for students to observe how a service or activity works prior to joining.

Woven throughout these considerations is the creation of flexible spaces that allow for both collaborative and individual learning. While some learners may prefer quiet spaces such as sensory rooms or escape spaces, many students increasingly seek collaborative spaces on campus that allow for small and large group work with their peers (Beckers et al., 2016). Desires for collaborative space fall along a spectrum from purely individual to purely collaborative spaces, so it is important to plan for learning spaces that allow for both, alongside any preferences that may fall in between, including those students who prefer to work individually within a collaborative space surrounded by others, which helps to create a sense of community and focused environment for them without peer interaction (Beckers et al., 2016). Learning spaces designed to meet diverse student needs in today's environment, crossing physical and intangible boundaries and intersecting various student populations, necessitate an element of flexibility in which students can participate in and take advantage of a variety of environments within a space or building, the development of a collaborative community for students to experience, and the technology to make all this possible (Watson, 2013).

DESIGN

Design principles and guidelines for neurodiverse spaces exist, and in the ideal situation, an entire campus would be redesigned with the needs of neurodiverse students, faculty, and staff at the forefront of space-planning decision-making. The reality of higher education is, however, that most institutions are retrofitting spaces that already exist or are redesigning their physical environments in stages and pieces. These spaces are often designed by specific teams within the institution, and there may not be a larger master plan that guides the design.

Universal Design for Learning

Universal Design for Learning provides a clear framework for instruction to ensure that in the educational environment, students of all learning abilities have an opportunity to receive instructional material and to comprehend it in a way that facilitates overall learning. As many academics are aware, however, it is not only the didactic instruction that is challenged by neurodiversity. The physical requirements of some instructional atmospheres (such as physically moving into classroom groups) can pose barriers to learning. Universal Design was first formally defined by a "working group of architects, product designers, engineers, and environmental design researchers" who "collaborated to establish the . . . Principles of Universal Design to guide a wide range of design disciplines including environments, products, and communications" (Connell et al., 2008, p. 97). The working group from North Carolina State University determined that these principles should serve as a guideline for those who are designing spaces, with the hopes that the design would support accessibility as a matter of course rather than as a retrofitting (Story, 1998). The seven principles identified by this group are:

1. Equitable Use: The design is useful and marketable to people with diverse abilities.
2. Flexibility in Use: The design accommodates a wide range of individual preferences and abilities.
3. Simple and Intuitive Use: Use of the design is easy to understand, regardless of the user's experience, knowledge, language skills, or current concentration level.
4. Perceptible Information: The design communicates necessary information effectively to the user, regardless of ambient conditions or the user's sensory abilities.
5. Tolerance for Error: The design minimizes hazards and the adverse consequences of accidental or unintended actions.
6. Low Physical Effort: The design can be used efficiently and comfortably and with a minimum of fatigue.
7. Size and Space for Approach and Use: Appropriate size and space is provided for approach, reach, manipulation, and use regardless of user's body size, posture, or mobility. (Connell et al., 2008, p. 97)

When designers take these principles into consideration at the outset of envisioning a space, then it is possible to create a truly welcoming space. Integration of UDL is ultimately intended to be less noticeable and taken as an aesthetic preexisting feature of a given space (Story, 1998). Certainly, a benefit to this aesthetic quality of the design demonstrates the welcoming nature of the space—all abilities, all neurodiversities are welcome in this space. At times, even unexpected benefits arise, such as the increased usability of a space for individuals who do not present with any physical limitation or neurodivergence. For instance, designing sidewalk spaces to include a dip at an intersection or in front of a storefront not only assists those in wheelchairs, but also those who are pushing strollers or other wheeled items (Damiani & Harbour, 2015; Story, 1998). Additionally, spaces that are designed to block certain stimuli "are good for people who are hypersensitive to visual and acoustical stimuli and for people who are hyposensitive to tactile stimuli" (Cassidy, 2018, p. 22). UDL can facilitate a welcoming environment in any space, and it does not limit or dictate those who are welcome.

When thinking of the potential users of a given space, it is important to consider all users and not only those who present with physical or learning limitations; however, space designers must not minimize challenges and barriers that may still exist for those with disabilities. Rappolt-Schlichtmann and Daley (2013) highlight that within UDL, "disability is understood as an artifact of limitations of the designed environment" and "is not situated within the person, but rather in the interaction between the person and the environment" (p. 307). Therefore, it is the responsibility of the physical environment (and its designers) to allow access for all. Speaking more directly on the design spaces that exist in museums, Rappolt-Schlichtmann and Daley found in their 2013 report that people experienced difficulty with design because the design of the space did not adequately anticipate the needs of the potential user. Museums represent an excellent foil for an academic institution. Both are spaces where it can be assumed that, regardless of ability, all are welcome. Users of these spaces, however, share different experiences, particularly in academic settings where even ADA compliance cannot be taken for granted. For example, in one university library, users pointed out that the signage and navigability of the library space were simply a barrier in and of themselves (Pionke, 2017).

When these barriers present themselves, they not only make the space unwelcoming but also may force the user into a position where they have to identify their disability when they otherwise would not have. While this may not seem problematic to those who are not disabled, users may have to face potential judgment where they have to prove that their disability does in fact require that a need be met. In the academic environment in particular, "students . . . fear that instructors assume that, rather than truly needing support, students are lazy or somehow faking their disability" (Chiang, 2019, p. 3). Spaces that put students into a position of self-reporting when they are not comfortable to do so are not welcoming and may be perceived as threatening, thereby discouraging students from utilizing the space entirely. Designers must consider how to create spaces, and users must decide how to operate within them, in ways that allow for privacy without forcing students to identify as neurodiverse. There is a need for balance between creating spaces of safety and community and ostracizing or outing neurodiverse students within the larger student population.

Designs that place neurodiverse spaces in separate areas that require travel through public, highly visible spaces put students' neurodiversity on display and may therefore discourage students from using them. At one institution, for example, the Office of Disability Services was located within the larger structure of the Learning Center. While this setup alone was not necessarily problematic, the sequencing and workflow of the space forced students to publicly identify themselves immediately upon entrance and inform the student staff at the front desk of the reason for their visit to the center. After checking in, students would then walk through the tutoring floor, past the offices for academic coaching and Learning Center staff, and enter a hallway that led to the Disability Services offices. Even if students in the area did not hear the student's reason for being in the space, it became clear as the students entered the hallway marked and used exclusively for Disability Services. Such forced identification does not allow for student agency, discretion, or safety. Spaces that house services for neurodiverse students should be located in an area that is easy to navigate but discreet so that students may choose when and to whom to identify their neurodivergence.

Sensory Design Theory

In addition to considering Universal Design to create spaces that are accessible across abilities, designers must consider Sensory Design Theory when developing spaces that will serve the needs of a neurodiverse student population. This theory "stipulates that favorably altering the sensory environment can be conducive to positive and constructive autistic behavior, particularly in learning environments" (Mostafa, 2014, p. 145). Sensory Design Theory focuses on not only the functional use of space but also the users' sensory experience within it, and provides a practical framework for creating spaces that increase attention span and response time, and improve behavioral temperament, as demonstrated through preliminary empirical support (Mostafa, 2014).

Kanakri et al. (2017) propose that Sensory Design Theory can be applied to the design of neurodiverse spaces through careful understanding of the needs of individuals with autism and how to favorably design spaces and environments conducive to their learning preferences. Neurotypical spaces are most often defined and sequenced by function, locating similar services and activities near one another. Neurodiverse-friendly spaces, on the other hand, sequence spaces with attention to sensory inputs and transitions between different types of sensory experiences. Kanakri et al. (2017) explains, "Differences in processing can lead to individuals with autism being overwhelmed by sensory inputs, which further encumbers coordination and autonomous control, disrupting routes of prediction and anticipatory control" (p. 848). Thus, "individuals with autism report frustration, annoyance, and physical discomfort as frequent outcomes" when sensory inputs are not accounted for in design and therefore lead to what Howe and Stagg (2016) refer to as "problematic environments" (Kanakri et al., 2017, p. 850).

Autism ASPECTSS Design Index

Among the design principles for neurodiverse spaces, the ASPECTSS model (Mostafa, 2014) offers a particularly promising one, with its specific, practical, and deliberate applications in an attempt to be generalizable to a variety of spaces. Mostafa (2014) developed the Autism ASPECTSS Design Index to combine the principles of Universal Design with Sensory Design Theory in an effort to direct the creation of neurodiverse spaces. While neurodiversity includes more conditions than autism alone, we are using the framework here because students with autism are uniquely impacted by sensory inputs, and, as with Universal Design, the creation of a space that would enhance the learning experience of students with autism would benefit all students. ASPECTSS provides a useful framework for creating neurodiverse learning spaces.

The Autism ASPECTSS Design Index provides framework for designers to consider the following elements when designing spaces for individuals with autism: **A**coustics, **SP**atial Sequencing, **E**scape Space, **C**ompartmentalization, **T**ransition Zones, **S**ensory Zoning, and **S**afety (Mostafa, 2014, pp. 147–148). The ASPECTSS elements create a space in which sensory stimuli are organized, spaces are sequenced and compartmentalized by both function and sensory experience, wayfinding is facilitated, and spaces are created for both escape and transition. Each element informs how designers plan the physical layout of the space, the functions within it, and the ways users will navigate it.

Note: The ASPECTSS elements will be addressed out of their regular order throughout the rest of this chapter to allow for connections to be made between elements.

Auditory

The auditory environment has been a topic of education studies for a long time. Auditory distractions can impact all learners, as evidenced by the common practice of creating quiet spaces in libraries and other academic spaces. In such spaces, noise is generally unwelcome, for neurotypical and neurodiverse learners alike. Kanakri et al. (2017) define *noise* as "the unpleasant sounds that distract the human both physically and physiologically, and that cause pollution in the acoustic environment" (Atmaca et al., 2005), which "is associated with reductions in attention and concentration" (Howe & Stagg, 2016, pp. 850–851). Research by the World Health Organization (2016) also suggests that noise levels can cause psychosomatic effects as well as adversely impact memory, high-frequency sound discrimination, speech functions, and school performance. Acoustics are particularly important in learning space design for individuals with autism, the majority of whom experience auditory hypersensitivity or related sensory differences (Kanakri et al., 2017). Research conducted by Nelson and colleagues (2002) provides specific guidelines for noise levels, noting that sound levels should not exceed 70 dBA, that background noise should remain lower than 35 dBA, and that speaker levels must be at least 15 dB louder than any accompanying background noises.

Compartmentalization

Compartmentalization, another element of the ASPECTSS Design Index, has an added layer of complexity within the current context of learning and workspace design. Based on Mostafa's (2014) model, spaces should clearly delineate "the sensory environment of each activity" (p. 147) so that space function and quality are clear to users. In recent years, both academic and corporate spaces have moved toward open, flexible designs. Kersh (2015) promotes this movement toward unbounded spaces because boundary-crossing allows students to transfer and utilize skills in different contexts within a singular space, which also encourages collaboration and productivity (for some). For neurodiverse learners, however, these open designs may lack the necessary boundaries and markers for wayfinding needed to easily navigate and operate within a space.

Learning spaces must be flexible and adaptable to change with ever-evolving pedagogies and demands for services. At the same time, the functions of each space should be clearly defined and separated. This harmony may be one of the more challenging to achieve within a learning space. Designers must strive to strike a balance between openness, flexibility, and compartmentalization. According to Mostafa (2014), the separations between compartments "need not be harsh, but can be through furniture arrangement, difference in floor covering, difference in level or even through variances in lighting" (p. 147), which should be achievable within an open design as well as within more traditional, static structures. The goal is to design the area so that sensory qualities of each individual space are unique and help to define the function of the space and its boundaries, providing "sensory cues as to what is expected of the user in each space, with minimal ambiguity" (Mostafa, 2014, p. 147). These compartments should include small-group work areas and visual cues for wayfinding through the compartmentalization scheme.

Sensory Zoning

Although compartmentalization of spaces is not unique, the ASPECTSS model also emphasizes the importance of both function and sensory experience in creating learning zones. According to Mostafa (2014), designers must create concepts that include not only functional zoning in an architectural sense but also a space's sensory qualities by "grouping spaces according to their allowable stimulus level, spaces are organized into zones of 'high-stimulus' and 'low stimulus'" (p. 148), which renders special attention to auditory inputs, as described above, as well as visual inputs.

Spatial Sequencing

Once the compartmentalization and sensory environment of the various areas within a space are determined, sequencing between these areas must be carefully considered to enhance navigation and ease transitions between sensory zones. Designers must consider how users will navigate the space. In particular, spaces should be sequenced in a way that is logical in relation to their function and also considerate of the sensory experiences within the space. Mostafa recommends "that areas be organized in a logical order, based on the typical scheduled use of such spaces" and that they "should flow as seamlessly as possible from one activity to the next through one-way circulation whenever possible, with minimal disruption and distraction" (Mostafa, 2014, p. 147). Thus, the function of the space should partially determine the placement of that space.

To further enhance wayfinding, spatial sequencing should be combined with sensory zoning to provide a gradual and clearly defined progression between types of sensory experiences in such a way to aid users in gaining independence and agency (Mostafa, 2014). When the space itself supports students navigating their way through the institution, faculty and staff also experience fewer disruptions in the form of navigational questions, and students experience fewer feelings of confusion, disorientation, and dependence. To support independent wayfinding, color and pattern should be employed in a consistent and meaningful manner, and pictorial language should be displayed with written language; textural signage can also be useful (Mostafa, 2014).

Transition Zones

Often, since institutions tend to retrofit existing spaces more than build new ones, the ways activities in a space interact with one another is not—or sometimes cannot be—considered. In this model, however, it is imperative that the connections between spaces are considered. To help students navigate the difference in sensory zones, designers should include transition zones that help "the user recalibrate their senses as they move from one level of stimulus to the next" (Mostafa, 2014, p. 148). These zones can vary in form, from a small nook, room, or cubicle area to a full sensory room, depending on the space available (Mostafa, 2014). The sensory rooms at the University of Tennessee–Chattanooga (West, 2019), which are part of a larger initiative to create a welcoming campus for neurodiverse students, serve as a strong example of how these spaces can be incorporated into various campus sites.

Escape Space

Learning spaces should also be updated to include areas that allow for "escape," used specifically in the ASPECTSS model, to increase accessibility for individuals with autism. Escape spaces are described as a "respite for the autistic user from the overstimulation found in their environment" (Mostafa, 2014, p. 147). Escape spaces can be added to preexisting structures on a variety of budgets, provided the goal is to remove sensory stimulators from the space that allow the autistic user to feel secure, safe, and able to rest from any overwhelming cognitive, social, or sensory experiences (Mostafa, 2014). Ideally, Mostafa (2014) recommends that "these spaces should provide a neutral sensory environment with minimal stimulation that can be customized by the user to provide the necessary sensory input" (p. 147).

Some institutions of higher learning may be following this advice unintentionally—the use of mobile furniture in libraries or learning commons spaces can allow the neurodiverse user to create private, quiet spaces through simple, unobtrusive means that do not call attention to the user's neurodiversity. For instance, allowing students to move chairs to quiet corners and turn desks so that they are facing blank walls rather than active walkways is one way to provide a simple escape from stimulation (Mostafa, 2014). In more intentionally designed areas, such as a private study space turned into an allocated meditative or quiet space with low lighting and soundproof walls, neurodiverse and neurotypical students alike can find a respite from external or environmental stressors.

These spaces also represent an ideal example of UDL because they support the full range of neurodiversity—from neurotypical students who become overwhelmed by a particular learning situation, to students with anxiety disorders, to students with all manner of sensory disorders. Depending on the design, they may also be able to serve additional roles as prayer rooms or nursing rooms, two private spaces that are often difficult to find on campus. Escape spaces can be used before and after learning activities to help students transition from one activity to another (Mostafa, 2014).

Challenges associated with adding escape spaces to a design are mostly related to safety and management. Since these are private, closed spaces, supervision of their use is challenging, and staff are tasked with determining how to make them available without allowing them to be abused. It is not uncommon for college students to, for example, seek a private place to sleep on campus or to study. These spaces, however, must be intentional, and policies around their use should be designed to make them as available as possible to students who need them without allowing them to be used in ways that would end up excluding the students for whom, and uses for which, they were designed.

Safety

Safety is the last element of the ASPECTSS model, and certainly one of the most important. Spaces must be designed with safety in mind, particularly with the removal of dangerous design items, which can be accomplished through comparatively simple solutions, such as "fittings to protect from hot water and an avoidance of sharp edges and corners" (Mostafa, 2014, p. 148). Other forms of safety are more difficult to achieve, particularly when considering privacy needs. For example, escape spaces should be private areas, but they also cannot be areas that remain outside supervision parameters that would place a student in a compromising or dangerous situation.

One method for ensuring the safety of all students is to consider ways to build what we will refer to here as passive supervision into the design of the space. When staff offices, front/welcome desks, and other areas in which supervisory staff work are located strategically to enable staff to see what is happening throughout the space without having to leave their work area, they are able to supervise the space effectively without causing the students to feel overly monitored. This type of setup enables students to feel ownership and agency within the space, without sacrificing their need for safety and security.

OTHER RELATED FRAMEWORKS

The activities taking place within a space, and their impact on student engagement is another important consideration to learning space design. Wilson (2009) provides a useful model for thinking about the purpose and structure of a space and explains that the "learning space continuum has two types of conditions at its extremities, wholly independent self-directed unstructured learning at one end and structured teacher-led didactic learning environments at the other" (p. 20). The continuum is provided in Figure 4.1 below. In general, learning spaces other than lecture halls fall near the middle-right of the spectrum.

Designers must consider how structured the space should be, considering its impact on student agency, flexibility, and accommodation. Once decisions about structure and flexibility are made, the next consideration is how the space and pedagogies implemented within that space will interact.

Radcliffe's (2008) Pedagogy, Space, Technology (PST) Framework provides a helpful guide to considerations of the connections between pedagogy, space, and technology. The three aspects of the PST Framework are reciprocal in nature, and thus, the desired pedagogy should influence the arrangement and use of the space. Similarly, the way the space is designed may

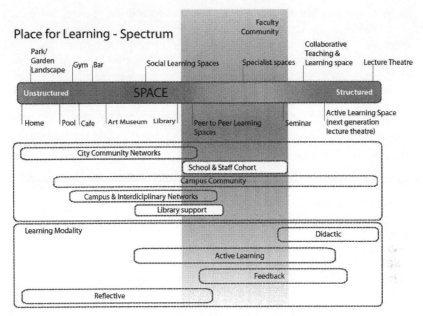

Source: **Wilson's Places for Learning Spectrum (Ellis & Goodyear, 2016)**

constrain or create pedagogical choices. The technology, in a similar way, may impact or be impacted by the pedagogy and space.

The PST Framework becomes particularly important when considering the role of neurodiversity in a learning space. If, for example, the space is designed to enhance collaborative learning and is outfitted with technology for screen sharing, shared writing spaces, and spaces that locate students within close proximity to one another, it would enhance the pedagogy but also pose challenges to students who may find the multiple focal points (multiple screens, writing surfaces, etc.) to be disorienting, or who may find the close proximity to—and forced eye contact with—peers to be uncomfortable. However, Griffin and Pollak (2009) offer encouraging evidence that trends in pedagogical best practices, including "visual and multi-sensory teaching methods" (p. 37), align well with the needs of neurodiverse learners and are gaining popularity among higher education instructors.

Because so many academic institutions reside within decades-old, if not centuries-old, buildings, many learning spaces must be reassessed to determine the extent to which these spaces are welcoming, offer accommodation of all levels of ability and neurodiversity, and integrate new assistive technologies which correlate with pedagogical aims. In their 2016 qualitative study, Siegel and Claydon interviewed instructors who were given access to an Active Learning Center (ALC) where "innovative classroom design and upgraded instructional technology [influenced] University professors' experiences and perspectives of teaching and learning in the classroom" (p. 31). The professors remarked on the connection between their instructional material, the available technology in the ALC, and the very design of the classroom space on their students' ability to learn as well as their enthusiasm to teach (Siegel & Claydon, 2016).

Being able to quickly and effectively rearrange the space to accommodate either of these activities enables a wide range of pedagogies within the space and ensures that the space supports the instructional strategies within it. Ideally, a learning space can accommodate a range of pedagogical activities but will have enough structure to clearly communicate the expectations of student engagement with the space. The following section offers practical tips to apply these theories and frameworks in today's learning spaces, with particular attention to inclusivity and the consideration of students' diverse needs and preferences.

PRACTICAL APPLICATIONS

For most higher education professionals charged with designing or redesigning a space, there are several inherent challenges that could impact choices about space, technology, and pedagogy. Primarily, there is generally limited space across campuses, as college enrollment increases but the physical and geographic boundaries of institutions do not. Including design elements that go beyond the primary use of the space may seem impractical, but as outlined previously, these considerations need to be made to welcome and help all students succeed. When designing spaces within existing structures, which is often the case for institutions of higher education, there will typically be constraints on the extent to which these elements are within the control of the designers. In such situations, it is necessary to remember that improving any element will have positive impacts for neurodiverse learners and that there is value in incorporating as many as possible.

Another challenge of higher education space design is the different types of expertise required to design learning spaces that are effective for all learners and well-suited to the pedagogical activities within the space. Often, spaces are either designed by education professionals who have a strong background in pedagogy and little professional expertise in design, or designed by architects and designers who have significant expertise in space and workplace design but do not necessarily have knowledge of the pedagogies and instructional activities that should inform the design of the space. In an ideal situation, a design team would include educators, disability service professionals, architects, and designers in a collaborative effort to develop spaces that are pedagogically effective, are universally accessible, and take into account the sensory environments created by the design. This section is designed as a guide for design teams and educators to practically apply some of the theories and frameworks above to learning spaces on their campuses with a wide range of budgets and capabilities. A shorter version of these considerations is also offered at the end of this chapter in list form.

Layout

Learning spaces, especially those designed for collaborative work, can become noisy and distracting quite quickly. Open floor layouts are generally favored by designers because they ease supervision and ensure the safety of students, but they often lack elements that enable neurodiverse students to use them comfortably and effectively.

To enhance the pedagogy within the spaces and support neurodiverse learners, designers should consider adaptable and flexible design elements, such as mobile furniture and reconfigurable walls. These elements enable changes in the structure of the space, allowing for flexibility and mobility for student-led activities and more structure and focus for more traditional instructional practices. For example, tables that are configured in a circle facing one another communicate that students will engage with one another, while tables facing forward toward the instructor podium communicate that the focus will be on the instructor. Moveable furniture and design elements can also help to compartmentalize spaces even in the absence of fixed elements.

The key to making such spaces work for neurodiverse learners is to ensure that the function of the space is clearly communicated in its setup, as well as signage (discussed in depth below). Quiet study spaces, for example, should have linguistic and pictorial indicators communicating to students that these are areas in which silence is expected. Seats should face away from one another, and dividers should be available when possible. Collaborative spaces, on the other hand, should have seats that face one another and should be sectioned off from quiet spaces, by either fixed or moveable dividers. Communicating the difference between the function of each space is crucial. Designers may also want to consider the use of textures, colors, and patterns to further enhance the visual communication about the function of a space and its compartmentalization.

It is also important to consider the spatial sequencing of a learning space, as described in the ASPECTSS model (Mostafa, 2014). When organizing spaces, designers may want to consider how and where activities are located in proximity to one another. Large group activities should not take place next to individual study spaces, as their level of noise and activity would be distracting and potentially even distressing. As students move through the learning space, they should ideally move from low-stimulus zones to high-stimulus zones, giving them the opportunity to adjust to the increase in stimuli and to make choices about how much stimulus they want to experience at that time.

When designing a space for neurodiverse learners, transparency and the adaptability of a space must also be balanced with attention to noise control. Noise-reducing retractable walls provide the flexible space use, while also assisting users of a space to block out unnecessary or distracting noises from other areas of a space. Soundproofing materials can also be added to walls and ceilings as unobtrusive design elements that are both functional and aesthetically pleasing. Exposed ceilings may also reduce noise reverberation within a space. To provide for better sensory zoning of a space (Mostafa, 2014), designers must also consider the impact of background noises, such as printers, keyboards, telephones, and video monitors in creating low-stimulus zones and spaces for student use. Low-stimulus and quiet zones should be designed far from frequently opened doors and staff offices that attract a lot of traffic.

Elements of welcoming and gatekeeping are also necessary to consider. A round welcome desk located centrally but near the entrance of a space may help to enable supervision as well as provide an inviting environment for the space. Sarrett (2018) describes how offices should consider any potentially off-putting or exclusionary gate-keeping practices for use of their space, in addition to thresholds for entry and use of their spaces and any activities taking place therein (Schendel et al., 2013).

Aesthetics

Aesthetic design elements can also serve practical purposes in creating neurodiverse learning spaces. The use of glass walls within a space aid in both supervision and noise reduction, although designers should be careful not to overuse them when creating low-stimulus sensory zones or escape spaces (Mostafa, 2014), as they do not prevent or block visual distractions. Similarly, the current use of large windows in space designs can be overly distracting or stimulating for some learners. To strike a better balance between an aesthetically pleasing environment and a welcoming one for neurodiverse learners, designers should consider locating windows above eye level to increase natural light and simultaneously decrease distraction and stimulation (Mostafa, 2014).

Aesthetic and sensory-pleasing elements may also prove particularly useful in the creation of escape spaces, as outlined by Mostafa (2014) in the ASPECTSS model. These may include cushions of various textures, brushes, sandpaper, small tents, blankets, fiber optic lights, and headphones (Mostafa, 2014).

Signage

Signage remains an issue in many publicly used spaces, including higher education learning spaces (Pionke, 2017). The use of signs is a simple gesture that empowers the user to independently determine the direction they wish to go, without requiring them to self-report their disability or neurodiverse need (Sarrett, 2018). Clearly defined pathways and emergency exit signage also ensure the safety of students within a space. As signage is important to creating a welcoming and accommodating space for neurodiverse learners in which they can exercise agency and ownership, designers must consider both the layout and implicit communication of its use through design elements, as well as explicit communication through signs and routes. Particular attention should be paid to issues of wayfinding, marking, route-planning, and contrast levels (Pionke, 2017).

In creating useful signage for all students, designers should consider the best font and size for legibility that is both clear and easy to read from a distance. Signs should also use colors with high contrast (light backgrounds and dark lettering/symbols or vice versa) to assist users with low visual acuity. Illustrations or symbols may also be helpful for dyslexic users or others (such as the use of Braille to assist blind users to independently navigate spaces).

Signage is a particularly easy and low-budget design change for many learning spaces to implement. A recommendation to any group looking to update their signage is to hold a survey or brief meeting with users of all abilities, "as people with mobility disabilities often have greater difficulty navigating spaces, [and] are perhaps more acutely aware of just how poorly spaces and architecture is designed" (Pionke, 2017, p. 53). A specialized focus group or survey of all users will provide insights to the stakeholders who are interested in redesigning a space to be more welcoming of users with all abilities.

Technology

It is also important that learning spaces are outfitted with strong connections to wireless internet, to make tools and programs that may help neurodiverse students navigate and engage in the classroom activities easily available. Assistive and multi-modal technologies should also be made available within learning spaces whenever possible (Griffin & Pollak, 2009). While this chapter focuses on physical space, it is also important to note that Radcliffe's (2008) framework also applies to virtual spaces and that learning support services and institutions of higher education in general should place an emphasis on creating appropriate virtual spaces for neurodiverse learners to engage in coursework, co-curricular activities, and social activities. There is evidence that "autistic students prefer online interactions with campus staff, peers, and each other" (Sarrett, 2018, p. 690). The ability to access assistive and other technologies without being tied to specific physical locations has also been demonstrated as useful in supporting neurodiverse students (Schendel et al., 2013).

Full renovations such as these can be costly, especially for individual units designing their own spaces, and even more costly when investments are made in quality materials that reduce noise and enable flexibility. Sponsorships are available to facilitate space and encourage innovative instruction for all learning abilities. Fairfield University updated 90 campus computer classrooms with technology provided by Apple and furniture supplied by Steelcase Education (Siegel & Claydon, 2016). Apple supplied Apple TVs to replace pull-down projector screens, "provided the entire full-time faculty with iPads, and upgraded the wireless connectivity so that professors and students bringing their own devices to the classroom could easily connect with Internet resources" (Siegel & Claydon, 2016, p. 26). Steelcase Education provided "multiple writing surfaces—whiteboard painted walls, large portable white boards (e.g., Steelcase's Huddle boards 23 x 32), and small portable white boards (e.g., Steelcase's Verb Boards 18 x 23)" (Siegel & Claydon, 2016, p. 26). The portable furniture, including mobile instructor stations, wheeled tables, and rotating chairs, also supplied by Steelcase (Siegel & Claydon, 2016), increased the flexibility of classroom instruction, where students and instructors are no longer required to sit in a static configuration but are able to move instructional materials to suit the needs of their own learning and physical abilities.

When stakeholders of academic spaces insist on accessibility for all users, the result can only be that users of all ability levels (but especially those whose disabilities are often neglected in design) will feel welcome and empowered to exist within the space independently and comfortably. In a space that utilizes Universal Design, the ASPECTSS model, and other theories and frameworks for inclusive learning space design, special features for neurodiverse students will hopefully "go unnoticed because they have been fully integrated into thoughtful design solutions that are used by a full spectrum of the population" (Story, 1998, p. 4). When this occurs, users of accessible spaces are not delineated according to ability. All are welcome to use the space equally. Although efforts to optimize learning spaces for neurodiverse learners may seem daunting and unrealistic when faced with outdated pre-existing structures and firm budgets, many small, immediate changes can be implemented without breaking the bank or requiring lengthy space closures for construction. Many of the helpful solutions offered here can be relatively cost-effective and simple to implement.

CONCLUSIONS

Ultimately, space redesign projects on campus should involve a number of interested and knowledgeable parties who can assist with various aspects of the design and usage. Before, during, and after the redesign process, decision-makers should consider utilizing campus partners to help plan and implement aspects of the redesign. These campus partners may include disability services offices, IT services, libraries, and other academic support offices on campus. By pooling their resources and knowledge about space, technology, and pedagogies, learning spaces can ensure they reach and meet the needs of a diverse student body, including those of neurodiverse students.

Depending on the type of redesign planned or underway, these offices and others can offer a variety of knowledge and impact on the design. For shorter-term, smaller-scale redesigns, Disability Services offices may offer audits on current spaces, as well as advice and input on longer-term overhauls. IT offices can offer input on any technology needs or interests for spaces, as well as offer training and support for installed equipment. Academic support offices and libraries can provide input based on their space design and the needs of learners from both a practical and pedagogical perspective, particularly those who might have undertaken similar redesign projects recently. Designers may also wish to reach out to peer institutions undergoing or completing similar projects for site visits, support, and expertise.

Materials that aid in noise reduction and effective design can be costly, but there are opportunities for institutions to seek grant funding and corporate partnerships to design such spaces. As with Fairfield University, sponsored support is an option (Siegel & Claydon, 2016), in addition to grant-funded space redesign competitions offered by Steelcase (https://www.steelcase.com/discover/information/education/active-learning-center-grant) and the Big 10 Student Design Challenge (https://btsdc.org), which partners with

Herman Miller to encourage student groups to redesign campus spaces for specific purposes.

Balancing the workflow and functionality of a space with the sensory and navigational needs of students in general, and neurodiverse students in particular, is not a simple task. It requires careful planning and consideration of the many ways students (current and future) will use the space and their sensory experiences within it. Ultimately, however, learning spaces designed with attention to students' sensory, emotional, cognitive, instructional, and social needs are spaces that communicate to students that the institution welcomes them and has been planning for their success.

Campus Essentials for High Impact

- *Consider structural and design elements in long-term planning and construction.* When creating multi-use and "unbounded" space (Beckers et al., 2016; Gormley et al., 2016; Radcliffe, 2008), ensure that the space has clearly defined markers and visual cues (such as color and texture changes) built into the environment to enhance wayfinding. Add sound barriers and noise-reducing options (such as soft touch keyboards in computer labs) wherever possible to reduce the amount of ambient noise and distraction in the space.
- *Explore the impact of sensory zoning and transitions areas.* Include gradual transition from areas of high sensory input to low sensory input, and guide the use and positioning of the space in design options (McAllister & Maguire, 2012). Plan for transitions between zones to help students move from one type of space to another (McAllister & Maguire, 2012).
- *Design with the future in mind.* Spaces should be designed with "future-proofing" (Radcliffe, 2008) in mind, accounting for how adaptable the space will be for today's and tomorrow's students.
- *Implement the use of sensory rooms and escape spaces.* Options for low sensory rooms should be added wherever possible (Sarrett, 2018) and escape spaces that include a door, "occupied" sign, and noise-cancelling headphones (Sarrett, 2018).
- *Purchase furniture with adaptation and mobility in mind.* Select furniture that can be adapted to multiple configurations and body types (Petit & Bielavitz, 2013; Schendel et al., 2013).
- *Consider the use of partitions and furniture to alter existing spaces.* Establish new spaces without extensive construction (DeAngelis & Neiman-Deschaaf, 2013).
- *Integrate visual clues for wayfinding.* Include visual identifiers such as graphics and colors on signage in addition to text (McAllister & Maguire, 2012).

- *Anticipate student needs in design elements.* Spaces should have a full suite of intuitive services that students can easily match to their needs (Schendel et al., 2013). Install soundproofing elements such as curtains, wall and ceiling coverings and materials, seating, and flooring to provide quiet spaces (Kanakri et al., 2017). Adjust lighting, particularly the selection of nonfluorescent lights to reduce noise emissions (Friedlander, 2009).

REFERENCES

Atmaca, E., Peker, I., & Altin, A. (2005). Industrial noise and its effects on humans. *Polish Journal of Environmental Studies, 14*(6), 721–726.

Beckers, R., van der Voordt, T., & Dewulf, G. (2016). Learning space preferences of higher education students. *Building and Environment, 104*(C), 243–252. https://doi.org/10.1016/j.buildenv.2016.05.013

Cassidy, M. K. (2018). *Neurodiversity in the workplace: Architecture for autism* (Doctoral dissertation). Available from ProQuest Dissertations & Theses Global database. (Accession Order No. AAT 10991788)

Chiang, E. S. (2019). Disability cultural centers: How colleges can move beyond access to inclusion. *Disability & Society*, 1–6. doi:10.1080/09687599.2019.1679536

Connell, B. R., Jones, M., Mace, R., Mueller, J., Mullick, A., Ostroff, E., Sanford, J., Steinfeld, E., Story, M., & Vanderheiden, G. (2008) What is Universal Design? *The Exceptional Parent, 38*(5), 97.

Damiani, M. L., & Harbour, W. S. (2015). Being the wizard behind the curtain: Teaching experiences of graduate teaching assistants with disabilities at U.S. universities. *Innovative Higher Education, 40*(5), 399–413. doi:10.1077/s10755-015-9326-7

DeAngelis, P., & Neiman-Deschaaf, M. (2013). Learning center: Case study for creating an active library. *Planning for Higher Education Journal, 4*(14), 122–125.

Ellis, R. A., & Goodyear, P. (2016). Models of learning space: Integrating research on space, place and learning in higher education. *Review of Education, 4*(2), 149–191. https://doi.org/10.1002/rev3.3056

Friedlander, D. (2009). Sam comes to school: Including students with autism in your classroom. *The Clearing House, 82*(3), 141–144.

Gormley, C., Glynn, M., Brown, M., & Doyle, J. (2016). Mobile learning spaces for a mobile generation: Redesigning the classroom. *European Conference on e-Learning*, 239–248. http://search.proquest.com/docview/1860071066

Griffin, E., & Pollak, D. (2009). Student experiences of neurodiversity in higher education: Insights from the BRAINHE Project. *Dyslexia, 15*(1), 23–41. https://doi.org/10.1002/dys.383

Howe, F. E. J., & Stagg, S. D. (2016). How sensory experiences affect adolescents with an autistic spectrum condition within the classroom. *Journal of Autism and Developmental Disorders, 46*(5), 1656–1668. https://doi.org/10.1007/s10803-015-2693-1

Kanakri, S. M., Shepley, M., Tassinary, L. G., Varni, J. W., & Fawaz, H. M. (2017). An observational study of classroom acoustical design and repetitive behaviors in children with autism. *Environment and Behavior, 49*(8), 847–873.

Kersh, N. (2015). Rethinking the learning space at work and beyond: The achievement of agency across the boundaries of work-related spaces and environments (Report). *International Review of Education/Internationale Zeitschrift Fur Erziehungswissenschaft/Revue Internationale L'education, 61*(6), 835–851. https://doi.org/10.1007/s11159-015-9529-2

McAllister, K., & Maguire, B. (2012). A design model: The Autism Spectrum Disorder classroom design kit. *British Journal of Special Education, 39*(4), 201–208. https://doi.org/10.1111/1467-8578.12006

Mostafa, M. (2014). Architecture for autism: Autism ASPECTSS in school design. *Archnet-IJAR: International Journal of Architectural Research, 8*(1), 143–158.

Nelson, P., Soli, S., & Seltz, A. (2002). *Classroom acoustics II: Acoustical barriers to learning.* Acoustical Society of America. http://mariobon.com/Corsi/Corso_ASA/ASA_booklet_2.pdf

Petit, J., & Bielavitz, T. (2013). Innovation on a shoestring: High impact space and technology updates in a low-funding environment. In R. G. Carpenter (Ed.), *Cases on higher education spaces: Innovation, collaboration, and technology* (pp. 248–264). Information Science Reference.

Pionke, J. J. (2017). Toward holistic accessibility: Narratives from functionally diverse patrons. *Reference & User Services Quarterly, 57*(1), 48–56.

Radcliffe, D. (2008). *A pedagogy-space-technology (PST) framework for designing and evaluating learning places.* Paper presented at the Learning Spaces in Higher Education: Positive Outcomes by Design, Proceedings of Next Generation Learning Spaces Colloquium, Brisbane, Australia. https://www.ntnu.edu/documents/1283650518/1283655368/A+Pedagogy-Space-+Technology+%28PST%29+Framework+for+Designing+and+Evaluating+Learning+Places/2852951b-7784-49cb-877f-aa4e860740fb

Rappolt-Schlichtmann, G., & Daley, S. G. (2013). Providing access to engagement in learning: The potential of Universal Design for Learning in museum design. *Curator: The Museum Journal, 56*(3), 307–321.

Sarrett, J. C. (2018). Autism and accommodations in higher education: Insights from the autism community. *Journal of Autism and Developmental Disorders, 48*, 679–693.

Schendel, E., Garrison, J., Johnson, P., & Van Orsdel, L. (2013). Making noise in the library: Designing a student learning environment to support a liberal education. In R. G. Carpenter (Ed.), *Cases on higher education spaces: Innovation, collaboration, and technology* (pp. 290–312). Information Science Reference.

Siegel, C., & Claydon, J. (2016). Innovation in higher education: The influence of classroom design and instructional technology. *i-Manager's Journal on School Educational Technology, 12*(2), 24–33.

Story, M. F. (1998) Maximizing usability: The Principles of Universal Design. *Assistive Technology, 10*(1), 4–12. doi:10.1080/10400435.1998.10131955

Watson, L. (Ed.). (2013). *Better library and learning space: Projects, trends, ideas.* Facet.

West, C. (2019, November 26). On the dean's list, with autism: Colleges add autism support services, but they're pricey. *USA Today, The Hechinger Report.* https://www.usatoday.com/story/news/education/2019/11/26/autism-autistic-spectrum-asd-college-student-services-awareness-university-tennessee/4303692002

Wilson, H. (2009) The process of creating learning space. In D. Radcliffe, H. Wilson, D. Powell, & B. Tibbetts (Eds.), *Designing next generation places of learning: Collaboration at the pedagogy–space–technology nexus.* University of Queensland.

World Health Organization. (2016). *Training for health care providers: Children and noise.* https://www.who.int/ceh/capacity/noise.pdf

Chapter 4: Campus Spotlight

Livingston Learning Center, Rutgers University

Stacey Blackwell and Anna Sandberg

Our Mission: Many of the above design elements were integrated in the overhaul of the Livingston Learning Center at Rutgers University–New Brunswick. Prior to the center redesign, the space was primarily an open floor with large, heavy tables and chairs. There were study carrels in the back and a few computers, with printers that were rather loud. Offices were located around the perimeter, removed from the tutoring floor.

Redesign Project: The design team integrated glass walls for office spaces and collaborative rooms off the main floor of the center. The large collaborative room also utilizes retractable dividing walls, which allows the space to be converted into three smaller rooms. The walls are composed of whiteboards, which further increases writing space within these rooms. Designers also implemented several noise-reducing elements in the center, including an open ceiling, thick soundproofed retractable walls, and both permanent and retractable divisions between spaces. All of these elements were chosen both for their functionality in a busy learning space and for flexibility of use.

Chapter Five

Classroom Supports

Cheryl L. Dickter and Joshua A. Burk

As the number of neurodiverse students attending post-secondary institutions increases, colleges and universities need to prepare and respond to student population changes to ensure that these students are supported. While these actions require many facets of the university to respond, one key component is the students' classroom experience. This chapter is designed to first provide an overview of the types of strengths and challenges of neurodiverse learners with several different conditions. Universal Design for Learning (UDL) is an approach to education that provides information in a manner that allows the opportunity for a broad proportion of society (ideally all individuals) to learn information. We describe evidence-based UDL approaches that support learners with several neurodiverse conditions and how these approaches benefit neurodiverse learners. Finally, we conclude by discussing how to move forward with faculty development to implement some of these strategies, along with potential barriers to faculty development. The goal is to offer some specific information and examples so that universities and, more importantly, faculty can implement elements of UDL in the classroom to support neurodivergent learners.

CHALLENGES AND STRENGTHS OF NEURODIVERSE LEARNERS

Autism Spectrum Disorders (ASD)

Autism is a neurodevelopmental disorder associated with social communication and social interaction deficits as well as restricted and repetitive behaviors, interests, or activities (American Psychiatric Association, 2013). The prevalence of autism has increased in the last several decades, likely due to increases in awareness, greater risk factors, and improvements in treatments (Charman, 2002; Fombonne, 2003). It is estimated that 1 in 160 children worldwide (World Health Organization, 2018) and 1 in 59 children in the United States has been diagnosed with Autism Spectrum Disorder (Baio et al., 2018). Below we review several challenges and strengths that autistic individuals may bring to the classroom and then focus on how to support these students through specific pedagogical techniques. Although this section focuses on general challenges and strengths associated with autism, it is important to remember that autism is a spectrum disorder, and therefore not every autistic student will display these characteristics. As autistic author and speaker Stephen Shore says, "If you've met one person with autism, you've met one person with autism" (International Board of Credentialing and Continuing Education Standards, 2018).

Classroom Challenges

Executive function deficits have been reported in children and adults with ASD, including with planning and cognitive flexibility (Hill, 2004). Regarding planning, autistic individuals often experience challenges with tasks and activities that involve planning multiple steps in the future (e.g., Ozonoff & Jensen, 1999). In addition, autistic individuals also often have difficulties in situations in which the rules or the situation at hand changes without warning. That is, autistic individuals perseverate on current rules and are less able to change strategies compared to neurotypical individuals (Hill, 2004). In the classroom, these challenges may lead autistic individuals to have difficulty focusing their attention on a new topic that comes up in a discussion or a lecture. Similarly, a change such as moving from a lecture to a group activity can be more challenging for autistic individuals in the classroom than non-autistic individuals.

Autism is also associated with social impairments that may lead to challenges in the classroom. Persons with autism are thought to have difficulties with theory of mind, which can make it difficult to read social cues such as when a faculty member wants to move on to a different topic or when an instructor or students are frustrated with the amount of questions that a student is asking. Another issue that might arise is the use of jargon, sarcasm, or metaphors, which may be difficult for autistic individuals to understand due to the subtlety of the cues to understand these forms of communication. Autistic individuals also tend to have a deficit recognizing and processing negative and complex emotions (e.g., surprise) (Baron-Cohen et al., 1993; Uljarevic & Hamilton, 2013). Picking up on subtle social cues may be a challenge for autistic individuals, which can lead to problems communicating with faculty or peers. For example, group work that requires students to coordinate with other students in the class and interact in an appropriate manner might be difficult for autistic students when no explicit instructions are given on how to communicate (e.g., whether to text, call, or go to someone's dorm room), or how to divide up the work among the group members, and so on. In addition, because autistic students might avoid eye contact or demonstrate signs of social anxiety, a condition that is often comorbid with autism (White et al., 2009), their peers may think that they are awkward or rude and thus respond poorly to them.

Autistic individuals can experience sensitivity to sensory stimuli in the environment (American Psychiatric Association, 2013). Overstimulation from lighting or noises in the classroom can be distracting and make autistic students uncomfortable, leading to attentional issues or discomfort. Skills such as planning and self-advocacy can be compromised when sensory environments are overstimulating (Adreon & Durocher, 2007). In addition, anxiety can be exasperated by situations involving overstimulation from sensory information in the environment. In these situations, anxiety regulation can be impaired (Adreon & Durocher, 2007), which may lead to challenges with classroom learning and performance in assessment (Shmulsky & Gobbo, 2013).

Classroom Strengths

Autistic students bring strengths to the classroom. Autistic individuals tend to have strong attention to detail in perception and memory (Mottron et al., 2003), which can lead them to be more focused on detailed information they are paying attention to and less distracted by surrounding stimuli than neurotypical individuals (O'Riordan & Plaisted, 2001). Therefore, especially when it comes to a topic in which they are interested, many autistic individuals can concentrate for a long time without getting distracted. In addition, autistic individuals tend to use a bottom-up, analytical problem-solving style that can offer unique contributions to class material. They often are able to assimilate and retain detailed information more easily than most neurotypical people. Autistic students often have advanced memory skills and also tend to be high in sincerity and integrity (Schindler et al., 2015).

UDL Options in the Classroom

The classroom is a place where autistic students may have unique challenges when it comes to organization, the structure of class sessions, implicit rules of engagement in the classroom, and social norms (Gobbo & Shmulsky, 2012).

These challenges may be particularly problematic in classes that involve discussions and group work. There are specific strategies suggested by the Organization for Autism Research (2006) that faculty can use to support individual autistic individuals such as helping them choose an appropriate seat, providing clear classroom rules, allowing lectures to be recorded, employing note-takers, providing access to notes prior to class, allowing extra time on tests, and facilitating study groups. However, offering accommodations to specific students requires these students to disclose their diagnosis to the disabilities support staff, which many students choose not to do (Matthews, 2009; Van Hees et al., 2015). Therefore, implementing UDL strategies in the classroom that may benefit autistic students, as well as other neurodiverse students, is imperative.

Executive Functioning Support

Autistic students, as well as most university students, benefit from a well-organized class in which clear instructions about expectations are provided throughout the semester. Faculty can support autistic students and other students who may have trouble with planning and organization by providing advice about scheduling for the semester and providing clear information about deadlines and assignments (Burgstahler & Russo-Gleicher, 2015; Gobbo & Shmulsky, 2012). Reminding students about upcoming deadlines can be useful, as can showing students how to use electronic or physical calendars or planners to schedule important deadlines (VanBergeijk et al., 2008). Large assignments such as long papers may be particularly difficult for students to know where to begin, so faculty can scaffold the assignment and provide advice for how to break these assignments into smaller parts (VanBergeijk et al., 2008). Furthermore, autistic students perform better when there is a predictable routine and perform worse when something changes unpredictably, such as a due date for a paper. Tips for reducing negative outcomes for these students in the classroom include describing the format of each class at the beginning of the class period and giving clear information when dates or assignments change (Burgstahler & Russo-Gleicher, 2015). For example, faculty can inform students that the first part of class will be lecture-based and that this will be followed by group work for the final part of class. Autistic students then can prepare for this change (Gobbo & Shmulsky, 2012).

Given the social skill challenges that autistic students may face, one issue that faculty may encounter in the classroom is a student not behaving in line with implicit social classroom rules such as not dominating the discussion and not interrupting the other students and the instructor. A UDL strategy that faculty can use to make these implicit rules more explicit is to set clear expectations for the classroom and to provide feedback to the entire class rather than to specific students (Burgstahler & Russo-Gleicher, 2015). Differences in social skills might also limit the ability of autistic students to engage in class discussions or group activities. Gobbo and Shmulsky (2012) suggest offering multiple mediums for participating including in-class discussions, online discussions, after-class office hours, and turning in discussion questions or comments to the instructor in an alternative format (e.g., note cards, app that allows students to participate from their computers or phones). In addition, they suggest explicitly providing instructions on how to engage in group work such as telling the students how to divide up work and make decisions and also to assign roles to each student within the group such as a recorder and a speaker; this can also reduce anxiety (Shmulsky & Gobbo, 2013). Defining rules for how students should communicate (e.g., via email vs. text) and how often (e.g., not more than once a week) may also be helpful. Faculty can also try to ensure that the language they use in the classroom will be understood by all students. That is, because some autistic students may have difficulty with figurative language, faculty can also try to avoid sarcasm, jargon, and innuendos. This can also be helpful for students from a variety of cultures and backgrounds.

To accommodate students with different sensory stimulation issues (e.g., sensitive to noises or fluorescent lights), faculty can point out different parts of the room that may be particularly loud/quiet, close to a door, or darker/lighter and encourage all students to sit where they feel comfortable (Burgstahler & Russo-Gleicher, 2015). In addition, faculty can be aware of other sensory stimuli such as odors resulting from cleaning supplies or noise from air conditioning units, heating devices, and projectors (Gobbo & Shmulsky, 2012). Allowing students to wear noise-canceling headphones to prevent auditory overstimulation in a testing environment can improve autistic students' ability to concentrate during an exam. Autistic individuals often engage in stimming, or repetitively moving parts of the body. As stimming can reduce discomfort due to sensory overstimulation, making it clear that students can engage in this behavior in the classroom can eliminate concerns about this behavior being disruptive. Persons with autism may also benefit from multitasking including using computers or other electronic devices rather than looking at the instructor, as it can reduce the amount of social stimuli they need to take in. Thus, making it clear that students are able to use electronics and move freely as long as it doesn't disturb other students can help autistic students feel more comfortable in class and focus on the class material rather than regulating their behavior. If behavior such as stimming is disruptive to other students in the class, announcing general rules about what behaviors not to engage in (and why) to the class may curb that behavior without being stigmatizing to the individual student. However, if the behavior continues, explicitly telling the student engaging in the disruptive behavior to try to reduce this behavior in a setting outside of the classroom may be necessary (Gobbo & Shmulsky, 2012). To prevent students from asking too many questions or speaking too much, faculty can set ground rules at the beginning of the semester for the number of questions that one student may ask during each class period. If more individualized directions are necessary, communicating specific rules—such as "You should ask no more than three questions per class"—can make implicit rules that other students naturally understand explicit.

Faculty can also strive to capitalize on the ability to use bottom-up analytic thinking that many autistic students bring to the classroom. Encouraging different styles of learning and emphasizing the unique contributions of different thinking styles can help everyone in the classroom feel supported and can increase the value of teamwork. Online courses may be beneficial to autistic students, as they typically provide detailed organizational structures and provide students the option of completing coursework in an environment comfortable to each individual. Indeed, research shows that students with disabilities get higher grades in online courses than in-person courses (Stewart et al., 2010).

ATTENTION DEFICIT HYPERACTIVITY DISORDER (ADHD)

According to the National Institutes of Health, ADHD is a disorder in which individuals experience challenges with staying focused, controlling behavior, and hyperactivity. ADHD symptoms can appear as early as 3 years old and can be mistaken for emotion or disciplinary problems if undiagnosed. The estimated prevalence of ADHD in children is 9.4%. Approximately 4.4% of adults are diagnosed with ADHD; this number is higher in males (5.4%) than females (3.2%) (Centers for Disease Control and Prevention, 2019). Students with ADHD are less likely to earn a college degree than students without ADHD (~12% vs. ~50%) and have lower grades than students without ADHD (Daley & Birchwood, 2009). The combination of cognitive, behavioral, psychological, and social challenges that students with ADHD face can affect classroom performance.

Classroom Challenges

One of the hallmarks of ADHD is a challenge with maintaining focus. During a class period in which students must concentrate for long periods of time in order to engage with the material, faculty, and classmates, concentration may be particularly challenging for students with ADHD. Issues with focus may also be related to the impaired time-management skills that are often seen in students with ADHD, which can affect the quality of their work or their ability to plan for academic tasks (National Resource Center on ADHD, 2019). University students with ADHD may also have difficulty maintaining focus on a specific task such as note-taking and can as a result have problems completing this task in the classroom (Centers for Disease Control and Prevention, 2019; Zwart & Kallemeyn, 2001). Indeed, note-taking is one task in which students with ADHD have challenges. In addition to issues with focus, the handwriting speed of individuals with ADHD tends to be slower than those without ADHD, although the quality of the notes does not differ between students with and without ADHD (Vekaria & Peverly, 2018). Note-taking deficits may also be compounded by the tendency for students with ADHD to be disorganized and to misplace things that are necessary for success such as notebooks or other important materials (National Institute of Mental Health, 2019; National Resource Center on ADHD, 2019). Together, these traits and behaviors may cause faculty to believe that individuals with ADHD are not following instructions. Hyperactivity can also be a symptom of ADHD and can cause students to constantly fidget or move their body (National Institute of Mental Health, 2019). Faculty and students in the classroom may be distracted by this movement.

Poor test-taking abilities have been demonstrated in university students with ADHD. One reason for these differences may be challenges with selecting main ideas that can come from an impaired ability to focus. Challenges with focus can also lead students with ADHD to make careless mistakes on exams. University students with ADHD have a harder time identifying key points, understanding the intent of test questions, and strategizing during an exam than university students without ADHD (Reaser et al., 2007). Another reason for test-taking challenges is that university students with ADHD have less accurate written recall, which is problematic since most classes emphasize studying from written notes in class (Vekaria & Peverly, 2018). Finally, students with ADHD tend to be spatial learners rather than language learners, which can be problematic in test performance, as schools often value learning styles that rely on language and logic (Schirduan et al., 2002).

Another challenge that students with ADHD may face is impulsivity, in which individuals may not take enough time to consider the consequences of their actions (National Institute of Mental Health, 2019). Thus, decision-making in the classroom about how to answer a question on an exam or what to say in class may be affected by the need that many individuals with ADHD have for short-term gratification. In the classroom, this may lead a student with ADHD to make impulsive decisions without considering the long-term consequences. It may also present as interrupting other students or the instructor.

One trait that is common in students with ADHD is an impairment in the motivation to reach goals through hard work; individuals with ADHD tend to prefer easy work and to persist less when attempting to complete difficult work (Carlson et al., 2002). They also tend to enjoy easy work more so than difficult work and are more extrinsically motivated (e.g., grades) rather than intrinsically motivated (Reaser et al., 2007). This can be problematic because research demonstrates that motivation is the strongest predictor of academic success in college (Rugsaken et al., 1998).

UDL in the Classroom

As with supporting autistic students, students with ADHD can benefit from a clear schedule and explicit rules for success in the classroom. Providing students with handouts or PowerPoint slides before class can help impart structure that students can easily follow (Wingert & Molitor, 2009). It is also important for faculty to be clear and explicit about rules for assignments or class activities. Communicating reminders for important deadlines can help disorganized students focus on upcoming assignments. Furthermore, breaking down longer assignments into smaller tasks can be beneficial in addressing planning deficits that students with ADHD may have.

Because students with ADHD can be distracted easily, using engaging and novel activities such as lab or small group activities has been shown to strengthen the performance of children with ADHD (Carlson et al., 2002). However, university students with ADHD reported less of a preference to work with peers, which can be limiting as they may not be receiving feedback from others about their study habits or performance (Simon-Dack et al., 2016). Encouraging group collaborations in the classroom may improve outcomes for students with ADHD in that they may acquire different approaches to learning class material and receive feedback on their performance (Simon-Dack et al., 2016). In addition, to support students with difficulties in focus, it may be helpful to break up lectures by introducing small activities such as posing questions to have students think critically about what they just learned, as suggested by Wingert and Molitor (2009). These activities may help all students to encode and apply the information they just learned. Another way to ensure that students with ADHD are encoding classroom content is to provide quick in-class assessments of the material that involve having students organize, recall, and apply the information that was taught (Wingert & Molitor, 2009). This way, the material is broken up into smaller chunks; this can also help the instructor identify content that may need to be re-emphasized or explained in a different way.

Because students with ADHD tend to be spatial learners, varying teaching techniques to appeal not just to students who learn based on language can be important. For example, having students create analogies with the information they are learning or applying the content to personal experiences can be effective (Reaser et al., 2007). In addition, students with ADHD tend to have strong knowledge of study skills and the use of study aids so emphasizing the use of study aids such as reviewing notes and making up test questions may be effective in improving test performance (Reaser et al., 2007). Faculty can also capitalize on the optimism and information processing skills that students with ADHD possess (Carlson et al., 2002).

University students with ADHD tend to be highly motivated by external markers of success such as grades (Simon-Dack et al., 2016). Thus, providing quick and specific feedback on assignments may improve the motivation and ultimately performance of students with ADHD. Another strategy may be to encourage students to adopt more intrinsic motivations. Reaser and colleagues (2007) recommend encouraging students to choose a topic for a paper that is interesting to them rather than selecting a topic because they think it will yield a good grade.

DYSLEXIA

The National Institutes of Health defines learning disabilities as disorders that affect the ability to understand or use language, conduct math calculations, coordinate body movements, or direct attention. Dyslexia is a learning difficulty that is associated with challenges with phonological processing, working memory, and processing speed. Estimates of the prevalence of dyslexia range from 4% to 15% in the United States, with the International Dyslexia Association estimating that as many as 15–20% of the American population has a symptom of dyslexia such as inaccurate reading, poor spelling, impaired writing, or confusing different words.

Classroom Challenges

Students with dyslexia can experience problems related to writing, math, concentration, listening, memory, synthesis, and organization (Olofsson et al., 2015). These issues are thought to be caused by weak phonological and orthographical coding (Callens et al., 2014) rather than issues with intelligence, problem-solving, or visual memory. That is, difficulties are thought to arise from deficits in the processing of speech sounds such as pronouncing a visual string of letters and less accuracy in analyzing the sounds of words. The main characteristics of adults with dyslexia are challenges with single-word recognition and spelling (Swanson, 2012; Wilson & Lesaux, 2001). These characteristics can result in slow reading, problems with recognizing errors, and spelling mistakes. Importantly, although dyslexic students may have difficulties with reading, the presentation of the same material in an auditory format may be easy to comprehend (Chodock & Dolinger, 2009). Writing problems specifically can manifest as issues with spelling, organization of sentences and paragraphs, and vocabulary choice (Olofsson et al., 2015). In the classroom, these challenges can appear in difficulties with note-taking, planning, written expression, text comprehension, expressing knowledge during assessment, and organization (Olofsson et al., 2015; Stienen-Durand & George, 2014).

Students with dyslexia may also experience difficulties with math. Although basic number processing is not a challenge, there appear to be deficits with math problems that rely on a verbal code rather than an analog code; as a result, students with dyslexia can have problems with addition and multiplication, although subtraction is not impaired (Göbel & Snowling, 2010). Challenges related to math as well as to other issues can lead students with dyslexia to be anxious or frustrated (Macdonald, 2010).

Classroom Strengths

Although there are significant challenges associated with dyslexia, the differences in cognitive style in dyslexic brains can lead individuals with dyslexia to be more creative, have better insight, and go about solving problems in more creative ways than nondyslexic students (Eide & Eide, 2012). In the classroom, students with dyslexia may be more top-down thinkers than other students in that they are more likely to see the holistic, big picture rather than focus on small details. Students with dyslexia may be better at finding patterns in places where other students might miss them. Individuals with dyslexia are also considered to have strong qualitative reasoning, or insight, and many have an ability to visually think about and share stories with others. Finally, as students with dyslexia have had to navigate a world that favors neurotypical people, they may bring strong problem-solving skills to the classroom.

UDL Options for the Classroom

There are several UDL options for the classroom that can benefit students with dyslexia with regard to learning in the classroom and assessment of knowledge (e.g., exams). Regarding learning strategies, research has demonstrated that using electronic portfolios or animation software to teach and reinforce course content can be beneficial (Dixon, 2004; Dziorny, 2012; Hughes et al., 2011). For example, Dziorny (2012) used Second Life to teach content to students rather than relying on text reading. Using digital media may be an effective strategy to reach students that learn better without reading. Presenting material in an auditory format may be helpful to students with difficulties reading text on a screen or in a book or handout. More research needs to be done, however, as these studies are limited by the small sample size of students with dyslexia included in this work (Pino & Mortari, 2014). Other studies have found that all students, including those with dyslexia, benefit from receiving printed handouts or electronic presentations of notes before the class which can help facilitate the balance of taking notes and listening to the instructor (Griffin & Pollak, 2009; Pollak, 2005). One study, however, found that approximately half of students with dyslexia surveyed reported difficulty reading online text and using learning technologies (MacCullagh et al., 2017).

As with most UDL best practices, it is recommended that faculty incorporate multiple formats of delivering course material and adjust to students' specific needs (Pino & Mortari, 2014). For example, presenting information in the classroom in both auditory and visual modalities is useful for different types of students (Pollak, 2005; Schnotz, 2002), as is presenting information in segments ranging from 5 to 20 minutes compared to longer durations (Wankat, 2002). For students who have difficulties with reading text, using text-to-speech technology can be helpful, as can providing lectures or other course material in a video format. A qualitative study that interviewed students with dyslexia found that they expressed appreciation for the availability of videoed lectures that depicted the instructor's face (MacCullagh et al., 2017). Information communication technology in particular can be helpful for students with dyslexia in that it supports students' ability to engage in mind-mapping and to use visual models (Dixon, 2004). Online courses can also support students with dyslexia, as they are well-paced and therefore slow down the speed at which verbal information is presented (Dziorny, 2012; Hughes et al., 2011).

Regarding assessment, the most common accommodations include allowing extended time on exams, providing a less distracting environment than a classroom for exams, and allowing the use of computers for the tests. Although extended time and alternate locations might reduce some of the difficulties that students with dyslexia face on exams, using alternative assessment modalities such as oral exams can be useful (Riddell et al., 2005). Some UDL experts suggest allowing all students, not just neurodiverse students, to decide how much time they need on an exam (Stretch & Osborne, 2005).

FACULTY DEVELOPMENT

Faculty development requires several stages. First, the group that is contacting faculty should include faculty members who can help the group understand the challenges that faculty experience in the classroom. A next step is that faculty must be aware of neurodiverse conditions along with the strengths and challenges articulated above associated with different forms of neurodiversity. Faculty workshops regarding neurodiversity can be an effective method for reaching faculty. In these workshops, it may be helpful, if possible, for some neurodiverse students to describe their experiences to faculty. Another approach is to provide information to department chairs and asking them to disseminate information about the challenges and strengths of neurodiverse students. Department chairs may benefit from the neurodiversity advocates on campus providing a short presentation about neurodiversity at a faculty meeting, especially if the concept of neurodiversity is new to a department chair. Finally, faculty development should include online resources for faculty. These resources may include simple steps or best practices for faculty to create an inclusive classroom for neurodiverse students. Strategies for interacting with neurodiverse students, particularly in situations where these students may be disruptive, would be beneficial. An example would be an autistic student who has a strong interest in a particular course and who may ask a disproportionately high number of questions in class compared with other students. In that case, the faculty member may ask to meet privately with the neurodiverse student and ask them to limit the number of questions to a set number in each class. The student could have, for example, three index cards and put one index card aside every time that the student asks a question. In summary, faculty development requires a multi-step process, which requires some organized group that includes members who can reach out to faculty. This group can then offer faculty specific strategies that can be employed in the classroom or in other interactions with neurodiverse students.

Access and Barriers for Faculty Implementation

One of the barriers to faculty implementation is knowledge about neurodiversity. This challenge is compounded by the fact that there are no clear lines for defining a student as neurodiverse, and that some neurodiverse conditions may be hidden (e.g., dyslexia). Also, even for conditions that are more clearly neurodiverse, the way in which issues are expressed in the classroom can vary. For example, research shows that the stimuli that neurodiverse individuals find irritating vary greatly across individuals (Mayer, 2017). Thus, faculty must attempt to be aware of students' individual sensory challenges, which may not be feasible in large lecture courses. In addition, there may be little that a faculty member can do about any structural aspects to the room (e.g., fluorescent lighting), other than perhaps allow the student to use a fidget when the student is feeling anxious due to the sensory environment. Even in these situations, the student may not want to appear different from other students by using a fidget, or the fidget may be distracting to other students in the class.

Faculty may also be concerned about whether any opportunities to assist neurodiverse students create an unfair advantage to succeed compared to other students in the class. The organization and focus of the neurodiversity message on campus can be an important step in mitigating these faculty concerns. Namely, it may be helpful for faculty to be informed that this is an issue of diversity and equity. The diversity of thought and experiences of neurodiverse individuals can lead to a broader range of perspectives and ideas during a class. Thus, by offering opportunities for neurodiverse individuals to succeed, it will enhance the classroom experience for all students.

A final limitation is the features of the classroom space. For example, fluorescent lighting or sitting very close to each other in a large lecture may be unavoidable, and there may be little that faculty can do with regard to the physical environment. However, by allowing things such as fidgets, it will hopefully alleviate the student's stress and give the student a better opportunity to succeed in class. Also, as faculty learn about the challenges of the physical classroom for some students, they can advocate to the administration for changes to the teaching spaces.

CONCLUSION

In this chapter, we describe the challenges and strengths that neurodiverse students who are autistic, who have ADHD, and who have dyslexia bring to the classroom. Although understanding the challenges that students with these conditions face is important, it is imperative to acknowledge that within each condition, students will display different traits and behaviors. Furthermore, many of these challenges may not be easily observable, such as difficulties with reading comprehension, executive functioning issues, and sensitivity to sensory stimuli. These challenges also may present as students appearing unfocused, rude, or apathetic.

Faculty can use the UDL practices presented in this chapter to ensure that all students are supported in their classrooms. Although different types of students will benefit from different strategies, there are some common UDL strategies reviewed here that can help students with autism, ADHD, and dyslexia as well as other neurodiverse conditions. First, all students can benefit from well-organized courses with explicit rules and clear explanations of class expectations. This includes being clear about the content and due dates of assignments and reminding students of upcoming deadlines. Second, several teaching strategies should be employed to support bottom-up analytic learners, top-down holistic thinkers, visual learners, auditory learners, and so on. Presenting course material in different formats that include visual, auditory, and digital components can be useful to different types of students. Third, faculty should consider using different types of assessments to allow all students to be able to demonstrate their understanding of the course material. For example, using oral exams, written exams, group work, and online assessments can give students with different strengths the opportunity to best express what they have learned. Finally, making sure the physical classroom is accessible to everyone can reduce anxiety, mitigate executive function deficits caused by overstimulation, and improve focus. Although getting buy-in from faculty may be difficult due to faculty members' lack of knowledge of neurodiversity, concerns about giving some students unfair advantages, or hesitation in putting in additional work, creating informational material with tangible, implementable UDL strategies that can be shared through workshops, departments, and digital mediums can help support all students.

Campus Essentials for High Impact

- *Implement UDL strategies in the classroom.* Neurodiverse and neurotypical students benefit from UDL practices infused into curriculum, lecture, and course assignments. Consider classroom redesign options including lighting, space, and furniture functionality.
- *Devote resources and time to faculty development.* Support training initiatives regarding neurodiverse student needs and UDL strategies. Invest in neurodiversity training programs for faculty on campus.
- *Consider infrastructure changes to address neurodiverse student needs.* Features of classroom space limit faculty options for addressing student needs.
- *Examine UDL options for classroom instruction and assessment.*
- *Encourage and provide opportunities for neurodiverse students to share their classroom experiences.*

REFERENCES

Adreon, D., & Durocher, J. S. (2007). Evaluating the college transition needs of individuals with high-functioning autism spectrum disorders. *Intervention in School and Clinic, 42*(5), 271–279.

American Psychiatric Association. (2013). Diagnostic and statistical manual of mental disorders (5th ed.). American Psychiatric Publishing.

Baio, J., Wiggins, L., Christensen, D. L., Maenner, M. J., Daniels, J., Warren, Z., Kurzius-Spencer, M., Zahorodny, W., Rosenberg, C. R., White, T., Durkin, M. S., Imm, P., Nikolaou, L., Yeargin-Allsopp, M., Lee, L., Harrington, R., Lopez, M., Fitzgerald, R. T., Hewitt, A., Pettygrove, S., Constantino, J. N., Vehorn, A., Shenouda, J., Hall-Lande, J., Braun, K. V. N., & Dowling, N. F. (2018). Prevalence of Autism Spectrum Disorder among children aged 8 years—autism and developmental disabilities monitoring network, 11 sites, United States, 2014. *MMWR Surveillance Summaries, 67*(6), 1–23. doi: 10.15585/mmwr.ss6706a1

Baron-Cohen, S., Spitz, A., & Cross, P. (1993). Do children with autism recognise surprise? A research note. *Cognition & Emotion, 7*(6), 507–516.

Burgstahler, S., & Russo-Gleicher, R. J. (2015). Applying universal design to address the needs of postsecondary students on the autism spectrum. *Journal of Postsecondary Education and Disability, 28*(2), 199–212.

Callens, M., Tops, W., Stevens, M., & Brysbaert, M. (2014). An exploratory factor analysis of the cognitive functioning of first-year bachelor students with dyslexia. *Annals of Dyslexia, 64*(1), 91–119.

Carlson, C. L., Booth, J. E., Shin, M., & Canu, W. H. (2002). Parent-, teacher-, and self-rated motivational styles in ADHD subtypes. *Journal of Learning Disabilities, 35*, 104–113.

Centers for Disease Control and Prevention. (2019). Attention-Deficit/Hyperactivity Disorder. https://www.cdc.gov/ncbddd/adhd/facts.html#SignsSymptoms

Charman, T. (2002). The prevalence of autism spectrum disorders. *European Child & Adolescent Psychiatry, 11*(6), 249–256.

Chodock, T., & Dolinger, E. (2009). Applying universal design to information literacy: Teaching students who learn differently at Landmark College. *Reference & User Services Quarterly, 49*(1), 24–32.

Daley, D., & Birchwood, J. (2009). ADHD and academic performance: Why does ADHD impact on academic performance and what can be done to support ADHD children in the classroom? *Child: Care, Health and Development, 36*, 455–464. doi:10.1111/j.1365-2214.2009.01046.x

Dixon, M. (2004). Disability as a vehicle for identifying hidden aspects of human activity: Inclusive design and dyslexia in educational software development. In C. Stary & C. Stephanidis (Eds.), *User-centered interaction paradigms for universal access in the information society* (pp. 254–261). Springer.

Dziorny, M. (2012). Online course design elements to better meet the academic needs of students with dyslexia in higher education. In P. Resta (Ed.), *Proceedings of SITE 2012—Society for Information Technology & Teacher Education International Conference* (pp. 332–337). Association for the Advancement of Computing in Education (AACE). https://www.learntechlib.org/primary/p/39585/.

Eide, B., & Eide, F. (2012). *The dyslexic advantage: Unlocking the hidden potential of the dyslexic brain*. Penguin.

Fombonne, E. (2003). Epidemiological surveys of autism and other pervasive developmental disorders: An update. *Journal of Autism and Developmental Disorders, 33*(4), 365–382.

Gobbo, K., & Shmulsky, S. (2012). Classroom needs of community college students with Asperger's Disorder and Autism Spectrum Disorders. *Community College Journal of Research and Practice, 36*(1), 40–46.

Göbel, S. M., & Snowling, M. J. (2010). Number-processing skills in adults with dyslexia. *Quarterly Journal of Experimental Psychology, 63*(7), 1361–1373.

Griffin, E., & Pollak, D. (2009). Student experiences of neurodiversity in higher education: Insights from the BRAINHE project. *Dyslexia, 15*, 23–41. doi: 10.1002/dys.383

Hill, E. L. (2004). Executive dysfunction in autism. *Trends in Cognitive Sciences, 8*(1), 26–32.

Hughes, J., Herrington, M., McDonald, T., & Rhodes, A. (2011). E-portfolios and personalized learning: Research in practice with two dyslexic learners in UK higher education. *Dyslexia, 17*, 48–64. doi: 10.1002/dys.418

International Board of Credentialing and Continuing Education Standards. (2018). *Interview with Dr. Stephen Shore: Autism advocate & on the spectrum.* https://ibcces.org/blog/2018/03/23/12748/

MacCullagh, L., Bosanquet, A., & Badcock, N. A. (2017). University students with dyslexia: A qualitative exploratory study of learning practices, challenges and strategies. *Dyslexia, 23*(1), 3–23.

Macdonald, S. J. (2010). Towards a social reality of dyslexia. *British Journal of Learning Disabilities, 38*(4), 271–279.

Matthews, N. (2009). Teaching the "invisible" students in the classroom: Disclosure, inclusion and the social model of disability. *Teaching in Higher Education, 14*(3), 229–239. doi: 10.1080/13562510902898809

Mayer, J. L. (2017). The relationship between autistic traits and atypical sensory functioning in neurotypical and ASD adults: A spectrum approach. *Journal of Autism and Developmental Disorders, 47*(2), 316–327.

Mottron, L., Burack, J. A., Iarocci, G., Belleville, S., & Enns, J. T. (2003). Locally oriented perception with intact global processing among adolescents with high–functioning autism: Evidence from multiple paradigms. *Journal of Child Psychology and Psychiatry, 44*(6), 904–913.

National Institute of Mental Health. (2019). Attention-Deficit/Hyperactivity Disorder. https://www.nimh.nih.gov/health/topics/attention-deficit-hyperactivity-disorder-adhd/index.shtml

National Resource Center on ADHD. (2019). ADHD in adults. https://chadd.org/for-adults/overview

O'Riordan, M., & Plaisted, K. (2001). Enhanced discrimination in autism. *The Quarterly Journal of Experimental Psychology: Section A, 54*(4), 961–979.

Olofsson, Å., Taube, K., & Ahl, A. (2015). Academic achievement of university students with dyslexia. *Dyslexia, 21*(4), 338–349.

Organization for Autism Research. (2006). *Life journey through autism: A guide for transition to adulthood.* Author. http://www.researchautism.org/resources/reading/index.asp

Ozonoff, S., & Jensen, J. (1999). Brief report: Specific executive function profiles in three neurodevelopmental disorders. *Journal of Autism and Developmental Disorders, 29*(2), 171–177.

Pino, M., & Mortari, L. (2014). The inclusion of students with dyslexia in higher education: A systematic review using narrative synthesis. *Dyslexia, 20*(4), 346–369.

Pollak, D. E. (2005). *Dyslexia, the self and higher education: Learning life histories of students identified as dyslexic.* Trentham. https://www.dora.dmu.ac.uk/bitstream/handle/2086/4089/DX220723_2.pdf?sequence=2

Reaser, A., Prevatt, F., Petscher, Y., & Proctor, B. (2007). The learning and study strategies of college students with ADHD. *Psychology in the Schools, 44*(6), 627–638.

Riddell, S., Tinklin, T., & Wilson, A. (2005). *Disabled students in higher education: Perspectives on widening access and changing policy.* Routledge.

Rugsaken, K. T., Robertson, J. A., & Jones, J. A. (1998). Using the Learning and Study Strategies Inventory scores as additional predictors of student academic performance. *NACADA Journal, 18*, 20–26.

Schindler, V., Cajiga, A., Aaronson, R., & Salas, L. (2015). The experience of transition to college for students diagnosed with Asperger's disorder. *The Open Journal of Occupational Therapy, 3*(1), 2.

Schirduan, V., Case, K., & Faryniarz, J. (2002). How ADHD students are smart. *The Educational Forum, 66*, 324–328.

Schnotz, W. (2002). Towards an integrated view of learning from text and visual displays. *Educational Psychology Review, 14*, 101–120.

Shmulsky, S., & Gobbo, K. (2013). Autism spectrum in the college classroom: Strategies for instructors. *Community College Journal of Research and Practice, 37*(6), 490–495.

Simon-Dack, S. L., Rodriguez, P. D., & Marcum, G. D. (2016). Study habits, motives, and strategies of college students with symptoms of ADHD. *Journal of Attention Disorders, 20*(9), 775–781.

Stewart, J., Mallery, C., & Choi, J. (2010). A multilevel analysis of distance learning achievement: Are college students with disabilities making the grade? *Journal of Rehabilitation, 76*(2), 27–39.

Stienen-Durand, S., & George, J. (2014). Supporting dyslexia in the programming classroom. *Procedia Computer Science, 27*, 419–430.

Stretch, L. S., & Osborne, J. W. (2005). Extended time test accommodation: Directions for future research and practice. *Practical Assessment Research and Evaluation, 10*(8).

Swanson, H. L. (2012). Adults with reading disabilities: Converting a meta-analysis to practice. *Journal of Learning Disabilities, 45*(1), 17–30.

Uljarevic, M., & Hamilton, A. (2013). Recognition of emotions in autism: A formal meta-analysis. *Journal of Autism and Developmental Disorders, 43*(7), 1517–1526.

Van Hees, V., Moyson, T., & Roeyers, H. (2015). Higher education experiences of students with autism spectrum disorder: Challenges, benefits and support needs. *Journal of Autism and Developmental Disorders, 45*(6), 1673–1688.

VanBergeijk, E., Klin, A., & Volkmar, F. (2008). Supporting more able students on the autism spectrum: College and beyond. *Journal of Autism and Developmental Disorders, 38*, 1359–1370.

Vekaria, P. C., & Peverly, S. T. (2018). Lecture note-taking in postsecondary students with Attention-Deficit/Hyperactivity Disorder. *Reading and Writing, 31*(7), 1551–1573.

Wankat, P. (2002). *The effective efficient professor: Teaching, scholarship and service.* Allyn and Bacon.

White, S. W., Oswald, D., Ollendick, T., & Scahill, L. (2009). Anxiety in children and adolescents with autism spectrum disorders. *Clinical Psychology Review, 29*(3), 216–229.

Wilson, A. M., & Lesaux, N. K. (2001). Persistence of phonological processing deficits in college students with dyslexia who have age-appropriate reading skills. *Journal of Learning Disabilities, 34*(5), 394–400.

Wingert, D., & Molitor, T. (2009). Best practices: preventing and managing challenging classroom situations. *Currents in Teaching and Learning, 1*(2), 4–18.

World Health Organization. (2018). Autism Spectrum Disorders. https://www.who.int/news-room/fact-sheets/detail/autism-spectrum-disorders

Zwart, L. M., & Kallemeyn, L. M. (2001). Peer-based coaching for college students with ADHD and learning disabilities. *Journal of Postsecondary Education and Disability, 15*, 1–15.

Chapter 5: Campus Spotlight

Neurodiversity Working Group, College of William and Mary

Cheryl L. Dickter and Joshua A. Burk

Our Mission: The William and Mary Neurodiversity Working Group has maintained a primary focus of supporting students on our campus. Characterized as a "grassroots" effort, led by faculty and others on campus, the Neurodiversity Working Group has the opportunity to gain knowledge about the experiences of neurodiverse students on the William and Mary campus.

Faculty driven, the Neurodiversity Working Group was initially developed in 2013 by a professor in the Department of History, Karin Wulf, and by the director of the Counseling Center at the time, Warrenetta Mann. From there, faculty in the Department of Psychology were included as part of the working group. Together the working group recruited members from many groups on campus, including students, staff, administration, advancement, alumni, Student Accessibility Services, the Career Center, and Residence Life.

Extending to Students: A student working group, comprised of neurodiverse and neurotypical students, was developed and has now grown to a listserv of over 150 students. The student working group has hosted a number of events, including "Autism 101" sessions and vigils for the Disability Day of Mourning along with numerous tabling sessions to promote their group. The student working group has offered leadership positions for students and has expanded to afford opportunities for the student leaders to speak at other institutions about creating their own student group.

Scholar in Residence Program: The Neurodiversity Initiative has been enhanced by the appointment of a scholar-in-residence, John Elder Robison, an internationally renowned advocate for neurodiversity. John's support includes meeting with the student group, talking with classes on campus about neurodiversity, and offering public community lectures. The addition of John

Robison has raised the profile of the William and Mary Neurodiversity Initiative, which has been instrumental in making stronger funding requests to administrators and donors.

Course Offering Added: A neurodiversity course, co-taught by four William and Mary faculty and the scholar-in-residence, was developed shortly after the beginning of the Neurodiversity Initiative. The team-taught approach has allowed the course to have an interdisciplinary perspective, including topics such as neurodiversity from a humanities perspective, neuroplasticity, social cognition, co-occurring medical and psychological conditions, and social relationships.

Course characteristics include:

- The course is offered for one credit and graded pass/fail so that students will focus more on engaging with the material rather than their final grade.
- It is kept relatively small (~15 students) to promote class discussion.
- There are no prerequisites for this course, and thus students typically have a range of majors, which often leads the class discussions to be interdisciplinary in nature.
- There are no exams in the class; instead, students write papers throughout the semester in which they reflect on class discussions and readings. They also write a final paper in which they identify a theme that has been highlighted throughout the semester and synthesize information that they have learned regarding that theme.
- The course is offered once per year on the main campus in Williamsburg and once in the summer at the William and Mary Washington, DC, Center.

Extending Best Practices: The Neurodiversity Working Group has reached beyond the campus community to offer resources and describe the William and Mary Neurodiversity Initiative. For example, online resources have been developed for faculty and students (https://www.wm.edu/sites/neurodiversity/resources/index.php).

1. ***For faculty,*** these online resources offer suggestions for developing a more inclusive classroom to support neurodiverse students. Faculty can use these resources in their classes at the beginning of the semester to provide information to students on how they can successfully navigate the course.
2. ***For students,*** resources are available to make implicit social rules more explicit during different situations. One of the resources describes "hidden rules" for interactions in a seminar course. This resource offers specific

examples of how to enter into a discussion to build on a point made by another student or how to respond when disagreeing with ideas presented by other students. Students can use these resources on their own to prepare for a class. Other resources include advice for navigating office hours and for ensuring success in a lecture class.

Hosting a Summer Bridge Experience: The Neurodiversity Working Group received feedback that a program to introduce neurodiverse students to campus before new student orientation would allow for a better transition to William and Mary. In July 2018, we offered our first Bridge Program. This event occurs over one weekend and gives neurodiverse students an opportunity to explore campus during a relatively quiet time of the academic year. Current and past members of our neurodiversity student group serve as mentors in the Bridge Program.

Bridge Program Curriculum: The Bridge Program Curriculum is largely developed by the student neurodiversity group and our Office of Student Accessibility. Sessions include:

- essential study tips and time-management strategies;
- introduction to the Office of Student Accessibility;
- mock lecture experience by a professor in the working group;
- optional social opportunities to foster peer engagement; and
- early exposure to the campus environment and community.

For more information, visit https://www.wm.edu/sites/neurodiversity/wm-bridge/index.php.

Future Directions for the Neurodiversity Initiative: Collaborating with other institutions on best practices and neurodiversity awareness. Our group has given talks about the Neurodiversity Initiative at several institutions, including Virginia Tech, University of Virginia, and Eastern Virginia Medical School, along with presenting at an Autism at Work conference. We recently hosted a Neurodiversity Summit in Washington, DC, to increase understanding about neurodiversity efforts at higher education institutions in Virginia. A future goal is to expand this summit to include institutions outside of Virginia.

Chapter 5: Campus Spotlight

Neurodiversity Connections, Duke University

Kimberly Blackshear and Tara Chandrasekhar

Our Mission: Duke University—in Durham, NC—is a world-renowned academic and research institute nestled in a vibrant college town. As a diverse community, Duke has historically valued differences and strives to be an inclusive space for all, including neurodiverse students. In 2016, an incoming graduate student requested to be connected with peers on the autism spectrum. No formal affinity group existed, though there was a shared understanding among Student Affairs members

Source: **Duke Neurodiversity Connections**

that students with autism and other neurodiverse conditions would benefit from coordinated efforts of support and inclusion. Thus, Neurodiversity Connections—a working group of Duke University faculty, staff, and students—was created.

Neurodiversity Connections Group: The group has organically grown to include individuals from both academic and student affairs who interface with undergraduate and graduate students during the entirety of their Duke experience, from admissions to graduation. Our members' expertise includes academic advising, case management, disability services, residential life, career counseling, and wellness. We have focused on outreach to the campus community via frequent on-campus presentations on how best to support neurodiverse students. We have disseminated tip sheets and other written materials for faculty and academic advisors via our website and outreach efforts. Neurodiversity Connections is included in the parent handbook and discussed at orientation events, and events are publicized throughout campus. In February 2019, in response to a student's request for support in navigating romantic relationships, we co-sponsored a viewing of the documentary *Autism in Love*, featuring a discussion with the film's director.

Meeting the Needs of Duke Students: Neurodiversity Connections is also aware of the needs of Duke students outside of the classroom, and nurtured the development of the Clubhouse, a student-led initiative for students who self-identify as neurodiverse. Students are provided with informal peer connection, mentorship, and sensory-friendly alternatives to campus activities (e.g., a low-stimulus Last Day of Class celebration) to meet their unique needs, while still creating opportunities for interpersonal connection. Open to both undergraduate and graduate students, the Clubhouse is not a treatment or social skills group, but rather a space for connection without the pressure to perform. Events are housed in sensory-friendly environments, and activities are selected to allow participants to engage and communicate at their level of comfort.

We have discovered that events that include volunteerism and a focused activity have been well received. A recent example has included making blankets for the homeless population, which included repetitive movement, pleasing textures, and low-pressure communication while working on a goal until completion. The Clubhouse members play an important role in developing and implementing grounded and impactful goals for Neurodiversity Connections. They informally serve as an advisory board for the group and guide the vision and implementation of activities at monthly meetings.

Future Directions of Neurodiversity Connections include outreach to students prior to matriculation, increasing career-related supports, and synergizing activities with other local and national universities focused on similar efforts. We anticipate that the Clubhouse members will continue to inform the greater campus community of the strengths and challenges of college students on the autism spectrum.

Find the Neurodiversity Connections Website at https://sites.duke.edu/neurodiversityatduke.

Neurodiversity Connections Membership, 2019:

Table 5.1. Neurodiversity Connections Membership, 2019

Academic Resource Center	Global Education Office
Academic Deans	Office of Biomedical Graduate Education
Career Center	Office of Student Conduct
Center for Autism and Brain Development	Office of Undergraduate Admissions
Counseling and Psychological Services	Residential Life
Dean of Students	Sanford School of Public Policy
Duke Reach	Student Disability Access Office
Financial Aid	Student Government
Fuqua School of Business	Student Health

Chapter Six

Tutoring

Abby Benzinger, Claytonia Boular-Woods, and James W. H. Howard

Effective strategies to engage students and increase retention are always high on the priority list for college administrators. As student populations change and more learners begin to identify as neurodiverse, traditional educational strategies need to be adapted for today's student. One way that colleges are able to provide academic assistance is through the use of peer tutoring. Although tutoring is not the only academic intervention being employed in institutions of higher education, it is often more cost-effective than other strategies offered (Pugatch & Wilson, 2018). Peer tutoring provides academic support for students struggling in course content and introduces study strategies that can assist in other coursework. Many neurodiverse students experience challenges with executive functioning, which impacts their mastery of collegiate study skills, including test preparation, note-taking skills, and comprehension. Students with learning differences have difficulty organizing material, can have low self-esteem, and struggle with social interaction (Michael, 2016). For neurodiverse students, peer tutoring programs can also provide the benefit of increased social engagement outside of the classroom.

Peer tutoring services differ on college campuses and are often dictated by available resources, campus size, and program offerings. Tutoring session delivery can vary, ranging from individual sessions to small-group sessions or class-wide assistance. The success of post-secondary tutoring services is impacted by the allocations of space, budget, and staff. In order to address the needs of neurodiverse learners, center administrators must explore the ways space, staff, and delivery of services intersect within the tutoring center. Readers are encouraged to reference chapter 4, "Welcoming Spaces for Learning," to identify elements of design and their impact on collegiate learners. Despite the abundance of tutoring services offered on many campuses, there is a gap in the literature regarding the effectiveness of services for students with learning differences. Research does suggest, however, that employing universal learning strategies can positively impact the academic success of college students (Michael, 2016).

This chapter explores how center leaders can redesign approaches that better assist neurodiverse students. Authors explore methods and best practices for effective tutoring, engaging students through Universal Design for Learning (UDL), and best practices for equipping tutors through training and evaluation processes.

SUPPORTING NEURODIVERSE STUDENTS

"Invisible scholars," those with learning disabilities that are not easily identified, are sometimes the hardest students to support. This isn't because resources are not available, but rather because the students themselves do not readily utilize campus resources. Vogel and colleagues (2007) credit low resource usage to a student's inability to self-advocate. For some neurodiverse students, connectivity to campus resources can be attributed to not having to initiate assistance in the past because of the easy accessibility of high school accommodations arranged by teachers and parents or guardians on their behalf. Fear of stigma can also impact use of services. Some students with learning differences will deny learning challenges once on the college campus. They want to separate themselves from the special education label they carried in elementary and secondary school (Janiga & Costenbader, 2002). Fear of stigma surrounding their learning challenges becomes an obstacle to their academic success in college. Lack of self-advocacy skills causes students to not seek the help they need. As reviewed in chapter 2, developing self-advocacy skills is vital for neurodiverse students so they feel empowered to seek the assistance they need to succeed in the collegiate environment. On post-secondary campuses neurodiverse students are challenged to adopt effective communication skills and to identify their learning strengths and weaknesses. Effectively communicating learning needs to faculty, tutors, and other support staff is essential to their success.

PEER TUTORING ASSISTANCE

The growth in the number of students in higher education with learning differences has created a need for additional support services (Vogel et al., 2007). On many campuses, it is not uncommon to find programs that offer free peer tutoring services to enrolled students. A survey by the U.S. Department of Education shows that 77% of 2- and 4-year post-secondary institutions provide tutors to support student success (Lewis, Farris, & Greene, 1999). Although tutoring is shown to support student academic success, how effective is this service for neurodiverse learners? In a survey of the PERACH peer tutoring project discussed by Vogel et al. (2007), both the tutee and tutor found these services to be beneficial and were highly satisfied with the tutoring relationship and would recommend the service to others. Although beneficial, some difficulties are encountered in peer tutoring services. There is a gap between the tutee's perceived ability to describe their needs and how well their tutor perceives these needs. The perceived gap in communication can be attributed to self-advocacy, which plays an important role in the success of tutoring services for neurodiverse students. Self-advocacy helps students effectively communicate their academic needs and correlates to their openness in utilizing available resources.

THE ROLE OF PEER TUTORS

Tutors play a fundamental role in providing effective academic support services in post-secondary institutions. For a student, their tutor functions as a bridge to faculty, class lecture, and understanding course content. We can expect that professional tutors would be more equipped to handle all types of learners, but this is not always true. When the tutor is a peer, it is of even greater concern. Although peer tutoring may help neurodiverse learners build academic competence and socialization skills, it is also important for higher education leaders to ensure the quality of the service provided. It is not safe to assume that just because a student has received a good grade in a course and possesses the desire to help others, that they will be effective at communicating and supporting the needs of another student. Tutoring a student with learning differences can present challenges for the peer tutor in teaching course content. In the peer tutoring project, Vogel et al. (2007) received feedback from both the tutee and the tutors that the greatest problem experienced was that tutors felt they did not possess the sufficient skills to meet the needs of tutees with learning differences. Many tutors observed the need for more training and expressed concern regarding their lack of skills to support neurodiverse learners. Specific areas of concern include challenges dealing with tutee learning differences, lack of resources for tutors when encountering difficulties in tutoring sessions, and the communication gap between tutor and tutee regarding learning needs (Vogel et al., 2007).

The research of Vogel and colleagues (2007) advocates that effort is needed to improve training for tutors to better equip them to help students with diverse levels of academic ability. Kiedaisch and Dinitz (2007) suggest one method of improvement is to incorporate Universal Design principles in tutoring sessions, making them accessible to the widest audience possible.

UNIVERSAL DESIGN AND EDUCATION

Universal Design (UD) was first developed by architect Ron Mace, who posed an architectural design process that was flexible and adaptable, with the goal of being more universally usable. Accordingly, the Center for Universal Design published seven principles (Connell et al., 1997) to guide the application of UD in design processes:

1. equitable use;
2. flexibility in use;
3. simple and intuitive use;
4. perceptible information;
5. tolerance for error;
6. low physical effort; and
7. size and space for approach and use.

Designing architectural spaces and tools using these principles of Universal Design goes beyond conventional accommodations for accessibility, such as those passed in Title III of the Americans with Disabilities Act (1990). Accommodation strategies tend to encourage repurposing designs after they are built, that is, adapting spaces originally designed for a hypothetically abled person so that they also serve the needs of a person with a disability. UD attempts to imagine usability without treating an average able-bodied person as the initial, default audience for design. Instead, in their design, architects should prioritize the benefit for all users. For example, as Jacobs (1999) suggests, affordances like *curb cuts* benefit people in wheelchairs as well as bikers, skaters, people who push strollers or carts, and people reading as they walk. Effective UD creates spaces and tools that increase access for everyone.

Educators have repurposed and applied UD to their classrooms. For instance, Zeff (2007) describes early educational programs that applied UD to instructional pedagogy. These revisions of UD targeted classroom dynamics, assignment design, the availability of information, options for participation, and other features specific to teaching. Universal Design in learning contexts creates strategies that promote the academic engagement of all learners and encourages academic success (Bublitz et al., 2015).

UNIVERSAL DESIGN FOR
LEARNING IN HIGHER EDUCATION

Like buildings and roads, education benefits from flexible and adaptable curriculum so that everyone can learn. Universal Design for Learning (UDL) or Universal Design for Instruction (UDI) emerged in this period as a system for rethinking not only the classroom but also institutional support for learning. Universal Design for Learning serves as an offshoot of Universal Design applied to learning contexts.

UDL practices influence the accessibility of educational environments and establish effective learning platforms for all students (Couzens et al., 2015). Following in line with the Universal Design for Learning (UDL), institutions of higher education are tasked with ensuring that all students have a safe space to learn and thrive. The three main components of UDL are a means of representation, engagement, and expression. In a classroom setting, it is not uncommon for instructors to offer their students a "variety of ways to interact with the materials because they often need multiple ways to process information before they can fully learn the material" (Webb & Hoover, n.d.). UDL assists teachers in reaching as many students as possible by offering multiple means of representation of the course material. Multiple representations of material formats allow the student to choose the representation that works for them and is especially helpful in supporting students with learning differences. When providing collegiate support services, the same UDL practices should be considered.

Rose and Meyer (2002) outlined the first complete version of UDL as developed by the Center for Applied Special Technology (CAST). CAST has since expanded UDL in successive editions, most recently in Meyer and colleagues (2014). UDL poses three guidelines for application in educational environments: (1) provide multiple means of engagement, (2) provide multiple means of representation, and (3) provide multiple means of action and expression (Meyer et al., 2014). These guidelines each include three kinds of practices that instructors, administrators, and tutors should provide, as summarized in table 6.1.

While UDL guidelines were initially designed for the classroom, tutoring administrators have observed success in applying principles of UDL within center services. Treating UDL as a general template through which administrators can reflect on their own practices in relation to tutoring, training, and space design, the specific recommendations they come away with are practices that would potentially benefit everyone who visits their center. For instance, asking questions at the start of a session is a common feature in tutor training manuals and guides, and applying UDL principles to reflect on them

Table 6.1. Universal Design for Learning Guidelines (adapted from Meyer et al., 2014)

Guidelines	Engagement	Representation	Action and Expression
Provide options for:	Self-regulation Sustaining effort and persistence	Comprehension Language, mathematical expressions, and symbols	Executive functions Expression and communication
	Recruiting interest	Perception	Physical action

may improve the quality of questions tutors ask at the start of a session. Other practices would require more change for many centers. While online tutoring has expanded greatly since 2007, using adaptive tools for in-person sessions would require further training and adaptation for many centers.

Although centers using Universal Design for Learning have investigated its effectiveness within their own services, the connection between UDL and students with learning differences may be harder to gauge. UDL should not merely be used to make changes in tutoring sessions but should change the institutional discourse around students. UDL is one way tutoring centers can raise awareness of what students need and lower the anxiety neurodiverse students experience regarding disclosing their learning challenges on campus (Sarrett, 2018). Students identifying as neurodiverse should not be singled out by a stand-alone Disability Services Office that sends a request for accommodation to an instructor; rather, the entire institution, from the classroom outward, should already be flexible and adaptable to all students, not just those who identify as having a learning difference. Those practicing UDL should treat all students as the target audience. The pedagogy of Universal Design for Learning has the capacity to assist all types of learners in higher education environments. UDL implementation in tutoring contexts has the potential to benefit all tutees, including neurotypical students as well as students with undiagnosed or documented learning differences.

Brizee and colleagues (2012) describe conducting usability testing for an online writing lab, the Purdue OWL. While much of their user testing focused on students with low vision or blindness, Brizee et al. (2012) introduced a specialist in learning disabilities to help train tutors on how to assist neurodiverse students. Black and colleagues (2015) combine UDL and UDI and investigate whether student perceptions of learning match UDL/UDI principles. Researchers framed tutoring as an important part of the UDI principle of "a community of learners" and the UDL principle of offering multiple means of engagement. Students rated tutoring highly, and the researchers found that tutoring helps with both coping skills and reflection. Burgstahler and Moore (2009) assess both student and staff perceptions of student success services through the lens of UD. They found that students frequently did not know how to perform tasks like getting a tutor or obtaining accommodations. Once students access support services, however, they report positive experiences.

UNIVERSAL DESIGN FOR
LEARNING IN THE TUTORING SESSION

The guidelines described in Universal Design for Learning are applicable when conducting effective tutoring sessions. Tutoring sessions are designed to foster close collaboration between student learners and tutors; practicing UDL helps ensure that many students benefit from use of tutoring services. At a glance, UDL guidelines (Meyer et al., 2014) provide three general questions for assessing the effectiveness of each tutoring session (exact wording from guidelines is in italics):

- Does the session provide *multiple means of engagement* in order to grow *purposeful and motivated learners*?
- Does the session provide *multiple means of representation* in order to grow *resourceful, knowledgeable learners*?
- Does the session provide *multiple means of action and expression* in order to grow *strategic, goal-directed learners*?

In turn, these questions can be rephrased into three primary learning goals that frame the work of an individual tutoring session or a sequence of tutoring sessions: (1) tutors should foster motivation and purposeful choices, (2) tutors should foster building knowledge and accessing available resources, and (3) tutors should foster setting goals and developing strategies. All three goals may recur throughout a tutoring session.

Tutoring sessions consist of three distinct periods of time: the beginning, the mid-session, and the ending. Deese-Roberts (2003) focuses on the engagement between tutor and tutee at the start and end of the tutoring session, leaving the middle to the development of content. Similarly, Ryan and Zimmerelli (2016) examine the tutoring session through a four-step process: (1) getting started, (2) setting the agenda, (3) mid-session practices, and (4) wrapping up a session. UDL principles align well with the stages or progression of a tutoring session:

- At the start of the session, tutor and student discuss the purpose for the visit and gauge motivation (prioritizing *engagement*).

- In the middle of the session, tutor and student work together to build knowledge using resources they both provide (prioritizing *representation*).
- At the end of the session, tutor and student set a plan for what the student will do before the completion of their assignment or before their next visit (prioritizing *action and expression*).

It is important to note that the alignment of session stages and UDL guidelines is imperfect. The time devoted to UDL integration does not correlate systematically to session stages. In the tutoring session, tutors need to be flexible with how they incorporate principles of engagement and action and expression, striving to represent information in multiple modes and ways.

Table 6.2 shows one example of mapping multiple means for promoting *engagement*, *representation*, and *action and expression* within a session. Experienced tutors may read a list like this and identify with several of the strategies. Tutors may also have strategies not listed that they regularly practice. Furthermore, tutors may have strategies that they apply selectively, without consciously recognizing why they employ specific strategies in some sessions and not in others. A tutor's attempt to represent these strategies is the first step toward understanding how that tutor *does* tutor. Consequently, it determines how they may strive to provide multiple means of engagement, representation, and action and expression to help neurodiverse students. As the next section will make clear, applying UDL to tutoring does not generate a single list of ideal practices. Such a list is impossible, or at the very least subject- and situation-specific. Rather, the goal for a tutoring session applying UDL should involve continually representing, reflecting on, and adapting tutoring strategies in order to successfully engage all types of learners.

TUTOR TRAINING WITH UDL PRINCIPLES

There is no better way to teach UDL principles to tutoring staff than to embed UDL strategies into the tutor-training program itself. Tutor trainers can teach and model multiple representations by presenting topics in multiple formats. For example, at East Carolina University's Pirate Academic Success Center, tutor training modules are presented in varying formats. Topics are introduced through engaging activities and collaborative discussions to demonstrate UDL pedagogical approaches. Center training staff utilize Canvas Learning Management System (LMS), videos, group assessment, and open discussions and introduce topics in written, electronic, and visual formats. Tutors are challenged to replicate strategies in their tutoring sessions through activities and role play.

Kiedaisch and Dinitz (2007) provide another example of training program redesign. Their goal was to help their tutors make sessions more accessible

Table 6.2. Best Practices for Tutoring Sessions Using UDL Practices

	Start of Session	Midsession	End of Session
Engagement	Ask open-ended questions to gauge task. Ask (within that task) what they know and what they want to work on. Suggest the goals and areas of focus for the session.	Provide positive feedback. Solicit check-ins in multiple ways (beyond "Do you have any questions?"). Ask questions designed to promote self-reflection at the end of learning tasks.	Ask about or summarize one to three learning takeaways. Ask to what extent they accomplished what they set out to do.
Representation	Ask students what reading format they prefer. Present options for directive or nondirective methods during the session.	Use multiple verbal/nonverbal strategies to work with student: open-ended and closed-ended questions, suggestions, explanations, instructions, direct modeling. Provide space or time for students to work: free writing, attempting to solve a problem, taking notes. Give multiple explanations and examples.	Ask whether they have a last question.
Action and Expression	Present options for where to work or what tools to use.	Use multiple tools and modes to promote learning. Ask students what they would try next with a simple or complex task.	Ask student what their plan is between now and the next class/due date/tutoring session. Suggest goals that fit their learning trajectory. Discuss how the student would prefer to monitor progress.

to multilingual writers and students with learning differences. They adopted the nine principles for UDI similar to Scott and colleagues (2003), by dividing them into *praxis, spaces, and services.* These principles and the examples Kiedaisch and Dinitz (2007) described are summarized in table 6.3.

Table 6.3.   Universal Design and Tutoring (summarized from Kiedaisch & Dinitz, 2007)

Principle	Example	Principle	Example
Simple and intuitive	Ask questions at the start of the session to gauge student experience.	Equitable use	Offer multiple options for using the center and its tools (e.g., in-person and online), and publicize them.
Flexibility in use	Offer multiple strategies for all stages of the writing process, including multiple tools like text-to-speech.	Perceptible information	Advertise availability of resources in multiple formats.
Tolerance for error	Discuss and reflect on alternative explanations for issues during a session.	Low physical effort	Allow work with students in hard copy or on a computer.
A community of learners	Bring relevant aspects of identity into a session (e.g., a tutor affirming that they also struggle with spelling rules).	Size and space for approach and use	Adjust layout of space and placement of resources to encourage their use by all individuals.
		Instructional climate	Consider diversity when selecting artwork and arranging/decorating the center.

   Tutor training provides an excellent opportunity for applying UDL principles in ways that reach *all* tutors and that will in turn help them work with the diverse learners who come into the center. UDL guidelines can be infused into existing training programs by revising three commonly used training phases:

- initial training, whether in a break-out session or a credit-bearing course;
- continuing training and professional development; and
- self-guided learning through reflection and research.

INITIAL TUTOR TRAINING

From the start of tutor training, programs should begin incorporating UDL practices. Initial training sessions are an opportune time to model how a tutor or instructor makes content-delivery decisions utilizing multiple means of *engagement, representation*, and *action and expression*. The outcomes of training program redesign are promising for both service delivery for tutees and meeting the learning needs of neurodiverse tutoring staff who are engaged in the training activities.

ENGAGEMENT

To promote engagement among tutors, combine several modes of training. For example, trainers could introduce new concepts in multiple ways, first having tutors read a short article, discussing it in small groups, and then discussing together as one big group. Training leaders could present a PowerPoint on specific practices or lead an activity where students practice mock tutoring and observation. Tutor trainers should seek new ways to highlight the goals and objectives of training, including the *whys* and the *hows* of tutoring. Introduce activities so that tutors know what learning objectives they will be meeting, and plan time after an activity for questions. Allow questions to be asked in multiple modes, including in writing and verbally. Create a post-training follow-up (an asynchronous survey or a staff meeting) to allow further reflection and provide another opportunity to contribute thoughts and suggestions.

Regarding content, in addition to modeling basic tutoring practices, find ways to scaffold for tutors how they would ask questions and offer choices to their students during a session. For example, some tutors excel at making these decisions on their own, and others require more mentoring or specific guidelines to feel comfortable introducing questions and options to their tutees. To meet the needs of both tutor groups, consider incorporating groups led by a more experienced tutor to collaboratively create guidelines or scenarios to work through the start-of-session and end-of-session procedures. Allow tutor-training groups to troubleshoot each other's work, and offer the revised results as quick references for tutors to use during the next semester.

REPRESENTATION

Within each content area of tutor-training programs, there are several ways to represent core content. For initial training, model common ways tutors and tutees interact with content within their subject area. For instance, writing tutors may want to learn strategies for working in a text document as well as on paper; math tutors may want to gain familiarity with both paper calculation and calculator use. Infuse assistive technologies available into training processes, and ask tutors to think through situations where these tools would be beneficial. Reframing training by introducing tools early will help provide what Conard-Salvo and Spartz (2012) describe as an "infrastructural framework" necessary for tutors to feel confident enough to introduce them in tutoring sessions.

Providing subject-specific guidance on how to represent core concepts is useful for helping tutors give multiple explanations to their tutees. Dinitz and Harrington (2014) observe that successful writing tutors can imagine how to apply general tutoring strategies and can effectively identify global issues, ask clarifying questions, and consider the tutee's perspective. For example, writing tutors might review concepts like *rhetorical awareness* or *organization*, which are likely to come up in a first-year writing course, while math tutors might review foundational concepts in first-year math courses.

Finally, tutors should become familiar with available resources that can help tutees learn key concepts. Centers may have access to physical resources like textbooks and handouts, digital versions of the same items, workshop presentations, lesson plans, models, or other materials. Trainers should ask tutors to map out the resources they would be likely to use, or to create a plan for reviewing and introducing these resources over the course of a semester in tutoring sessions.

ACTION AND EXPRESSION

For modeling principles of action and expression in tutoring sessions, ask tutors to set their own goals and expectations around training. New tutors may have many of these goals given to them, but leave room for tutors to self-identify elements of tutoring they anticipate having to focus on in their sessions. This may involve interpersonal skills, tutoring techniques, or mastery of subject knowledge. If returning tutors participate in training, have them set personal goals for improvement, and involve them in helping new tutors identify strengths and weaknesses.

When teaching tutoring strategies, emphasize multiple means for providing *action and expression* to students. For example, Mackiewicz and Thompson (2015) provide a list of strategies in three broad categories: (1) instruction (telling, suggesting, explaining/exemplifying), (2) cognitive scaffolding (pumping questions, reading aloud, responding as a reader/listener, referring to a previous topic, forcing a choice, prompting, hinting, and demonstrating), and (3) motivation (showing concern, praising, reinforcing student writers' ownership and control, being optimistic or using humor, and giving sympathy or empathy). Incorporating these or other strategies allows tutors to think about how to offer tutees both *questions* and *statements*. Through *tutor modeling* and *training activities*, trainers can introduce the use of both *open-ended questions* and *closed-ended questions* and equip tutors to foster both *directive* (tutor leads) and *nondirective* (tutee leads) engagement within their sessions.

Tutor-training programs can better prepare tutors and provide ways tutors can use the practice of giving a variety of tutees the opportunity to express both what they want to work on (start of session) and what they plan to work on later (end of session). Some tutees may show up to a session with a clear plan for what they want to work on, whereas others may come with only a general idea that they need help. The relative abilities, skills, personalities, and day-to-day circumstances of tutees will vary widely. In the start of semester training, trainers should begin by giving specific examples of different types of learner needs or session formats by emphasizing the general range of learning difference they can anticipate as a tutor.

UDL IN CONTINUED
TRAINING AND SELF-GUIDED LEARNING

Training does not stop after a tutor starts working. Rather, tutor training is an ongoing activity. Common avenues for continued training include staff meetings, periodic breakout sessions or workshops, online training modules in a learning management system, assigned readings or activities, and professional development meetings with a center administrator. Alongside tutoring experiences and training activities, center administrators can create opportunities for tutors to learn from their ongoing activities. Many centers feature post-session client reports where tutors summarize what they focused on during a session. They may also have peer observations, where observing tutors take notes, answer a series of questions about the session, or offer verbal suggestions to observed tutors. Sometimes observations and similar activities are done by a mentor who is a more experienced peer or professional tutor who can listen to concerns and share practical advice. Centers may also schedule time for tutors to do research or present at conferences. Because tutors learn from all of these activities, and especially because they may affect how tutors interact with students, UDL applies to them too.

Table 6.4 summarizes training activities and includes suggestions for how to apply principles of engagement, representation, or action and expression.

Table 6.4. Sample Practices for Increasing Engagement, Representation, and Action and Expression in Tutor Training and Learning Opportunities

	Engagement	Representation	Action & Expression
Staff Meetings, Workshops, and Breakout Sessions	Give tutors choices for setting the agenda. Foster discussion about expectations and beliefs toward tutoring and learning.	Use handouts/presentations/other media to display information. Keep notes, minutes, or record sessions.	Model use of assistive tools and technologies. Solicit periodic assessment of center strategy.
Online Training	Create tasks that allow for active participation and exploration. Make goals and assessment guidelines transparent.	Provide transcripts of any video or audio content. Ensure training is accessible on multiple platforms and browsers.	Provide multiple means for navigating content (browser menus, document checklist). Provide multiple ways to assess progress (self-reflection prompts, peer feedback, checklist).
Assigned Reading	Select readings that highlight multiple approaches to tutoring. Select multiple kinds of reading (empirical research, training writing, tutor reflections).	Ensure that readings are available in print or PDF. Process PDFs so that they are searchable and screen readers can access them.	Vary methods for reporting on reading (summary, discussion group, visualization, role play). Help more experienced tutors select or curate readings for group.
Individual Meetings	Give tutors options for setting the agenda of a meeting (tutoring, professional development, research). Provide specific and individualized feedback using reports, surveys, observation notes.	Offer both online and in-person meetings, using the affordances of each. Meet in a space with multiple means for representation (a screen, a board, a table and paper).	Help tutors set appropriate goals for the next month, semester, or year. Assess with tutors their relative competencies in tutoring, tools and media, and work performance.

Post-Session Reports	Discuss with tutors what to mention and how to include it in a report. Represent to tutors the goals (why) for reports.	Encourage tutors to explain or exemplify what they do. Have tutors workshop their reports with target audiences (administrators, other tutors, focus groups).	Discuss whether and how to share tutor reports with students or faculty. Encourage tutors to look at reports for returning students.
Peer Observations	Develop clear expectations for why and how tutors observe. Clarify observation as formative assessment and as collaborative learning—both the observer and the observed tutor should learn.	Define what aspects of the tutoring session the observer should note. Encourage highlighting patterns, like similarities and differences between peer approaches.	Develop clear guidelines for soliciting student permission to observe. Use notes from observations to inform other forms of feedback.
Mentoring	Provide mentoring to mentors in how to build and maintain a mentoring relationship. Provide options for how mentees engage with their mentors (individual meeting, observation, discussions during shared shifts).	Encourage the mentor to share resources or consult them together with their mentee. Encourage the mentee to ask content-related questions of the mentor.	Have mentor/mentee pairs collaborate to master the use of tools and technologies. Ask mentors and mentees to set appropriate goals for what they want to get out of their working together.
Research	Encourage research as an extension of tutoring practice, rather than a specialized and exclusive activity. Suggest specific topics and venues for research based on a tutor's interests and abilities.	Provide options for what mode to disseminate research in—poster, presentation, article, handout, website. Clarify the research process, including how to manage time and how to find sources.	Provide—and let tutors set—reasonable deadlines and goals for their own work. Assess periodically that research activities stay within the confines of work and do not encroach on academic or personal lives.

The larger goal of tutor-training programs is to ensure content delivery promotes reflection and learning for tutors. Not every tutor will find the interpersonal stakes of mentoring equally significant; some tutors will view session reports as busywork and engage minimally in reflection. Tutors sometimes need help in learning how to plan for, participate in, and get the most out of a meeting or workshop. Center administrators know that these activities work to promote reflection and improve the tutor's ability to effectively support tutee needs. When using reflection activities, trainers should focus on increasing tutor understanding of the importance of reflection processes. Giaimo and Turner (2019) found that training tutors in end-of-session notes increased the rate tutors were completing notes to 96% from a low of 20%; Blazer (2015) promotes inclusive transcultural practices through actively involving tutors in activities, like providing discussions, blog-writing activities, reading groups, and resource development. By providing multiple activities and carefully attending to how tutors participate in them, centers model multiple options for engagement, representation, and action and expression.

UDL IN TUTOR EVALUATIONS

Assessing the effectiveness of UDL strategies in tutoring centers can be difficult, but annual or bi-annual evaluations for tutors provide measurable data on the successful implementation of these best practices. A peer evaluation process is often encouraged, because it provides multiple means of engagement and promotes a collaborative learning environment. Collaborative skills and the ability to give and receive professional feedback are important job-ready skills that industry professionals seek in future employees. Gueldenzoph and May (2002) suggest five best practices when conducting peer evaluations, as illustrated in table 6.5. Practical examples of how to apply each practice in a learning center evaluation are also included.

UDL principles provide a quality framework for assessing the effectiveness of high-impact learning strategies (Craig et al., 2018). UDL practices provide measurable guidelines for assessing tutors during tutoring sessions. An example of a UDL evaluation tool is seen in textbox 6.1. The evaluation tool focuses specifically on tutor communication strategies and the use of learning resources during sessions. The goal of the evaluation is to effectively rate how a tutor demonstrates information through multiple platforms for both neurotypical students and neurodiverse students. The evaluation includes both quantitative and qualitative measures, which allows a supervisor to better relay the summative assessment to the tutor at the conclusion of the evaluation process.

Table 6.5. Tutor Evaluation Best Practices and Example Strategies

Best Practices for Collaborative Evaluations	Example Strategy
1. Building a foundation to support collaborative learning	Allow students to participate in peer tutoring observations, and provide written and verbal feedback to peers. Students learn strategies based on examples of other tutors during the process and how to give and receive professional feedback.
2. Creating effective evaluation tools with specific criteria that allow honest student feedback	Utilize UDL principles to define learning objectives or evaluation criteria.
3. Implementing formative feedback during the collaborative process	Make sure to include both quantitative and qualitative measures in evaluation process.
4. Formulating summative feedback at the conclusion of the experience	Set face-to-face meetings with tutors to provide professional feedback from supervisors as well as peers. All final summative assessments should be approved by the tutoring supervisor.
5. Assessing the collaborative evaluation process	At the end of each evaluation process, reassess evaluation criteria to make sure it effectively measures the intended purpose and if the process was fair and equitable.

DL Tutoring Evaluation Tool, East Carolina University

TutorName_____ NameofEvaluator_____

Date and Time of Evaluation_____

Please circle tutor evaluation rating and include written feedback below.

1. *Tutor responded professionally and was composed when working with the tutee.*

   Unacceptable   Needs   Development   Proficient   Excellent

2. *Tutor utilizes technology, white boards, or other visual aids in order to expand on topics covered in the session.*

   Unacceptable   Needs   Development   Proficient   Excellent

3. *Tutor exhibits good listening skills and pays close attention in what others are saying, and expresses genuine interest. Tutor asks open-ended questions.*

Unacceptable   Needs   Development   Proficient   Excellent

4. *Tutor conveys information in both verbal and written formats.*

Unacceptable   Needs   Development   Proficient   Excellent

5. *Tutor smiles and shows patience. Tutor is encouraging to the tutee throughout the appointment.*

Unacceptable   Needs   Development   Proficient   Excellent

6. *Tutor uses questioning techniques to stimulate critical thinking. (The tutor should not be re-creating lecture.)*

Unacceptable   Needs   Development   Proficient   Excellent

7. *The tutor provides study tips and techniques to connect to the material, as applicable.*

Unacceptable   Needs   Development   Proficient   Excellent

8. *The tutor talks to the student about their personal learning style and what learning strategies fit them best, in order to personalize the appointment to the student's individual needs.*

Unacceptable   Needs   Development   Proficient   Excellent

9. *The tutor discusses learning goals at the beginning and end of the session. The tutor suggests goals to fit learning strategies for each tutee.*

Unacceptable   Needs   Development   Proficient   Excellent

10. *Comments about Tutor Communication and Demonstration of Course Material (please give detailed responses addressing any areas of concern or positive remarks)*

_____

_____

_____

_____

RAISING TUTOR AWARENESS OF NEURODIVERSITY

We close this section by briefly introducing College Reading and Learning Association (CRLA) certification for tutors. Many centers participate in their International Tutor Training Program Certification (ITTPC). In order to achieve certification status, CRLA representatives thoroughly evaluate a center's training program, topics, structure, and delivery process. Setting specific guidelines for training best practices, CRLA accreditation guidelines are referenced on their association's website: crla.net. The tutor-training program certification offers three training competencies: Level 1, Level 2, and Level 3. Level 1 emphasizes basic practices in tutoring, techniques for beginning and ending a session, working with adult learners, learning theory and/or learning styles, and communication skills. Levels 2 and 3 emphasize greater theoretical knowledge of tutoring and more engagement in mentoring, training, leadership, and supervising.

CRLA does not require a UDL approach or highlight neurodiverse learners. One of the few explicit focuses on neurodiverse students occurs in Level 2 training, and a loosely recommended topic involving "Cultural awareness, inter-cultural communications, diversity, and/or special needs students" ("Standards, Outcomes, and Assessments," 2015). Therefore, it would be possible to utilize CRLA's own guidelines and reach Level 2 competency before neurodiversity was introduced into the training curriculum.

Level 1 training guidelines encourage a variety of activities and formats that could arguably involve principles of UDL. Presenting training concepts in varied ways facilitates a CRLA-certified training program that works well for neurodiverse learners. For instance, Topic 4, "Adult learners and/or learning theory and/or learning styles," encourages tutors to differentiate their learning strategies "to meet various needs of learners based on learner preferences, strengths/weaknesses, background, or prior knowledge" ("Standards, Outcomes, and Possible Assessments," 2013). Many of the start-of-session and mid-session activities already discussed in this chapter would meet the expectations for this topic, such as asking questions and offering options at the start of a session to gauge what a student needs and then using multiple modes and explanations to convey information based on that assessment. These topics also fold into more general sections like learning "techniques for beginning and ending a tutoring session" ("Standards, Outcomes, and Possible Assessments," 2013). Ultimately, any stage of a session or any subtopic of training can be presented in such a way that it provides multiple options for learning.

Revisions of current tutor-training programs are warranted. Center administrators and tutor trainers need to consider program training through the lens of neurodiversity and UDL. Current CRLA-accredited programs should revise delivery methods and introduce topics related to neurodiversity beyond CRLA requirements. Raising tutor awareness of learning differences and the tutor's role in providing academic success resources is paramount to establishing a neurodiverse-friendly tutoring center.

CONCLUSION

Students who are neurodiverse continually face academic challenges that hinder their collegiate success. As educators, it is our responsibility to mitigate those challenges as best we can by creating adaptable learning environments where all students can thrive. Often in academia, students learn via traditional lecture models, which can further magnify difficulties, anxiety, and lower grade point averages for students with learning differences (Proctor et al., 2006). Higher education needs to meet the demands of this growing population by employing strategies that personalize the educational experience and ability for every student to succeed academically. The Universal Design for Learning standards give tutors a prescriptive set of guidelines for creating learning environments that are adaptable, collaborative, and suited for students at all stages of learning development. In addition, the CRLA and ITTPC training program provide certification for tutors who work directly with neurodiverse students. Despite the limited research on the effects of tutoring for students with learning differences, it is imperative that tutoring center leadership review, redesign, and envision new methods of delivery and support on their campus. What we do know is by utilizing peer tutoring in higher education settings, we can increase the opportunity for students with diverse learning needs to receive effective academic support services.

Campus Essentials for High Impact

- *Consider the use of UDL principles in your campus tutoring sessions.* In what ways would your students benefit from new approaches to tutoring services?
- *Transform tutor training with UDL.* Model UDL for tutoring staff by revising training modules and presenting topics in multiple formats and materials.
- *Access tutor competencies with UDL measures in evaluation processes.* Reconsider evaluation processes by infusing UDL measures and competencies for tutors.

- *Explore digital platforms to support neurodiverse students.* Work with campus partners to integrate digital formats and tools for tutor use in campus tutoring sessions.
- *Support neurodiverse tutoring staff.* Administrators should never assume that only tutees have learning differences. Changes to tutor-training practices assist neurodiverse tutors as well as produce positive outcomes for tutees.

REFERENCES

Black, R. D., Weinberg, L. A., & Brodwin, M. G. (2015). Universal Design for Learning and instruction: Perspectives of students with disabilities in higher education. *Exceptionality Education International, 25*(2), 1–26.

Blazer, S. (2015). Twenty-first century writing center staff education: Teaching and learning towards inclusive and productive everyday practice. *The Writing Center Journal, 35*(1), 17–55.

Brizee, A., Sousa, M., & Driscoll, D. L. (2012). Writing centers and students with disabilities: The user-centered approach, participatory design, and empirical research as collaborative methodologies. *Computers and Composition, 29*(4), 341–366. https://doi.org/10.1016/j.compcom.2012.10.003

Bublitz, D., Wong, V., Donachie, A., Brooks, P. J., & Gillespie-Lynch, K. (2015). Applying universal design to build supports for college students with autism spectrum disorder. *Progress in Education, 36*, 1–24.

Burgstahler, S., & Moore, E. (2009). Making student services welcoming and accessible through accommodations and Universal Design. *Journal of Postsecondary Education & Disability, 21*(3), 155–174.

College Reading and Learning Association. (2013). *Standards, outcomes, and possible assessments for ITTPC certification.* https://crla.net/images/ITTPC/ITTPC_Standards_Outcomes_Assessments_Level_1.pdf

College Reading and Learning Association. (2015). *Standards, outcomes, and assessments: Levels 2 & 3 tutor training programs.* https://crla.net/images/ITTPC/ITTPC_Standards_Outcomes_Assessments_Levels_2_and_3.pdf

Conard-Salvo, T., & Spartz, J. M. (2012). Listening to revise: What a study about text-to-speech software taught us about students' expectations for technology use in the writing center. *The Writing Center Journal, 32*(2), 40–59.

Connell, B. R., Jones, M., Mace, R., Mueller, J., Mullick, A., Ostroff, E., & Vanderheiden, G. (1997, April 1). *The principles of Universal Design.* NC State University, the Center for Universal Design. https://projects.ncsu.edu/ncsu/design/cud/about_ud/udprinciplestext.htm

Couzens, D., Poed, S., Kataoka, M., Brandon, A., Hartley, J., & Keen, D. (2015). Support for students with hidden disabilities in universities: A case study. *International Journal of Disability, Development and Education, 62*(1), 24–41. doi:10.1080/1034912X.2014.984592

Craig, S. L., Smith, S. J., & Frey B. B. (2019): Professional development with universal design for learning: Supporting teachers as learners to increase the implementation of UDL. *Professional Development in Education*, 1–16. DOI: 10.1080/19415257.2019.1685563

Deese-Roberts, S. (Ed.). (2003). *CRLA: Tutor training handbook (Rev. Ed.)*. College Reading and Learning Association. http://www.lsche.net/?page_id=4526

Dinitz, S., & Harrington, S. (2014). The role of disciplinary expertise in shaping writing tutorials. *The Writing Center Journal, 33*(2), 73–98.

Giaimo, G. N., & Turner, S. J. (2019). Session notes as a professionalization tool for writing center staff: Conducting discourse analysis to determine training efficacy and tutor growth. *Journal of Writing Research, 11*(1), 131–162.

Gueldenzoph, L. E., & May, G. L. (2002). Collaborative peer evaluation: Best practices for group member assessments. *Business Communication Quarterly, 65*(1), 9–20. https://doi.org/10.1177/108056990206500102

Jacobs, S. (1999). *The electronic curb cut.* The Center for an Accessible Society. http://www.accessiblesociety.org/topics/technology/eleccurbcut.htm#012

Janiga, S. J., & Costenbader, V. (2002). The transition from high school to postsecondary education for students with learning disabilities: A survey of college service coordinators. *Journal of Learning Disabilities, 35*(5), 463–470.

Kiedaisch, J., & Dinitz, S. (2007). Changing notions of difference in the writing center: The possibilities of Universal Design. *The Writing Center Journal, 27*(2), 39–59.

Lewis, L., Farris, E., & Greene, B. (1999). *An institutional perspective on students with disabilities in postsecondary education, NCES 1999-046.* Washington, DC: U.S. Department of Education, National Center for Education Statistics.

Mackiewicz, J., & Thompson, I. K. (2015). *Talk about writing: The tutoring strategies of experienced writing center tutors.* Routledge, Taylor & Francis Group.

Meyer, A., Rose, D. H., & Gordon, D. (2014). *Universal Design for Learning: Theory and practice.* http://udltheorypractice.cast.org/home?3

Micheal, R., (2016). The perceived success of tutoring students with learning disabilities: Relations to tutee and tutoring variables. *Journal of Postsecondary Education and Disability, 29*(4), 349–361.

Proctor, B. E., Prevatt, F., Adams K., Hurst, A., & Petscher, Y. (2006). Study skills profiles of normal-achieving and academically-struggling college students. *Journal of College Student Development, 47*, 37–51.

Pugatch, T., & Wilson, N. (2018). Nudging study habits: A field experiment on peer tutoring in higher education. *Economics of Education Review, 62*, 151–161.

Rose, D. H., & Meyer, A. (2002). *Teaching every student in the digital age: Universal Design for Learning.* Association for Supervision and Curriculum Development.

Ryan, L., & Zimmerelli, L. (2016). *The Bedford guide for writing tutors.* Bedford/St. Martin's.

Sarrett, J.C. (2018). Autism and accommodation in higher education: Insights from the Autism community. *Journal of Autism and Developmental disorders, 48*(3), 679–693. https:// doi.org/10.1007/s10803-017-3353-4

Scott, S. S., Mcguire, J. M., & Shaw, S. F. (2003). Universal Design for Instruction: A new paradigm for adult instruction in postsecondary education. *Remedial and Special Education, 24*(6), 369–379. https://doi.org/10.1177/07419325030240060801

Vogel, G., Fresko, B., & Wertheim, C. (2007). Peer tutoring for college students with learning disabilities: Perceptions of tutors and tutees. *Journal of Learning Disabilities, 40*(6), 485–493.

Webb, K. K., & Hoover, J. (n.d.). *Universal Design for Learning (UDL) in the academic library: A methodology for mapping multiple means of representation in library tutorials.* College and Research Libraries. https://crl.acrl.org/index.php/crl/article/view/16441

Zeff, R. (2007). Universal design across the curriculum. *New Directions for Higher Education, 2007*(137), 27–44. https://doi.org/10.1002/he.244

Chapter 6: Campus Spotlight

Pirate Academic Success Center, East Carolina University

Elizabeth M. H. Coghill

Neurodiverse learners demand a new approach to academic learning environments. Students benefit from learning spaces that foster facets of Universal Design for Learning (UDL) and are designed to heighten academic engagement and encourage collaborative learning. The Pirate Academic Success Center (PASC) at East Carolina University (ECU) integrates technology tools to transform the learning environment within the campus learning center.

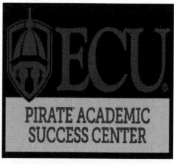

Source: ECU Pirate Academic Success Center

The Pirate Academic Success Center provides tutoring, mentoring, and academic support services for a high volume of students, averaging 32% of the 23,000 campus undergraduates using its services annually. Since 2011, the PASC has been integrating technology tools in order to advance tutoring platforms by blending face-to-face services with digital services, foster a welcoming collaborative learning environment, and enable learning center staff to better meet the educational demands and learning needs of neurodiverse students.

PASC services reach a large population of students, and the use of technology devices significantly impacts the ability to serve high numbers of students and address their individual learning needs. For tutors, it fosters a collaborative learning environment, allows tutors to apply tenets of UDL in sessions, increases options when addressing student learning differences, and promotes engagement opportunities. Technology tools cultivate fresh approaches to learning support, promote the integration of UDL principles, and address the needs of neurodiverse learners.

The PASC combines technology and students in precisely the right formula. It is perhaps the most positive learning environment I have ever witnessed. I marvel at the digital tools that have been assembled and the quality of the Center experience. The technology is clearly an important part of this welcoming environment.

—ECU interim chancellor and provost Dr. Ron Mitchelson

Seeking to provide a network of academic and social supports for students who historically have been underserved by the post-secondary education system, in 2011 PASC began to incorporate UDL into programming and academic support services. The integration of UDL supports the goal that all students should have access to teaching and academic support in a way that meets their individual learning needs and fosters an open and accepting learning environment. Through the blending of innovative technology applications and center design, PASC provides a welcoming learning environment fostering digital engagement, incorporating UDL principles into center activities, and cultivating a collaborative learning space for neurodiverse learners.

On an average day, the PASC serves 250-plus students with tutoring and mentoring services, each student requiring the assistance of different learning resources and approaches. PASC center design supports the integration of technology devices and applications that, combined, allow tutors to choose their approach and tailor services to meet student learning needs. UDL is supported by an open learning environment, multiple technology tools, LCD monitors and touchscreen tablets, interactive white boards, wireless connections using Air Media, and collaborative learning tables. A collaborative learning environment is cultivated when students communicate as equals and technology tools combine to increase interaction between peer educator and tutee, allowing them to address different learning styles, needs, and preferences. In daily tutoring sessions, PASC tutors utilize tablets to ensure greater collaboration, review materials, and provide resources designed to help reinforce course concepts. Tablets, monitors, and collaborative technology tables have become a lynchpin in achieving optimum student engagement for all learners.

Noteworthy on the East Carolina University campus is the creation of digital support through peer-produced videos designed to supplement learning

Technology Devices at the PASC	Center Application
Think Pad Tablets/ Yoga Touchscreen, Helix Tablets	Used for content in tutoring sessions, academic mentoring session notes, class presentations, and course support workshops.
Air Media/Display Monitors	Allows for wireless connectivity for tutoring sessions, workshops, and presentations.
Knapp Smart Boards	Allows tutees to download white board notes from tutoring session.
Lecture Capture/Videos	Supports 13 STEM courses for tutors to produce digital support content.
Ipad/Applications	Interactive applications for tutoring, mentoring and study skills support.
One Note	Allows tutors and mentors to share session notes directly with tutees or mentees or professional staff members.
Digital Forms and Document Sharing	All center services preformed and documented digitally.
LCD Monitors	Fosters small group collaboration, displays One Note, connects to E-text books, and online resources.

Source: Technology Devices at the PASC

materials for 13 high-demand STEM courses. Course content is created by undergraduate tutors with faculty input and then offered digitally to students enrolled in 13 science courses in the areas of chemistry, biology, and physics. Utilizing Canvas as a learning platform, tutors produce content that is specific to the courses and faculty members offered at East Carolina. Videos are made available all semester for unlimited viewing at any time of day. When grades are compared, there is a positive grade impact for students who combine face-to-face tutoring and digital services above students who did not seek assistance. Historically, these students achieve 30% higher passage rates (A, B, or C grade earned) in chemistry, 25% in physics, and 10% in biology (Coghill, 2017–2020).

STUDENT IMPACT

The integration of technology in the PASC provides the ability for tutors to present materials with varied UDL approaches and helps address the learning differences of our students. PASC tutors are empowered to make content delivery choices and are trained to engage students in a welcoming learning environment. The training and exposure to technology devices and applications enhances the student user experience in meaningful ways. When learning centers use technology to support campus learning, all students benefit.

REFERENCE

Coghill, E. (2020, 2019, 2018, 2017). Pirate Academic Success Center Annual Report. https://pasc.ecu.edu/about-us/annual-report/

Chapter Seven

Learning Supports

Morgan James, Alysha Gray, Emily Johnson, and Sarah Williams

Colleges and universities today are enrolling more diverse student populations on a variety of metrics, including neurodiversity. This necessitates a change in how we do business, and we must learn to anticipate and embrace the increasing variability in learners who now fill our classrooms. Post-secondary campuses are learning to offer high-quality academic programs, while simultaneously providing students access to appropriate supports. For the past several years, we have been exploring best practices for serving students with learning and attention challenges who trust us during their college years with their time, talents, and resources.

SPECIALIZED LEARNING SUPPORTS AND PROGRAMS FOR NEURODIVERSE STUDENT POPULATIONS

The authors of this chapter are connected with programs on public university campuses that support students with learning and attention differences. Each day, we watch capable and motivated students succeed in a rigorous post-secondary environment, but nationally, university graduation and retention rates for students with learning differences are lower than those of their peers (Katsiyannis et al., 2009; Kosine, 2007; Murray et al., 2000). Some students with learning differences transition to college smoothly, develop support systems or strategies as necessary, and thrive in the university setting. For others, learning and attention challenges can make the transition to new educational environments difficult.

The majority of students who participate in our programs have Attention Deficit/Hyperactivity Disorder (ADHD), specific learning disabilities

(SLDs) such as dyslexia, dysgraphia, dyscalculia, and/or executive functioning challenges (EFCs). These neurodiverse groups constitute a large
proportion of students who receive special education support in the K–12
setting and additional services on college campuses (Newman et al., 2011;
U.S. Department of Education, 2017). Each of our programs is different in
regard to our administrative location, funding model, structure, and size, but
we have worked together over the past 7 years to share resources and best
practices, understand the college experience for neurodiverse learners, and
connect with other like-missioned student support programs to expand our
network and ability to learn together. This is creating a unique opportunity
to research collaboratively and share best practices for a group of students
who have historically been anonymous on our college campuses. See table
7.1 for example student support programs that serve students with learning
and attention challenges.

Essential Elements to Support Student Learning

In preparation for writing this chapter, we came together to identify essential
elements for high impact that have emerged across all of our programs (regardless of our differences). Many of these elements are grounded in research
and best-practice routines for students with learning and attention differences.
That said, individuals with disabilities must choose whether to self-disclose
to instructors and disability support providers, and only an estimated 25% of
students do so (Newman et al., 2011), making for an under-researched population of students. Some of what is included here comes from our collective
experience working day-to-day with neurodiverse students in the college
environment.

Serving neurodiverse students requires a balance. On the one hand, we
must anticipate learner variability and create educational spaces (in our
classrooms, advising offices, tutoring centers, libraries, etc.) that increase
opportunity for learning and reduce unintentional barriers for students who
have historically been marginalized in the college setting. Universal Design for Learning (UDL, addressed more fully in chapter 5) has provided
critical guiding principles for our teams. On the other hand, we must learn
to find and effectively support students with learning and attention challenges who need direct and specialized support to reach their potential in
the post-secondary setting. The first part of that balance is addressed by
our colleagues in several other chapters in this book. This chapter focuses
on lessons learned together in identifying and providing support to neurodivergent learners.

Table 7.1. Example Student Support Programs

College/University	Program Name	Student Population
Appalachian State University	As-U-R	Students with executive functioning challenges
Auburn University	SKILL	Students with documented learning differences, ADHD, and/or executive functioning challenges
Beacon College	Beacon College	Students with diagnosed learning differences and/or ADHD
Curry College	PAL	Students with ADHD, executive functioning challenges, and/or language-based learning disabilities
East Carolina University	STEPP	Students with learning disabilities
Fayetteville State University	Bronco STAR	Students with executive functioning challenges
Landmark College	Landmark College	Students with specific learning differences, ADHD, and/or Autism Spectrum Disorders
Louisburg College	Learning Partners	Students with specific learning differences and/or ADHD
Marshall University	H.E.L.P.	Students with specific learning differences and/or ADHD
	West Virginia Autism Training Center	Students with Autism Spectrum Disorders or Asperger's Syndrome
Mercyhurst University	Learning Differences Program	Students with specific learning, physical, and/or sensory disabilities, Autism Spectrum Disorder, and/or chronic health conditions
University of Arizona	SALT Center	Students with specific Learning Differences, ADHD, and/or students who have a history of learning differences
University of Central Florida	Student Accessibility Services (SAS)	Any UCF student who experiences barriers in the academic environment due to a disability
University of Denver	Learning Effectiveness Program	Students with specific learning differences, ADHD, Autism Spectrum Disorders, and/or a history of learning differences
University of North Carolina at Greensboro	ACCESS	Students with ADHD

Identifying and Connecting Students to Support Services

Disabilities that impact learning and attention are *invisible* disabilities. It is easy for educators (and the students themselves) to fall into the habit of "blaming" the student rather than understanding the very real impact the disability can have on student access and performance in the classroom. Years of living with stigma and misconceptions about learning differences can leave students hesitant to self-disclose and seek educational support and accommodations available to them. This makes awareness-building across campus, as well as partnering with the K–12 setting, essential to ensure students connect with programs that are equipped to provide appropriate support.

Strengthening connections with our K–12 colleagues is essential if we are to help students with different learning profiles make a seamless transition to college. High school guidance counselors, teachers, and transition specialists can be valuable partners, especially for students who have received support through special education legislation throughout their K–12 experience. Additionally, recruiting during times when parents are on campus (at events like new student orientation, new student advising, weeks of welcome, and open house) provides another source of encouragement for students to proactively seek and access support. Colleges and high schools alike can point students to resources that are designed for students with different learning needs and can help them prepare for the transition to the college setting (e.g., College Bound curriculum: https://www.ecu.edu/cs-acad/stepp/curriculum.cfm).

Once on campus, student interactions with peers and professionals all across campus are beneficial if students are equipped for them, and these people can be excellent allies in connecting students to support. For example, first-year seminar instructors, student organization leaders, advisors, transfer-student services, early college, counseling services, disability services, and peer tutors can all be valuable partners in the recruitment process. Some of our programs have found that a brief training and awareness-building experience can help colleagues across campus recognize and refer students who may need support. Additionally, an efficient way to reach students is through social media platforms (Facebook, Twitter, Instagram, and Snapchat), videos, testimonials, and giveaways. These tools assist in relating to others and foster a sense of being approachable to our students. For example, student video testimonials can catch the attention of other students who may be experiencing similar challenges and help them feel less embarrassed about seeking support.

Building a system of tiered services or varying levels of intensive support can be helpful for both accommodating larger numbers of students and addressing individual student needs with varying risk levels. Coordinating a tiered system of services (either across campus or within an individual program) helps meet students where they are and personalizes their support needs and reduces duplication of services in various campus offices. In decentralized service operations, however, it is critical for a student to have one point person or program for guidance, even if some direct services come from multiple sources on campus.

Moreover, student support needs may change during key transition points in their college career. By anchoring key identification efforts and supports to common transition experiences, students receive reoccurring opportunities to connect, assess, and design the support services they need. Common transitions include high school to college, general college courses to major-specific courses, full-time coursework to full-time internships, and undergraduate to graduate school, or after college to the workforce. During each of these transitions, students face unique challenges that require individualized support. For example, a student may need support in utilizing new note-taking strategies as courses become more difficult, staying organized and keeping track of internship/job applications, and applying study skills as they prepare for graduate school admission exams.

Providing Support

The remainder of this chapter will focus on lessons learned in programs specifically designed for students who demonstrate learning and attention challenges. We consider a combination of the following elements to be essential in our day-to-day work with neurodivergent students:

- community development and building a sense of belonging;
- connections to campus resources and organizations;
- attention to the social and emotional aspects of learning;
- well-timed parallel curriculum interwoven through the program;
- establishment of structured learning environments;
- provision of support for executive functioning; and
- direct support with study techniques.

Community Development and Belonging

Feeling a sense of belonging through relationships and connections with others can be extremely important to students who may otherwise feel marginalized on a college campus (Vaccaro et al., 2015). Support programs can facilitate meaningful communities that offer opportunities for students with similar learning profiles to interact and learn from each other, share successes and frustrations, swap helpful strategies, and develop a peer support network that can benefit them throughout their college experience. Our programs each take different approaches to scheduling opportunities for community-building among students and staff. Events such as family weekends, stress management workshops, soup day, movie nights, and so on not only provide a different way for students to connect but are also a lot of fun. Furthermore, within the larger campus community, opportunities for students to engage, connect, and feel a sense of belonging through being a part of learning communities, joining student organizations, and attending campus events can create organic and natural results of bringing bright and talented college students together who have similar interests and commonalities (Ribera et al., 2017).

Connections to Campus Resources and Organizations

Universities often provide students with a rich array of resources and experiences designed to help students pursue academic success, stay healthy, meet new people, and have fun! Some college students may be hesitant to take advantage of these campus opportunities, and others may not realize their availability. For students with learning and attention differences, the sheer volume and size of campus offerings can be overwhelming. Even knowing where to begin can be a hurdle, so one of the essential elements of a student support program is actually the ability to connect students to other support services on campus. Being intentional about helping students connect to resources is just as important as having them available. Strategies for supporting connectivity include:

- *Semester goal-setting and action plans*: semester goal-setting and action plans, resource-finding events, connection events, guided connections, and crisis connections. An important part of our goal-setting with students each semester includes identifying key campus resources that are most applicable for helping them meet their goals. For example, a student with a goal to reduce social anxiety and become more engaged with campus activities may include action items to visit the counseling center and the student activities office.
- *Resource-finding events*: Programs find ways to engage students with campus offices before a challenge arises and to raise awareness of their locations. Scavenger hunts can range from "old school" to highly technical and can be a fun way for students to work together to become oriented to campus support in a proactive and nonthreatening way. In addition, hosting resource fairs can be effective. These fairs can be different from the large resource fairs at campus-wide orientations or open houses; student support programs can develop smaller and more tailored resource fairs for students with learning differences and their families. These fairs offer a chance for

students to meet office representatives, ask questions, and establish connections with key support staff on campus.

- *Connection events*: Some programs schedule campus connection events throughout the year, for example, featuring one program each month. This format provides an opportunity for students to have in-depth conversations with representatives of each office and supports the development of relationships that may be helpful later on.

- *Guided connections*: For students, connecting with some campus support offices can be accompanied by hesitation and a fear of the potential stigma associated with that office. For example, students who have negative experiences in the K–12 setting associated with learning challenges and teasing from other students may be nervous about connecting with the campus disability support office or disclosing a disability to their instructors. While sharing this information is always voluntary for students, support programs can assist students in establishing connections in various ways, such as role-playing, previewing emails to campus staff or faculty, providing reassurance, and accountability. Help students practice with disclosing their disability in a way that will be perceived as they intend. These practice sessions not only may assist students while they are seeking resources on campus but also may help them successfully disclose their disability as they enter the workforce and prepare for life after graduation.

- *Crisis connections*: The availability for ongoing as-needed support may be one of the most essential elements of student support on large college campuses. Regardless of how proactive students try to be, there are simply times when they need immediate help. Instead of becoming crisis moments, minor daily challenges (e.g., the learning management system crashes in the middle of a test, an argument with a roommate, difficult email from instructor) can become teachable moments if students have developed a relationship with key personnel who can provide front-line regular support with ongoing routines, or critical in-time guidance and encouragement during times of crisis or insecurity. Academic coaching is addressed more fully in chapter 8, "Academic Mentoring and Coaching Services," which addresses the need for immediate support.

SOCIAL AND EMOTIONAL ELEMENTS OF LEARNING

While social and emotional elements of learning are important to consider in general on a college campus (Stocker & Gallagher, 2019; Wang et al., 2012), they are essential factors when designing supports for students with learning and attention challenges. Students with learning and attention differences will likely experience more academic, social, and emotional challenges than their peers (Grieve et al., 2014), Support programs can help neurodivergent students identify methods for coping with the new pressures of college and the routines that will at times feel tedious and overwhelming. By helping students identify their strengths and leverage those assets academically and socially, mentors on campus can help students develop problem-solving and self-advocacy strategies for working through difficult situations that can otherwise paralyze or stifle progress toward course or semester goals. Additionally, creating positive, trusting, inclusive communities is critical. Students will need individuals they can seek out during times of crisis or trial. Students also need to understand that they are not alone, but instead have opportunities to connect with other students with similar needs and who face similar learning challenges.

PARALLEL CURRICULUM

Neurodivergent students can benefit from two types of "curriculum" in the college environment. The first, their academic curriculum, is provided through their general education and major courses, and many students come to college well prepared for this curriculum. Our programs infuse a second parallel "curriculum" that is integrated strategically throughout the college experience. Designed to help students develop the knowledge, skills, and dispositions needed to successfully "do college" and prepare for life after graduation, this curriculum may or may not be attached to specific courses, but it is intentionally infused into each program. It is grounded in best practices for students with learning and attention challenges. The parallel curriculum is focused on equipping students with the skills to be successful in their academic courses. While some of these elements are included in a typical freshman-seminar-style course, many students require more intensive support. Despite possessing the necessary capacity, content knowledge, high motivation, and strong work ethic, neurodiverse students may need explicit instruction in how to navigate the college environment (Meltzer, 2018). Student programs can provide instruction focused on developing personalized learning routines needed to cope with classrooms that may not be welcoming for different learning profiles.

Parallel curricula can be grounded in seminars or courses and can facilitate the development of metacognitive awareness that serves as a foundation for effective academic strategies (Meltzer et al., 2015) and daily habits. In our experience, the following instructional topics are essential during key transition experiences and can be tailored to the specific needs of student populations:

- self-advocacy skills;
- planning and time-management skills;
- study skills;
- research skills;
- learning strategies;
- leadership training; and
- workforce-readiness skills.

Our course facilitators use experiential and active learning as the foundation for skill acquisition and reflection, create common learning experiences in the seminar environment, and help students generalize new skills and strategies to their current academic coursework. Student success courses, combined with other supports for students such as academic coaching, provide a scaffolded holistic model of support that pinpoints a student's strengths, needs, and how those impact successes in and out of the classroom (Getzel, 2008).

All students learn differently, and some may require more practice and experience using strategies and developing skills and techniques than their collegiate peers. Over time, students require different levels of practice, instruction, and coaching as they progress through their degree program. For some, generalization of skills and incidental learning may take time, while others become confident and proficient with new skills quickly. Student support programs have the opportunity to scaffold support for each student as needed, enabling a focus on *what* students need as opposed to how quickly students can acquire and implement new skills.

Naturally, neurodiverse students who have greater areas of needs will require more intensive support and higher levels of structure. For example, a student with dyslexia might be well prepared to master content in his major but may need to learn how to adjust to the increased volume of reading required for college courses. Assistance with selecting technology resources that assist with decoding, finding supplementary study resources, and establishing pre-/post-class study routines may provide sufficient understandings that the student can generalize to future courses. Another student may need more intensive or longer-term support and work longer with a mentor or coach to gradually be able to independently select and refine study strategies. Each student is practicing the self-advocacy needed to understand and connect with the appropriate type and level of support, a skill that will be needed during and after college.

When building a program curriculum, program staff must (1) determine *what* areas of support are needed for the student, (2) define the *amount* of support needed in that area, and (3) identify the best *method* for administering the support. Providing paths for individualized methods of learning support can increase the overall effectiveness of the program and reduce the likelihood that students will feel either lost or "boxed in" to supports that are not a match for their specific needs. By offering a variety of support options for all students, we not only benefit our students by anticipating the variability in their learning profiles but can also help reduce the stigma associated with utilizing supports for neurodiverse learners who must have them to be successful.

STRUCTURED LEARNING ENVIRONMENT

As students transition from high school learning environments that are often highly structured and consistent to the unstructured college setting, the task of making good use of newfound "free time" can be overwhelming. For example, a characteristic of students with ADHD can be difficulty with self-regulation, and the transition to college requires an immediate and significant adjustment to higher demands for this skill (Parker et al., 2013). As students enter the collegiate environment, everything is new. Previous support systems are gone, and knowing where to start with new academic routines can feel ambiguous. For some students, consistency of routine, the availability of support, and opportunity for encouragement and accountability are critical. This can take many forms, but ideally it is a place on campus where a student feels comfortable, safe, and productive.

Access to a structured and consistent learning environment can be an essential element for students who need external support to practice and perform their academic routines such as planning, studying, completing assignments, and meeting with support personnel. Beyond simply making a variety of options *available* for students on campus, we provide learners with the opportunity to connect with intensely scaffolded and individualized supports with professionals who can provide a balance of encouragement and accountability. Space can be limited on college campuses, so while some campuses are able to allocate and tailor environments for students with varying learning profiles, others must be creative by using the campus library, student union, or space used by living/learning communities. Offering locations with reduced distractions in close proximity to support like academic advisors, academic coaches or tutors, and resources is ideal for neurodivergent students. Others may prefer to study in a place that has some background noise and a more public feel. Regardless of the location, support programs can help students create a personalized learning environment to accommodate the unique needs for structure, support, and accountability.

In addition to physical space, a support structure can include access to a specific *point person,* a mentor, an advisor, or staff member who can establish accountability, track student success, direct the student to the campus resources, and provide strategies and suggestions for workload and organizational needs. Identifying a point person who maintains a relationship with a student in a long-term capacity that is greater than one semester is effective in helping the student to value the relationship and keeps from them "sliding off the radar." Chapter 8, "Academic Mentoring and Coaching Services," provides more detail about work that coaches and mentors can do with students.

SUPPORT WITH EXECUTIVE FUNCTIONING CHALLENGES

Executive functioning refers to the cognitive abilities that work together to facilitate self-control, displayed through skills such as inhibition, working memory, emotional regulation, planning, and attention (Barkley & Lombroso, 2000). Difficulty with executive functioning skills can be a characteristic associated with neurodivergent students (Grieve et al., 2014). Students with executive functioning challenges (EFCs) often have difficulty with tasks involving time management, goal follow-through, long-term tasks, and self-monitoring. A disconnect between awareness of learning strategies and their application in academic settings can cause difficulties for college students with EFCs (Petersen et al., 2006). Students may experience stress and higher levels of distraction due to the inability to self-regulate and to engage in independent, purposeful, self-serving behaviors (Grieve et al., 2014; Petersen et al., 2006). Additionally, the characteristics of EFCs themselves may limit student awareness of and follow-through with help-seeking behaviors. Fortunately, we can teach explicit strategies to improve EFCs (ECRA Group, 2011). Planning systems, goal-setting, and cognitive flexibility are three examples of areas of emphasis important for many students with EFCs.

PLANNING SYSTEMS

The emphasis on independent learning and long-term, multi-step assignments is prevalent in the college environment, and helping students build a strong and personalized system for time management is critical for their college success. Planning systems can take several forms, from elaborate notebooks to electronic apps. Many contain a variety of ways to record/view information: monthly view, week-at-a-glance, daily, or hour-by-hour. Some planning systems do not allow for enough detail to be helpful for college students with EFCs, while others are so intricate and cumbersome that students lose interest quickly. We have learned over time that students with EFCs may need external support early on to find the system that works best for them.

More important than the format selected for a planning system is the consistency with which it is used. Therefore, the system must be one that is easily accessed, convenient, and one that the student will use throughout each day. This may take some experimentation, supported by someone who will provide both guidance and accountability. For example, some students may be encouraged by the university to use an online planner that integrates with the school's email system or other electronic resources, but a student may notice that interacting with the daily calendar as frequently as needed during the day offers too many opportunities for becoming distracted or overwhelmed with other online activities that are just "one click away." These students may prefer to print their daily calendar to use as a guide and stay away from their phone or email system during time allotted for studying.

Teaching students how to design and use an academic planner is critical during the first year since high school and home support networks may have previously provided this structure. Helping students to plan their week fully—taking into account class sessions, meals, meetings, sleep, study time for each subject, exercise, and so on—not only helps students learn to create a balanced schedule but also forces direct attention to six considerations:

1. Time on task: how long specific tasks actually take (e.g., reading a chapter in a psychology text, getting ready for school, completing math homework, a trip to the gym). This sense of elapsed time may be difficult for some students with EFCs (ECRA Group, 2011); therefore, first-year students may not know how to effectively allot time for daily tasks.
2. Realistic task goals: what can realistically be accomplished in a day. Building a growing to-do list can become overwhelming, especially when it begins to contain more than anyone could accomplish in 24 hours. This can be more paralyzing than helpful for some students. Balancing academic and nonacademic activities on a calendar can help students with EFCs focus on what is reasonable to expect to accomplish each day, balanced with other activities needed to stay healthy. By planning a week at a time, students can see where they have "guilt-free free time" because they know they have allotted sufficient time for both work and play.
3. Identify daily rhythms: the most effective rhythms for before-class, during-class, and after-class study activities for each course in their schedule.
4. Establish learning practices: how to build distributed learning/practice into their schedule each week and, if possible, touch each class almost every day.

5. Connections to support networks: how to synchronize learning activities with available support (e.g., planning to study physics when they know a tutor for their course is available in the campus tutoring center).
6. Establish communication routines: routines each day for checking key academic communication sources such as emails and announcements in a learning management system.

While this sort of strategic approach to time management comes naturally to some college students, we work with many students with EFCs who need explicit instruction and support to develop a proactive and productive time-management system.

GOAL-SETTING

Goals are what drive people to engage in independent and purposeful behavior (James, 2019), and setting goals enables a student to visualize accomplishments, anticipate possible challenges, and create life-school balance. Goals are always individualized and can range from short term ("get an A in English this semester") to long term ("increase my grade point average by half a point"). Goals may center around personal priorities such as academics, career exploration, personal endeavors, and spiritual fulfillment. Whatever the goals may be, creating and sharing goals with other people (friends, teachers, family members, and co-workers) can help a student create more concrete steps to achieve their potential (Willis, 2007).

Goal-setting can feel daunting for college students who bring a history of learning challenges to the educational setting. We can help students engage in activities that identify their interests and strengths, make the goal-setting process concrete, divide it into small action-oriented steps, and build in time for reflection and iterative adjustment. During one-on-one goal-setting meetings, support team members can help students identify their goals, assess the difficulty of achieving each one, and create an action plan (Matthews, 2015; Schunk, 2006).

See chapter 8, "Academic Mentoring and Coaching Services," for additional tips on academic coaching, goal-setting, and progress-monitoring.

COGNITIVE FLEXIBILITY

Students who have trouble with cognitive flexibility have difficulty switching from one task to another and often get "stuck" on something for an extended period of time, or repeat the same mistakes (LD@School, 2019; Roth et al., 2005). Additionally, they may have difficulty:

- shifting from main ideas to details when reading, writing, and taking notes;
- interpreting questions in different ways on quizzes and tests;
- self-checking (e.g., asking "Does this make sense?" when completing math problems);
- recognizing and reducing rigidity in social situations;
- adjusting to new situations, classes, groups or friends, or schedule changes; and
- developing coping mechanisms to enlist in situations they find overwhelming or stressful (e.g., deep breathing, meditation, exercise, and positive self-talk).

Even with proactive goal-setting, effective planning, and ongoing support, students with EFCs still may struggle with the management of day-to-day tasks. It is essential for students to have a safe place where, when meetings are missed or assignments are forgotten, they can find support and encouragement to reflect, adjust their plan, and move forward. This blend of accountability with acceptance is crucial to creating a space where ongoing routines with the goal of long-term success can be developed.

DIRECT SUPPORT WITH STUDY TECHNIQUES

Students who struggle with concentration or persistence with tedious tasks many find it hard to follow through with consistent study routines (Reaser et al., 2007). Students who enter the college environment with limited confidence may abandon potentially effective study techniques quickly with the assumption that they are just "not good at" a certain subject or a type of learning environment. Study tools and tactics vary based on a student's unique learning profile, and a one-size-fits-all approach will not work. On post-secondary campuses, students encounter many different courses and a multitude of teaching styles from professors. Therefore, having an arsenal of study tools prepared for use in these different types of educational settings is essential. Staff can play a role in helping students find what works best for them in the context of a particular course's content, expectations, and resources.

Studying with Peers

Study groups in college environments are nothing new. From loosely constructed study groups formed primarily to provide accountability and bring a social element, to study sessions, to intentionally formed cooperative learning groups (Dudley et al., 1997; Johnson & Johnson, 2008), studying with peers can have a positive impact on academic achievement and confidence (Cançado et al., 2018). Students have multiple opportunities to interact and engage with peers in their classes, creating organic opportunities to find study groups or partners to share in the learning process. Group studying can create a necessity for students to voice course content aloud, quiz each other, or share examples of how to apply what they are learning to the real world—all things that can aid in understanding and mastery of course goals. Students are able to compare notes, create study guides, and review course content together, providing the opportunity to check the accuracy of notes and understanding from class lectures. The accountability, comradery, and resources in a peer group can be valuable in the college setting, yet we cannot assume that all students come to campus prepared to connect with peers and approach group study opportunities with the intentionality that will help them be productive. This is something that can be directly taught in student support programs, and in some cases, the programs themselves can become a place where students connect with others with whom they feel safe and encouraged to explore and utilize different study techniques.

Test-Taking

Taking good notes (see chapter 8), completing study guides, creating study materials, and pausing after each class to apply what has been learned are just a few methods students can use to prepare for tests and exams. Support programs can help students learn and effectively align their course content, instructor expectations, and learning preferences, as well as build them in to daily academic routines. For example, while many students like to use flashcards to study, that is not always the most appropriate study technique for some content and courses. Program staff can teach students to be strategic while taking tests, such as helping them with cues and strategies for fully reading test directions, planning their time during a test, eliminating incorrect answers, and reviewing their answers (Dodeen, 2008). See chapter 8, "Academic Mentoring and Coaching Services," for an example of a test-taking strategy.

Paraphrasing

Learning and properly using a paraphrasing strategy can help students avoid plagiarism. Paraphrasing encourages students to read more carefully and note important details within texts, while also expanding their vocabulary (Wormeli & Stafford, 2018). We can help students identify when they have possibly plagiarized text, help them to utilize paraphrasing strategies such as the RAP strategy (see chapter 8), explain the importance of academic integrity, and help students identify the difference between summarizing and paraphrasing. It is important that we show students why their paraphrasing is incorrect and how to correctly cite sources. For more intense needs, we may refer students to campus resources such as the university's writing center or writing lab.

Vocabulary

As students improve their paraphrasing skills, they will also need to improve their vocabulary. Vocabulary development is important, as there is a positive correlation between academic vocabulary and college performance (Turner & Williams, 2007). We can help students build their vocabulary by helping students learn new words as they encounter them. We may teach students how to use strategies such as LINCS to help build their vocabulary (see chapter 8). Students should be encouraged to make vocabulary development a part of their study routine by underlining and/or highlighting words they are unfamiliar with when reading a text. Students can then look up the word at a later date by using a dictionary or the textbook's glossary. Students may need the definition read to them and made relatable to their lives. In addition, students may need help to determine the meanings of words from their context. As students learn new words, they will then be able to access more of the college curriculum, which could lead to better goal attainment.

CONCLUSION

This chapter outlined various elements that student support programs can utilize to help students with learning differences achieve academic success. While not recommending a cookie-cutter method of supporting students, over time common elements have emerged in our programs that have helped to foster student success. Our student programs, networks of support, and campus offices can help students in their initial transition, identification of campus resources and programs, and development of community belonging. We can work together to provide support curriculums, structured learning environments, and connections to campus resources and organizations.

Campus Essentials for High Impact

- *Increase awareness about learner variability on campus.* Promote understanding of neurodivergent students.
- *Provide multi-tiered support services for neurodivergent students.* Work to help students who have traditionally struggled to build the confidence and skills needed to fulfill their potential.
- *Program and plans for connecting neurodiverse students to support services.* Encourage connectivity to support services beyond disability services or accessibility offices.

REFERENCES

Barkley, R. A., & Lombroso, P. J. (2000). Genetics of childhood disorders: XVII. ADHD, Part 1: The executive functions and ADHD. *Journal of the American Academy of Child & Adolescent Psychiatry, 39*(8), 1064–1068.

Cançado, L., Reisel, J. R., & Walker, C. M. (2018). Impact of first-year mathematics study groups on the retention and graduation of engineering students. *International Journal of Mathematical Education in Science & Technology, 49*(6), 856–866. https://doi.org/10.1080/0020739X.2017.1423120

Dodeen, H. (2008). Assessing test-taking strategies of university students: Developing a scale and estimating its psychometric indices. *Assessment & Evaluation in Higher Education, 33*(4), 409–419.

Dudley, B. S., Johnson, D. W., & Johnson, R. T. (1997). Using cooperative learning to enhance the academic and social experiences of freshman student athletes. *Journal of Social Psychology, 137*(4), 449–459. https://doi.org/10.1080/00224549709595461

ECRA Group. (2011). Addressing executive function at the secondary level. *Journal of College Reading and Learning, 36*(2), 59–67.

Getzel E. (2008). Addressing the persistence and retention of students with disabilities in higher education: Incorporating key strategies and supports on campus. *Exceptionality, 16*(4), 207–219. https://doi.org/10.1080/09362830802412216.

Grieve, A., Webne-Behrman, L., Couillou, R., & Sieben-Schneider, J. (2014). Self-report assessment of executive functioning in college students with disabilities. *Journal of Postsecondary Education and Disability, 27*(1), 19–32.

James, M. B. (2019). *Nurturing student engagement and personal achievement through goal setting: A strategy evaluation of the About2Be Program for probationary college students* [Unpublished doctoral dissertation]. East Carolina University. http://hdl.handle.net/10342/7214

Johnson, R. T., & Johnson, D. W. (2008). Active learning: Cooperation in the classroom. *The Annual Report of Educational Psychology in Japan, 47*, 29–30.

Katsiyannis, A., Zhang, D., Landmark, L., & Reber, A. (2009). Post-secondary education for individuals with disabilities: Legal and practice considerations. *Journal of Disability Policy Studies, 20*(1), 35–45. doi:10.1177/1044207308324896

Kosine, N. R. (2007). Preparing students with learning disabilities for post-secondary education: What the research literature tells us about transition programs. *Journal of Special Education Leadership, 20*(2), 93–104.

LD@School. (2019). *An in-depth look at executive functions.* LD@School Learning Module. Learning Disabilities Association of Ontario. https://www.ldatschool.ca/learning-modules/executive-functions/eight-pillars/cognitive-flexibility

Matthews, G. (2015). Goal setting research. Proceedings of the 9th Annual International Conference of the Psychology Research Unit of Athens Institute for Education and Research; 25–28 May 2015, Athens, Greece.

Meltzer, L. (2018). Creating strategic classrooms and schools: Embedding executive function strategies in the curriculum. In L. Meltzer (Ed.), *Executive function in education: From theory to practice* (2nd ed.; pp. 263–299). Guilford Press.

Meltzer, L., Greschler, M., Kurkul, K., & Stacey, W. (2015). Executive function and peer mentoring: Fostering metacognitive awareness, effort, and academic success. In K. R. Harris & L. Meltzer (Eds.), *The power of peers in the classroom: Enhancing learning and social skills* (pp. 1–32). Guilford Press.

Murray, C., Goldstein, D. E., Nourse, S., & Edgar, E. (2000). The post-secondary school attendance and completion rates of high school graduates with learning disabilities. *Learning Disabilities Research and Practice, 15*(3), 119–127.

Newman, L., Wagner, M., Knokey, A.-M., Marder, C., Nagle, K., Shaver, D., & Wei, X., with Cameto, R., Contreras, E., Ferguson, K., Greene, S., & Schwarting, M. (2011). *The post-high school outcomes of young adults with disabilities up to 8 years after high school: A report from the National Longitudinal Transition Study-2 (NLTS2).* NCSER 2011-3005. SRI International. https://ies.ed.gov/ncser/pubs/20113005/pdf/20113005.pdf

Parker, D. R., Hoffman, S. F., Sawilowsky, S., & Rolands, L. (2013). Self-control in post-secondary settings: Students' perceptions of ADHD college coaching. *Journal of Attention Disorders, 17*(3), 215–232. https://doi.org/10.1177/1087054711427561

Petersen, R., Lavelle, E., & Guarino, A. (2006). The relationship between college students' executive functioning and study strategies. *Journal of College Reading and Learning, 36*(2), 59–67. doi:10.1080/10790195.2006.10850188

Reaser, A., Prevatt, F., Petscher, Y., & Proctor, B. (2007). The learning and study strategies of college students with ADHD. *Psychology in the Schools, 44*(6). https://doi.org/10.1002/pits.20252

Ribera, A. K., Miller, A. L., & Dumford, A. D. (2017). Sense of peer belonging and institutional acceptance in the first year: The role of high-impact practices. *Journal of College Student Development, 58*(4), 545–563. https://doi.org/10.1353/csd.2017.0042

Roth, M., Isquith, P., & Gioia, G. (2005). *BRIEF—a behavior rating inventory of executive functioning—adult version professional manual.* PAR Inc.

Schunk, D. H., & Zimmerman, B. J. (2006). Influencing children's self-efficacy and self-regulation of reading and writing through modeling. *Reading & Writing Quarterly, 23*(1), 7–25. https://doi.org/10.1080/10573560600837578

Stocker, S. L., & Gallagher, K. M. (2019). Alleviating anxiety and altering appraisals: Social-emotional learning in the college classroom. *College Teaching, 67*(1), 23–35. https://doi.org/10.1080/87567555.2018.1515722

Turner, H., & Williams, R. L. (2007). Vocabulary development and performance on multiple-choice exams in large entry-level courses. *Journal of College Reading and Learning, 37*(2), 64–81.

U.S. Department of Education, National Center for Education Statistics. (2017). *Digest of education statistics, 2017*. NCES 2018-070. https://nces.ed.gov/programs/digest/d17

Vaccaro, A., Daly-Cano, M., & Newman, B. M. (2015). A sense of belonging among college students with disabilities: An emergent theoretical model. *Journal of College Student Development, 56*(7), 670–686. https://doi.org/10.1353/csd.2015.0072

Wang, N., Wilhite, S. C., Wyatt, J., Young, T., & Bloemker, G. (2012). Impact of a college freshman social and emotional learning curriculum on student learning outcomes: An exploratory study. *Journal of University Teaching & Learning Practice, 9*(2), 1–20. http://search.ebscohost.com/login.aspx?direct=true&AuthType=ip,shib&db=ehh&AN=89049780&site=ehost-live&scope=site

Willis, J. (2007). Brain-friendly strategies for the inclusion classroom. Association for Supervision and Curriculum Development (ASCD). http://www.ascd.org/publications/books/107040/chapters/Success-for-all-Students-in-Inclusion-Classes.aspx

Wormeli, R., & Stafford, D., (2018). *Summarization in any subject: 60 innovative, tech-infused strategies for deeper student learning* (2nd ed.). ASCD.

Chapter 7: Campus Spotlight

As-U-R Program, Appalachian State University

Ellen Bunn

Our Mission: The As-U-R program is an intensive support program for students with executive functioning challenges (EFCs). As-U-R serves approximately 100 traditionally enrolled college students at Appalachian State University and provides a network of individualized support through accountability, one-on-one mentoring, academic strategy instruction, and community. The ultimate goal is to create academically independent students by providing intensive support in the beginning of their

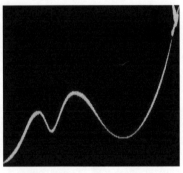

Source: As-U-R

As-U-R program acceptance, with the intention that students will develop the necessary executive skills to increase academic independence during their education at Appalachian State University. As part of the Student Learning Center at ASU, As-U-R assists students with connecting with campus resources, such as tutoring services, counseling, and advising, in addition to the supports provided through the As-U-R program.

As-U-R program services:

- *Accountability:* As-U-R provides intensive academic accountability to students through weekly one-on-ones with an As-U-R mentor, as well as assistance in creating weekly study times. As-U-R is located in Study Central in Edwin Duncan Hall, Suite 213, and is designed to serve as a private library space and mentor meeting space for our students. Using Study Central as a primary study space gives students direct access to assistance from support staff and mentors, as well as an ability to engage with the As-U-R community of students.

- ***Weekly Academic Mentor Meetings*:** All As-U-R students are matched with a support staff member to work with on a weekly basis throughout the semester. Every As-U-R student is required to have one academic check-in (minimum) per week with an As-U-R staff member. These weekly, regularly occurring meetings are mandatory support for As-U-R students where they will receive individualized organizational support for the week, which includes creating a weekly plan for completion of assignments that are due. Additionally, students have access to intensive executive skill coaching with As-U-R's learning specialist as well as with their trained As-U-R mentor. Lastly, As-U-R collaborates with other campus resources to ensure all As-U-R student needs are being met.

> After 5 years in this program, As-U-R has taught me a lot of life skills and has helped me grow into a successful person who is going to succeed in the post-college life. As-U-R helped push me through.
>
> —Dylan, Class of 2019, import operator for Epes Logistics

- ***Individualized Academic Support Plans and Learning Profiles:*** The As-U-R director and learning specialists work hard to create individualized support plans for each As-U-R student, and academic needs are reassessed each semester. The amount of support each student receives varies on a semester-to-semester basis.
- ***College Transition Support:*** Students apply to the As-U-R program once they have been admitted to Appalachian State University through the traditional admissions process. Applications for As-U-R are accepted on an ongoing basis from high school seniors, transfer students, and current ASU students. Students receive coaching based on their transition needs, for both incoming students as well as students who are approaching graduation.

> As-U-R helped me cultivate the skills I needed to succeed in school and everyday life. Since entering As-U-R, I have discovered strength and confidence I never knew I possessed. Through emotional and academic support, As-U-R always got me to the finish line.
>
> —Allison, Class of 2018, youth care worker in the Psychiatric Residential Treatment Center at Grandfather Home for Children

- ***Drop-In Assistance:*** In addition to weekly mentor meetings, we recognize that crises do occur. Students are always welcome to seek support from the As-U-R director or As-U-R learning specialist on a drop-in basis if issues arise. Additionally, students seeking further assistance with learning strategy development may make an appointment with the As-U-R learning specialist to further dive into these skills.
- ***Study Materials and Learning Assistance Technology:*** As-U-R students are given access to necessary study tools, such as highlighters, notecards, Cornell note-taking paper, and list and planner tools. Students also have the option to use Livescribe Smart Pens to assist with note-taking. Students can rent a Livescribe 3 Smart Pen with a notebook at any point during the semester from the As-U-R director. Additionally, Study Central provides access to free printing and access to desktop computers, as well as PC laptops and MacBooks. Students can rent these from As-U-R while completing homework in Study Central.

Community and Peer Engagement: Along with the intensive academic support that As-U-R students receive, the community is also a large contributing aspect that makes this program successful. As-U-R produces an environment that is always positive and inclusive, allowing As-U-R students to motivate

Source: **Courtesy of the authors**

one another on a daily basis. Students are encouraged to participate in wellness and social activities together outside of academics, which is an important part of student stress relief.

- *Seminar Experiences:* As-U-R provides an ability for students to further engage with the As-U-R community, as well as learn relevant skills related to EFCs, through access to semester-long seminars. These seminars are offered for elective credit and taught by the As-U-R director and learning specialists. While these courses are not mandatory, they are strongly encouraged.

Chapter Eight

Academic Mentoring and Coaching Services

Morgan James, Ellen Bunn, and Sarah Williams

Academic coaching is not new to post-secondary education, but rather it has been used in various versions since the early 1990s. Academic coaching emerged from corporate mentoring models, where experts in the field guided new employees with advice and encouragement on how to achieve success in the workplace (Richman et al., 2014). In the academic context, coaching occurs through one-on-one interactions between a coach and a student in an effort to help the student examine and address academic concerns and perceived barriers to success. Coaches provide students with semester-long or year-long academic support in areas such as time management, test preparation, note-taking, and reading strategies. They often work individually with students, assess their strengths and needs, and devise a personalized plan of action to achieve academic success (Prevatt & Yelland, 2015).

Research shows that students who receive academic coaching are more likely to see things through to completion, ask others for feedback, experience higher levels of self-esteem, receive higher grades, successfully navigate transitions, talk to school officials, improve their study skills, and employ organizational processes (Bellman et al., 2015). Coaching shows promise for increasing retention and academic success rates among college students and has become popular in the academic setting for students with diverse learning profiles (Bettinger & Baker, 2011; Dalton & Crosby, 2014; Hoover, 2011; Parker et al., 2011; Robinson & Gahagan, 2010).

Academic coaching has been aligned with "wellness models" (Bettinger & Baker, 2011; McWilliams & Beam, 2013; Richman et al., 2014), and overlaps considerably with models for mentoring and advising. Deiorio and Miller (2016) distinguish between these three common models of student support in post-secondary education by emphasizing that, while mentoring and advising share several characteristics of coaching (grounded in relationship, pairing between more experienced and less experienced individuals, etc.), mentoring and advising are more directive and mentor/advisor-driven. Coaching, on the other hand, is considered to be driven more by the learner who works over time with a coach to co-construct, refine, and carry out goals and action plans. Our goal in this chapter is not to take a stance about a certain terminology, and we have heard the terms used interchangeably during dialogues with colleagues on various college campuses. We use the term *coach* with the idea that college-level student-support programs can equip students to take the lead relative to their goals and educational steps. We hope that the strategies and resources in this chapter will be beneficial to coaching, mentoring, or advising programs.

Academic coaches prompt students to reflect and plan by asking thought-provoking questions that guide the development of goals, provide distinct interventions, and build strategies for success. Academic coaches are advocates who help students focus on their personal and professional goals through the development of self-awareness, strength-building, and academic planning (National Academic Advising Association, 2017). Effective coaching is collaborative, as the coach, student, and other professionals on campus work together to address goal-setting, self-regulated learning, and (in some cases) behavioral changes (Prevatt & Yelland, 2015). A strong relationship between the coach and student is needed and can be developed through regular meetings designed to establish consistent academic routines and an atmosphere that balances support and accountability (Parker et al., 2011). Each student's coaching session is unique in nature, and some level of flexibility may be needed in order to maintain a holistic approach to student support. Coaching sessions can take place in person (e.g., coach's office or campus meeting space) or from a distance (e.g., telephone or web conference) (Parker et al., 2011). The academic coach can also connect students to additional resources on campus (Parker et al., 2011).

A central component of academic coaching is aiding a student's development by promoting understanding about personal learning profiles. Often referred to as *metacognitive awareness*, students must become familiar with what works for their specific academic strengths and needs in order to be strategic in matching study routines with specific course/assignment expectations. "Metacognitive awareness, a concept originally defined by Flavell (1979) and Brown, Bransford, Ferrara, and Campione (1983), refers to each student's understanding and beliefs about how he or she thinks and learns, as well as the strategies that can be used to accomplish specific tasks" (Meltzer, 2018, p. 268).

Academic coaches can vary from campus to campus. In our programs, coaches are primarily paid graduate assistants who are trained by full-time staff members. Coaches can also be full-time staff who have permanent positions working with students within a support-program model. Additionally, some campuses have coaches who are using academic coaching as a required internship or practicum experience. These coaches are typically students who plan to work with special populations and are seeking experience working with students who learn differently. Other options include volunteers, both on and off campus, faculty members, peers, and others. Campuses may want to consider cost, training, student needs, space, and so on when determining who their coaches will be.

ESTABLISHING RELATIONSHIPS, SETTING GOALS, AND DEVELOPING ROUTINES

In the next sections, we describe strategies and resources that can be selected and designed based on individual student strengths, needs, and preferences. While specific strategies will be personalized for each student, and specific formats/models will vary, academic coaches can begin with activities such as gathering and synthesizing background, developing rapport, and establishing shared expectations (Deiorio & Miller, 2016; Swartz et al., 2005).

Gathering Information

We recognize the wide variety of viewpoints that surround the notion of learning styles, intelligences, and learning preferences (Husmann & O'Loughlin, 2019; Pinto et al., 1994; Price, 2004; Sfrisi et al., 2017; Torres, 2014). That said, from our experience working with students who have learning and attention challenges, helping students develop an understanding about the academic strategies, resources, and routines that are a good fit with their personal learning strengths, needs, and preferences is essential. For students who commonly do considerable background work in a course, taking a strategic and systematic approach to studying can enable more efficient and effective uses of their time. Students who have a strong awareness of their personal learning profile can be more strategic when matching study techniques to different kinds of classes, content, and assignments (i.e., the old adage "study smarter, not harder"). A wide variety of resources are available for the practical task of helping students develop an understanding about the environment, activities, and tools that produce the best results for their personal learning strengths and needs, and students can continue to refine those approaches over time.

Coaches can help students begin to form an understanding about their specific learning profiles using tools such as interviews (see example intake questions used in one student support program in appendix 1), short-answer or essay-style survey questions (see example in appendix 2), self-report assessments (e.g., BRIEF-A Behavior Rating Inventory of Executive Function—Adult Version or the LASSI-Learning and Study Strategies Inventory) (Roth et al., 2005; Weinstein et al., 1987), existing documentation and assessment results (e.g., formal psychoeducational testing), and feedback from others (e.g., family members, teachers, or peers). Gathering information over time and with a blend of assessment techniques is essential. For example, self-report selection-style instruments (e.g., checkboxes or multiple-choice options) can be used to gather quick information but should be supplemented with open-ended and more detailed answers that provide time for more thoughtful input and/or seek input from parents, teachers, or counselors. Giving students the option to write, type, or speak (e.g., in recorded or interview format) will help to ensure that one mode of responding does not raise an unintentional barrier to the accuracy and depth of information collected. The use of multiple measures up front provides academic coaches the opportunity to observe how students interact with different types of assessment formats. For example, interview responses and writing samples can provide useful information about a student's ability to self-express through verbal or written communication, both of which are important in the classroom.

Some neurodiverse students arrive at college with detailed and informative documentation. This may include notes from therapists, counselors, teachers, or doctors, assessment results from formal testing, Individualized Education Programs (IEPs), or 504 Plans. Often, this documentation is used to qualify for academic accommodations (e.g., extra time on tests, distraction-free/reduced settings, note-taking accommodations, and other necessary accommodations), but these records may also include valuable information about a student's educational history and needs in school. Students may or may not want to disclose such resources to academic coaches or mentors, but if not, they can be encouraged to consult the existing documents themselves to aid in an understanding about their learning profile.

All types of information come with assessments regarding strengths and limitations. Assessments conducted while a student is in grade school may be outdated and less aligned with post-secondary education settings but may include parent and teacher perspectives that are helpful to educational professionals. Both standardized instruments (e.g., LASSI or BRIEF-A) and home-grown assessment tools often rely heavily on self-reported perceptions of students, something that may not be well-developed for students with some learning differences or who are just building metacognitive awareness. Instruments developed by and for specific student-support programs may be narrow in scope and may not have been subjected to validity and reliability testing.

These assessments do provide insights that can directly inform support and match students to services provided by that program. In combination, all can provide useful information, and assembling background information from a variety of sources may help to mitigate some of the challenges of each.

Pulling It All Together

By synthesizing and documenting a student's experience throughout a college semester, an academic coach can help a student see patterns and impacts of their learning activities and outcomes over time and can use that information to make decisions about future action plans. Students who are overwhelmed might not immediately see connections between the many factors that affect their academic success (e.g., pre-, during-, and post-class routines, disability and accommodations used, eating and sleeping habits, down time, exercise, style of instructor, format of course, emotional state, level of content). A coach can help students bring this information together to use to set goals and establish action plans. Moreover, tracking basic information such as a student's major, grade point average, course schedule, probation terms, and other campus involvement that may be significant to their academic experiences can be important if a student transitions between several coaches throughout their college experience.

A synthesis of information collected from a variety of methods such as those described in the previous section can provide coaches with three primary resources:

1. a "quick look" at a student's general strengths and challenges;
2. detailed descriptions, where needed, to help guide coaching strategies, academic routines, or areas that need support and/or encouragement; and
3. a baseline for helping students track progress and on which to build action plans.

Students and academic coaches can work together to co-construct learning profile descriptions and advocacy in supporting a transition from a time when parents, teachers, and counselors may have reviewed formal and informal assessment information *on behalf of* their students to a time when students must build the self-awareness and agency to be able to guide their own academic path. Goudreau and Knight (2018) explain that "when students are aware of the neurological differences in their brain, it creates an 'ah-ha' moment, removing the possible stigma associated with the diagnosis, and allowing the student to be more receptive to receiving services" (p. 380). See appendix 3 for an example format that one student-support program uses to record and update student profile information.

Over time a student's learning profile can change, and learners often adjust their behaviors and preferences depending on the learning context or class (Pinto et al., 1994; Gurpinar et al., 2011; Powell & Kusuma-Powell, 2011). Additionally, given the transient nature of the college setting, students may have different academic coaches as they progress through their college degree or program of study. Therefore, profiles need to be updated frequently (e.g., at the end of an academic calendar year or each academic semester). If possible, an in-person briefing during periods of transition can provide important and nuanced information for new coaches. Former coaches who have developed close working relationships and become very familiar with the individualized needs of their students can help ensure that unsuccessful strategies are not reattempted and that effective strategies continue to be emphasized and encouraged.

Regardless of how a learning profile is developed and organized, it is a vital resource for academic coaches working with neurodiverse students. The information available in a learning profile can be used to articulate student strengths and needs as well as drive the identification of personalized study tactics or techniques. Coaches can also use this information when developing productive relationships with students by incorporating information from the profile to guide their coaching methods.

Building Meaningful Student-Coach Relationships

The student-coach relationship is a cornerstone to effective academic coaching, and a collaborative relationship is essential for success (Richman et al., 2014). Coaching relies on student buy-in, and students must view their coach as reliable, knowledgeable, and trustworthy. According to Richman and colleagues (2014), coaches don't tell students what to do, but rather they listen to students and help them discover themselves through asking questions designed to engage the student in deeper thinking and problem-solving. Therefore, students must be comfortable with their coach before they disclose information that may be sensitive and must feel respected by the coach before they can be receptive to advice and constructive criticism. Coaches must treat students with respect and understanding, and students should not view coaching as forced, a punishment, or remediation. A healthy student-coach relationship creates a climate of positive accountability.

Relationship-building is one of the most important aspects of academic coaching. Like many other relationships in our lives, a relationship between an academic coach and a student requires three basic elements to be successful: respect, trust, and communication (Killion et al., 2014). When positive relationships are created, students can more easily share their needs and experiences, and coaches are better able to guide and relate to the students (Rimm-Kaufman & Sandilos, 2019). From the first meeting to navigating difficult situations, this relationship can influence the ability for a coach to make a positive difference in a student's achievement of academic and personal success.

In our experience, most coaches develop their own personalized style. Whether outgoing, extroverted, warm, soft-spoken, direct, or gentle, each coach will bring a different background and skill set. While training for academic coaches is always recommended, there is not a one-size-fits-all model for student-coach interactions (McWilliams & Beam, 2013). Some schools may have the capacity to take steps to match coaches and students in areas such as personality, interests, skills, experiences, and interaction styles. Some examples of strategies that have been promoted for facilitating student/coach matching or early relationship-building include scheduling mixers, team-building exercises, and program orientation events.

Before the first meeting, academic coaches should review any available information that will contribute to their understanding of each student's learning context and learning profile (e.g., student's course schedule, major, and existing assessment data). Then, the goal of the first meeting between a student and an academic coach is to develop a shared understanding of what the academic coaching process entails. The academic coach can set the tone for future interactions and establish a foundation that will be important to facilitate respect, trust, and communication as the relationship continues to grow. The coach should also articulate programmatic rules, boundaries, and expectations guiding the student-coach engagement. In return, students can use this time to express what they hope to get from the coaching relationship and respond to information provided by the coach. From there, the student and coach can co-create descriptions of the student learning profile, goals, action plans, and support needs, as well as establish a consistent meeting schedule.

Students should leave their first meeting with a better understanding of why the coaching sessions are important and how they will help improve their academic outcomes. They should know what is expected of them and what they can expect from their coach. Examples of student expectations include: attending meetings, arriving on time, being prepared with the necessary materials (e.g., computer, notes, grades, etc.), following up with use of strategies taught during the coaching sessions, exhibiting a good attitude, and remaining engaged. Examples of expectations for the academic coaches may include attending meetings, arriving on time, being prepared with the necessary materials, preparing for the meeting beforehand, bringing a good attitude, keeping up-to-date records, and staying engaged. Some coaching programs include an opportunity for students and coaches to sign an agreement that outlines common expectations, such as:

1. Both students and academic coaches turn their cell phone to silent when the session starts and refrain from checking their device during the session.
2. Students and academic coaches practice active listening for the duration of the session.
3. Students and academic coaches keep multitasking to a minimum.

An hour-long first meeting between a student and an academic coach may have the following agenda:

1. 5 minutes—unstructured conversations
2. 10 minutes—guidelines, expectations, and boundaries
3. 20 minutes—student profile (e.g., current needs, syllabi, learning style inventory, etc.)
4. 15 minutes—student goals
5. 5 minutes—expectations and objectives for the next meeting
6. 5 minutes—unstructured conversation

Rapport-Building

Starting and ending each meeting with a brief time for open and unstructured conversation can be a way for a student and the academic coach to build rapport. These periods of relaxed dialogue allow students to share what is going on in their daily life and simply connect on a personal level with their academic coach. They may share information about extracurricular activities, family updates, hobbies, new opportunities, or upcoming activities. They can also provide updates about recent accomplishments or current challenges and ask for practical advice from their coach. These conversations provide insight about a student's life or current circumstances outside of academics that are likely to have a strong impact on their academic success.

Beyond being a useful way to gather important information that may help engage students and construct high-quality learning plans, these brief times of conversation may simply help students to relax and know that they are being heard. That said, more reserved students may find times for relaxed conversations or "small talk" more anxiety-producing than helpful. Over time, coaches can personalize their meeting style with each student, and may want to build a repository of open-ended conversation starters to have on hand (e.g., funny YouTube videos, memes, news stories, etc.) for when conversation does not flow naturally.

Boundary-Setting

A healthy and productive relationship between a coach and a student also includes appropriate boundaries (Killion et al., 2014). We have found that it is important for a student and an academic coach to maintain a professional distance, as well as to be intentional about defining those relationship parameters clearly and early. Various coaching programs may define these guidelines differently, depending on the model used, but the key is to be intentional about developing these guidelines. As students and academic coaches work together and grow their relationship, there may be times when students forget the professional nature of their connection. In these instances, students may over-share information, share information that a coach would be required to report, or ask their academic coach to engage in activities that are outside the realm of professional duties. In these instances, it is important to have a baseline understanding of boundaries established early on.

Creating a successful relationship may be challenging with some students and may require more time and persistence than others. Academic coaches must remember the importance of meeting students where they are and tailoring each session for each individual student. Each meeting presents a new opportunity for meaningful engagement. Students who have the most difficulty with follow-through will need a coach who stays diligent and persistent. This may mean that the coach will need to reevaluate study plans, rework expectations, reinforce positive behaviors, and reteach important skills and strategies multiple times during an academic semester.

COMMUNICATION, ACCOUNTABILITY, AND MOTIVATION

The way that coaches communicate and hold students accountable may vary. Many students agree that being held accountable by their coach through providing frequent updates about their goal-directed efforts in between sessions is helpful in maintaining focus on their goals and staying motivated in working on them (Richman et al., 2014).

In some campus programs, communication extends beyond face-to-face meetings. Coaches stay connected through emails and text messages. Coaches have also utilized more personal approaches such as a quick phone call or video chat using FaceTime or similar digital platform. Some coaches establish preferred shared technologies or to-do lists in technology such as Wunderlist, Google Tasks, Habitica, or MyHomework. These digital resources provide another connection to the student's progress, and coaches can maintain accountability as the monitor when a student has completed a task and can check it off their list.

During meetings, coaches make progress checks and gather information about grades and ongoing assignments and can use this information to gauge student progress toward goals and suggest adjustments accordingly. Using time during regular meetings to reinforce behaviors, strategies, and skills that students are effectively using can help students connect their actions to a successful outcome. This kind of dialogue supports the development of metacognitive skills and can increase motivation to continue using effective study strategies. Coaches and students establish a system of rewards and/or consequences to help maintain motivation and follow-through for especially challenging or tedious goals (Goudreau & Knight, 2018). Similarly, coaching sessions can help students identify ineffective strategies or habits. Sometimes students will continue to fall back on behaviors that impede their success. When coaches work with students to identify these habits and determine alternatives more likely to increase success, they are assisting students in refining their metacognitive skills and strategically modifying and adapting their approach to different academic tasks and environments. Clear and consistent communication between coaches and students will be critical for identifying successful strategies and those that hinder progress, as well as for helping students become more independent and intrinsically motivated to continue to refine their approach to college-level learning (Richman et al., 2014; Goudreau & Knight, 2018).

Academic coaching can help students pinpoint their academic challenges and maximize their strengths to strategically approach the learning process. Critical skills such as time management, planning, organization, self-advocacy, problem-solving, and coping can be addressed through personalized coaching in specific and manageable strategies for common academic tasks. Example strategies will be explored and can be addressed by academic coaches and their students in the common areas of time management, organization, problem-solving, goal-setting, and self-advocacy.

TIME MANAGEMENT

Time management is an often-cited challenge for neurodivergent students who experience executive functioning challenges (Serry et al., 2018; Kredier et al., 2019). The demand for students to utilize strategies to effectively use unstructured time productively increases exponentially in the transition from high school to college. Support from academic coaches can be critical for helping students harness this newly found *free time* and use it productively through organization, prioritization, and self-regulation (Parker et al., 2011).

Some students can become overwhelmed with the temptation for over-scheduling of the college environment. Coaches can help students find a balance between academic and nonacademic responsibilities through the use of planner systems. Whether in electronic or paper format, using a planner helps students collect information they are given (syllabi, scheduling, due dates, appointments, etc.) and pull it together in an organized system. Students can be guided to use a planner system that not only records all of their due dates, meetings, and activities in one location but also can sequence them in such a way to stay ahead of tests and deadlines and synchronize those with support opportunities. For example, after recording the due date for a major paper in a planner, coaches can help students think through the process of working backward to block time in the planner to work on each step of the paper, and schedule those activities to be done in the library or close proximity to the campus writing center (during their operating hours) in case the student needs support along the way. We cannot presume that all students will come to campus automatically using these strategies, nor can we assume that students who do not have this level of awareness are not ready for college. Coaches can provide students with the ability to start from scratch with the time-management process in this new educational setting and learn to effectively plan ahead (Kader & Eissa, 2015).

An academic coach can use meeting times early in the semester to help students schedule weekly goals, due dates, and action items right in the planner system. Weekly check-ins can provide a chance to revisit the "to-do" items that need to be completed that week and/or assignments that may be due during the week. When students agree to academic coaching, they are agreeing to accountability to their coach and the expectation that they provide frequent updates about follow-through with goal-directed efforts in between sessions. This external accountability is important for maintaining focus and motivation for working toward their goals (Richman et al., 2014). Regularly scheduled check-ins with coaches can facilitate a relationship that balances both support and accountability (Capstick et al., 2019). Over time, the academic coach can scaffold support for students, so they become more independent with the backward planning process. This process of starting with an end goal and working in reverse chronological order to plan the steps needed to accomplish the goal can lead to improved motivation, less time pressure, and better performance (Park, Lu, & Hedgcock, 2017) and is a skill that will serve them well long term.

ORGANIZATION

Time isn't the only thing that students in college must quickly learn to organize. Given the myriad of information that students receive in college, coupled with the expectation that students quickly learn to access, process, and make good use of that information, an academic coach can be a critical source of support for helping students with learning and attention challenges organize their time and manage their collegiate expectations. For example, adding color-coding to the backward planning process in a calendar can help students group together and organize information for their classes. Students may extend these color codes to their schedules, folders, notebooks, binders, and email. Academic coaches help students develop a personal system that matches with a student's learning profile but also one that would be realistic for that student for follow-through until the end of the semester. This process will differ with each student. Regardless of the model used, a period of thorough up-front planning/organization can transition to ongoing routines and check-ins that become automatic and much less time-consuming.

Academic coaches should adapt to student learning preferences. Some students will prefer physical copies of class materials (e.g., notes, syllabi, handouts, etc.), while other students will prefer to maintain and interact with digital formats. If organization is a challenge for a student, the academic coach may consider creating a checklist that students can complete at the end of each day or at the end of each academic coaching session as a reminder for what needs to be completed in order to get or stay organized. Some students work better with tangible items. In this instance, physical class materials (e.g., binders, notebooks, textbooks, and folders) may work best. Other students prefer to stay organized with the help of technology. Therefore, computer folders, online planners, and eBooks may suit them best. Coaches can help students understand that there is no one "right" or "wrong" method. Neurodiverse learners, like all students, benefit from multiple approaches to stay organized, and coaches can help students be systematic and confident about finding the one that works for them.

PROBLEM-SOLVING

As students experience new things and encounter new issues in college, they may realize they have limited experience problem-solving when new issues arise. Academic coaches can help students improve their problem-solving skills by listening and communicating effectively with the student, modeling the problem-solving process, navigating problem-solving strategies, and helping students connect to key campus resources.

Academic coaches are in an ideal situation to listen for problems or dilemmas students are facing during their regularly occurring discussions. A habit of active listening to the students will make it more likely that coaches can help students identify and address challenges they are facing. From there, the academic coach can probe for an understanding of steps the student has already taken, and where students are in their problem-solving abilities. Typically, students fall into one of two types of problem-solvers: They are either *impulsive problem solvers* or *avoidant problem solvers* (Nezu et al., 2012), and each student will need varying degrees of guidance depending on their problem-solving tendency. For example, an academic coach working with an avoidant problem-solver may need to ask more probing questions (e.g., *What can we do about this problem? How can we fix this?*) before moving right into a strategy.

Treating problem-solving in the academic setting is a learned skill, and a coach can model the problem-solving process rather than simply solving the problem for the student. Modeling allows the student to understand appropriate and inappropriate ways to problem-solve and see that everyone (even coaches) must go through this process at times. This transparency not only helps students see how to strategically address a challenge but also may help reduce feelings of inadequacy or worry that experiencing this challenge means something is "wrong with me." If a student has attempted to problem-solve but has not been successful, the academic coach can help identify missed steps and also alternatives. For example, if a student is having trouble with a class and has only been stopping by the faculty member's office with no luck in connecting, the academic coach can guide the student toward a different strategy (e.g., email to make an appointment, looking up office hours). It will be important for academic coaches to remember that some students may lack confidence with school-related problem-solving and therefore must remain sensitive to student needs for reassurance, encouragement, and positive reinforcement.

Sometimes students just need a safe space to vent, problem-solve, or seek wisdom. They may need a word of encouragement or some reassurance. Academic coaches can provide these reinforcements to students, as well as share healthy coping skills like engaging in positive self-talk, saying affirmations, exercising, seeking social support from family and friends, and participating in leisure activities (Pierceall & Keim, 2007). These coping skills are reactive in that they help students deal with challenges they are actively facing in the present or have faced in the past.

Academic coaches may also assist a student in engaging in proactive coping. *Proactive coping* is defined as "efforts to strive actively to seek new challenges, create new opportunities, and facilitate promotion toward challenging goals so that they will be less negative" (Gan et al., 2010, p. 644). If a student is experiencing any issues that may be out of the realm of the services that an academic coach can provide (i.e., coping with a sexual assault or coping with difficult family matters), then the academic coach will need to refer the student to other campus resources that are more equipped to provide the student with the right tools (e.g., the campus counseling center). Schools should be sure to equip coaches with the information and contact information they need to follow up in moments like these. For example, they may help students set up the appointments, role-play what to say when contacting the counseling center, or help the student locate the counseling center on campus.

GOAL-SETTING

Some students may not set realistic expectations for themselves or others. Having a coach to guide long- and short-term goal-setting efforts may be necessary for students who may lack confidence in setting academic or professional goals. Parker and Boutelle (2009) explain that coaching can help students "maintain focus to achieve identified goals, translate abstract goals into concrete actions, and build motivation and learn to use those rewards effectively" (Goudreau & Knight, 2018, p. 385). For students who have difficulty with executive functioning tasks related to academic success, this may be critical for long-term motivation. Coaches can frequently refer back to broader goals to help keep smaller (possibly less desirable) tasks in perspective. The coach can help students see small actions that will be important and necessary stepping stones toward larger goals, as well as assist students in clarifying goals and ensuring they are realistic and attainable.

For example, long-term goals, such as career or life goals, can be brought into a shorter-term focus by selecting a major or identifying a potential internship opportunity, and then further segmented into more manageable actions. Coaches can support students who may be overwhelmed with larger goals (e.g., passing a course or improving a student's overall GPA), through the process of breaking them into smaller, concrete tasks (e.g., writing a final paper, studying for exams or tests, and reading assignments). Even within these tasks, there are specific steps that students must take to be successful, and those can become the focus of regular initial coaching meetings. For example, if a student has an upcoming test, the coach and student may break up the content into more manageable steps that can be accomplished each day during the upcoming week. If helpful, these steps can even be assigned a specific day and amount of time in a planner as well as a specific study strategy that aligns the expectations of the test with the learning characteristics of the student. While the coach can help the student see how daily actions are contributing to their advancement toward long-term goals, a layout brief and concrete daily tasks can make reaching those goals (and even knowing where to start) feel more attainable.

Coaches can help students proactively plan goals and the action steps needed to achieve their academic goals. Coaches help students identify times and spaces for students to study or complete schoolwork that are conducive to their learning profile. During regular meetings, coaches help students continue to refine their understanding about study strategies and spaces that work for them. While these thought processes related to organization, planning, and time-management skills come naturally for some students, they may be very challenging for others. Thus, academic coaches who help students effectively use goal-setting strategies and planning tools (e.g., planners, calendar systems) can be critical supports for promoting future independence and academic success.

SELF-ADVOCACY

Students enter college with varying levels of skill and comfort with self-advocacy and the ability to take the lead on being proactive about their approach to college life, addressing challenges, and communicating (to support staff, professors, or academic coaches) how they learn best or what support they need to be successful. Academic coaches have exclusive opportunities to help students become self-advocates by working on self-awareness and self-reflection, as well as helping to equip students with the tools necessary to communicate effectively. After working with students to understand their background and skill level with self-advocacy skills, an academic coach can meet students where they are and determine next steps. For example, students who experience challenges with social anxiety may struggle when having to talk to professors or ask for help (Farrell, 2007). Coaches can work behind the scenes to encourage, role-play, and otherwise help students find good ways to make connections (Swartz et al., 2005). Other students may assume that *self-advocacy* only refers to reactive behaviors, such as "sticking up for yourself" when an instructor fails to provide an accommodation. Coaches can work with these students to understand a broader picture of self-advocacy to include proactive and collaborative steps they can take to effectively use campus resources, develop relationships with faculty, and establish a personal support structure.

Role-play provides another way to make transparent the thought processes behind strategic approaches to academic situations. Taking the time to work together and practice situations or encounters that may be common among college students might be what a student needs to anticipate and plan for situations that might otherwise take them off guard. For example, students will likely not want to be composing the words to describe their learning profile and support needs for the first time while standing in front of their first college instructor. Yet avoiding these discussions might mean an inability to access accommodations (like extended time on exams, testing in a quiet location) that have been critical in their educational experience thus far.

Academic coaches have a unique opportunity to provide a safe space for the student to practice different types of descriptive language that enables them to explain their learning profile in such a way that communicates the necessary information to instructors while still painting the student in a positive light. Coaches can also help students find terminology that will likely be recognized in the college setting by a typical instructor. For example, if a student is not sure a professor will be familiar with the term *dyscalculia*, a coach can help the student find a different way to describe this math-affected disability, the impact it has on their academic performance (e.g., "I often switch numbers around" or "I skip steps when trying to solve a math problem"), and what the student does to compensate (certain study approach, using specific note-taking format, etc.), and support or advice that may be needed from the instructor. This type of practice session with an academic coach will help better prepare students for meetings with professors in which they have to self-advocate and describe not only their disability but also how they learn and what they may need from the course or professor to aid them toward success.

Using a broad view of self-advocacy, coaches can also help students be proactive about the kinds of resources they access for different learning situations. For example, students who have ADHD may struggle in lecture-heavy courses, yet most students will find themselves in these courses more than once in a typical post-secondary environment. Use of assistive technologies that make an audio recording of the lecture that is synced with notes taken during class (and at times the instructor's slide deck) can help students actively engage with the content of the lecture and leave with both auditory and typed notes. These will be extremely helpful for later studying, especially if the student's mind wandered at any point during the lecture. The academic coach has the potential to be extremely valuable in providing one-on-one support for students with different learning profiles, providing individualized instruction to aid the student toward success.

LEARNING STRATEGIES FOR ACADEMIC SUCCESS

In addition to the more overarching skills described above, academic coaches can also provide valuable support for helping students find specific study techniques and resources that most effectively enable them to meet their academic goals each semester. Some students arrive on the post-secondary campus with a rich "toolkit" of strategies and tools for tackling college-level learning. Others may come from school environments that have never been a good fit with their learning strengths and needs. For those students, successes and failures may have felt random or externally facilitated, especially when reliance on external supports and structures from parents and teachers was critical. These students may need to develop the internal locus of control (Aquino, 2017), confidence (National Center for Learning Disabilities [NCLD], 2017), or knowledge needed to be intentional and strategic about how they approach each class. Coaches can be valuable sources of just-in-time encouragement and strategies that will help students build and refine their toolbox (and confidence with taking risks) over time. While there are too many to capture in one chapter, we will discuss some examples in the areas of: learning strategies, note-taking, and assistive technologies.

Learning Strategies

Coaches can provide support with the development of metacognitive skills in the college setting by helping students try new strategies, embark on an iterative process of reflection, and adjust student process throughout the semester to maximize the efficiency and impact of how they spend their academic time. Learning strategy instruction has long been utilized to ensure student success in academic settings (Weinstein et al., 2011; Weinstein et al., 2004). Researchers have classified learning strategies by type, such as rehearsal, elaboration, mnemonics, and organization (Weinstein & Mayer, 1986; Riding & Rayner, 1998). Coaches help students—who come with the aptitude, motivation, and content readiness to succeed in college—build the strategies necessary to develop learning routines and study strategies necessary for meeting their potential (see table 8.1). These strategies go beyond general study techniques and apply specific processes (often accompanied by mnemonic-style reminders) to frequent study routines using one manageable step at a time.

Although the strategies summarized in table 8.1 below can be very effective, coaches can help teach students *when* and *how t*o use each strategy. For example, rehearsal may be effective when trying to remember basic information such as a mathematical equation or years and dates for key events but may not be effective when applying the equation or describing/analyzing what happened during the historical event. In this case, a mnemonic or elaboration strategy may be better suited. Students also may need help personalizing the strategy for their individual needs. The strategies give students the benefit of going "back to the beginning" when learning a study technique and can be taught relatively quickly. That said, they can be tedious to use for maximum benefit—especially early on before students reach automaticity

Table 8.1. Sample Learning Strategies

Strategy Category	Sample Strategy Spotlight
Rehearsal Strategies Rehearsal strategies utilize repetition to learn new information. As students continue to revisit and repeat new information, the content stays in their working memory (Woolfolk, 2017). Rehearsal strategies are effective when students are tasked with learning concrete and discrete information, such as a list of terms or a play script. Rehearsal strategies alone are not sufficient when trying to learn complex and applied information that must be retained long-term (Santrock, 2017).	**Flashcards** Familiar to most students, and inexpensive to develop, flashcards require rewriting and/or reframing information learned in class. Both developing and using flashcards requires rehearsing information. This long-used strategy enables students to pull information from multiple sources into one portable study resource that divides learning material into bite-sized chunks. Flashcards can be developed to include text, images, mnemonics, and applied examples. It generally takes time to create a well-developed set of flashcards. Therefore, they are most useful when developed over time after each class or unit of study and then used to study for a test. They are less useful for learning a lot of new or detailed information in a short amount of time. Emerging technologies are providing more variety and efficiency with developing flashcard-style study resources that may be more engaging for some students.
Elaboration Strategies Elaboration strategies involve expanding newly learned material by connecting new information with previous knowledge. When students connect what they already know to what they are learning, they are able to encode and remember information more effectively (Ashcraft & Radvansky, 2018). This type of strategy helps students add a distinction to new material that can aid with later recall (Hofmeister & Vasishth, 2014; Santrock, 2017).	**LINCS** LINCS is a vocabulary building strategy developed by the University of Kansas Center for Research on Learning (KU Center for Research on Learning, n.d.). The strategy is designed to help students remember complex terms by connecting the term with existing knowledge. When using this strategy, students connect a new vocabulary word to a similar-sounding word, image, and story/scenario to help them remember long-term. For example, if students are trying to learn the word *fief*, their reminding word might be *chief*. This reminding word is then used to help create a "story" or sentence that links the reminding word to the term being defined. After creating the story, students draw a picture that provides a mental image of the story, which encourages students to link the new complex term to its meaning.

Mnemonics Strategies

Mnemonics are memory aids that help students remember large sets of information, including lists, steps, stages, or characteristics (Rummel et al., 2003; Soemer & Schwan, 2012). Mnemonics can be helpful when students are trying to learn new or novel information that cannot be connected to prior knowledge (Homa, 2008). Instead, they attach meaning to new information by creating or identifying a rhyme (e.g., "*I* before *E* except after *C*"), acronym (e.g., SMART or Specific, Measurable, Attainable, Relevant, Time-Bound), key word, or mental imagery (Santrock, 2017; Woolfolk, 2017).

Organization Strategies

Organizing new content in meaningful ways can help students better understand and remember the information. New material becomes connected and more manageable, as recalling one aspect of the information can prompt memory of other elements. Students may organize information in various ways, such as creating an outline or mind map, using hierarchy to connect information, or chunking information into groups or units (Santrock, 2017; Schneider, 2015; Woolfolk, 2017).

Strategy Spotlight: PIRATES

The PIRATES test-taking strategy, developed by the Center for Research on Learning at the University of Kansas, provides a mnemonic device paired with specific steps for taking a test. While not applicable to all types of test, PIRATES can help students systematically work through a test, apply what they learned when studying to test questions, pace themselves appropriately, check back over their work, and guess when needed—but not too quickly (KU Center for Research on Learning, n.d.).

RAP

This paraphrasing strategy, designed by the KU Center for Research on Learning, helps students improve recall of main ideas and facts presented in course readings. RAP requires students to pause after reading short passages and rephrase the content in their own words. This process requires students to actively engage with the content they are reading and regularly test their understanding. It also enforces the idea of organizing or chunking information into small sections to aid in recall and attention (KU Center for Research on Learning, n.d.).

with the strategy. External encouragement and accountability are necessary. We have found that, without initial support, many students with learning differences quickly jump to a familiar academic routine (e.g., flashcards), even if it is not the most effective or efficient approach for the learning goals for a particular course or unit of content. Coaches can help students learn to identify study tools and tactics that are more suited for their learning profile and that may more effectively improve their academic performance.

NOTE-TAKING

Students often tell us that the transition from a high school environment, where much of the active learning occurs *in the classroom*, to a college environment, where much of the active involvement with content occurs *independently*, constitutes a major adjustment. In college, leaving a class session with an adequate record of content, context, examples, and so on, is critical for effective studying. An early and intentional focus on effective note-taking can be a good starting point for coaches. It addresses a predictable transition focus, and if a student identifies a good system early on, it will provide high-quality class notes that can be used for other studying support and strategies later on.

By the time students get to college, pen-and-paper note-taking might be something they take for granted. However, it requires the coordination of a myriad of cognitive and physical skills that range from working memory to attentiveness to grip strength, areas that can be a source of significant challenge for some students with learning and attention issues (Boyle, 2001; Suritsky, 1993; Boyle et al., 2015). Challenges include keeping pace with the speed of the lecture, recognizing important versus supplemental information, capturing a full lecture without omitting key information, using legible handwriting, and more. Fortunately, with the range of technologies and note-taking strategies available, it is a "fixable" problem that a coach and student can address together to find the most effective system. For example, although research suggests that writing notes with traditional pen and paper helps students remember the material better (Smoker et al., 2009), the traditional method of note-taking may not be plausible for some students (i.e., students with dysgraphia). These students may want to speak with their instructor or the disability support specialist on campus to ensure they can use a computer or recording device for note-taking. While having a recording of the class lecture can be an incredibly valuable resource, it is only useful if built into after-class study routines. This is where coaching and advance planning can be just as critical. Moreover, students may need coaching to understand appropriate ways to approach their instructor about recording class settings and ethical uses of those resources.

Transitioning from often-explicit course materials provided in high school to more conversational-style lectures in a college environment may be a challenge for students with learning and attention challenges. The cognitive load of maintaining attention and actively participating in class, grasping the organization and structure of what can sound like a free-flowing lecture, and recording sufficient information in legible and complete notes can be overwhelming. Students who are often fully capable of mastering course content with the appropriate study materials may need direct support learning to "take notes" in the post-secondary setting. This is not a new challenge, and literature that addresses the challenges students face with note-taking spans decades (Locke, 1977).

Coaches can help students broaden their repertoire of note-taking strategies, as well as apply the most effective and efficient approaches for specific courses. For example, the note-taking system used for a science course like biology may not be the same system utilized for a math or psychology course. For students with atypical slower processing speed or working memory, developing a comprehensive set of notes during class may be exhausting, and may not be the best use of their mental energy and attention. Instead, these students can utilize technology to find the right balance of active participation in class and note-taking, from basic recording devices to well-designed software that syncs recordings of a lecture to typed notes and presentation slides (Sonocent Ltd., 2019). Coaches can play an essential role here. New technologies can feel like "one more thing" to students who are already overwhelmed with a very new learning environment. Having a coach to help match new technologies to their learning and study patterns can make the difference between finding an effective solution and premature abandonment tools that take time to learn or do not produce immediate results.

ASSISTIVE TECHNOLOGY

The ever-changing technologies available to students today create both an opportunity and an educational need for student-support programs. First-year students may find themselves using technology for academic purposes that, although familiar to them, was previously used primarily for social or informal reasons (e.g., email, phone apps). We cannot simply assume students will make this transition naturally, and direct instruction in appropriate communication and use patterns with these resources is essential. Some direct and well-timed support up front can save time and challenges in the long run for students who are well-intentioned but find difficulty navigating this transition. Academic coaches may find themselves in an ideal position to offer this support.

Students may have access to technologies in college that are new and unfamiliar. Without direct support in adopting these resources, however, students may avoid taking on the task of learning about a new tool during the time when the technologies might actually be the most beneficial (e.g., general education courses, courses with large numbers of students, etc.). Assistive technologies like text-to-speech or speech-to text software, note-taking software, recording devices, or planning applications can help students in both academic and organizational pursuits. Access to some technologies may require working with the campus disability support office, and some must be purchased. Just in the past few years, we have seen technology that was once very expensive or difficult to obtain become ubiquitous in phones and common software. While this has the potential to reduce the stigma around various forms of assistive technology, some students may not know about their existence or even where to begin looking. Coaches can help. Below are some of the technologies commonly used by our students today. While lists of specific electronic resources can quickly become outdated, the examples in figures 8.2–8.4 can provide a sense of the functions that are most helpful to students with learning differences in the college environment and resources that coaches can revise and build over time.

Reading is an area most commonly affected by learning disabilities (Shaywitz, 2003). Disabilities such as dyslexia can make decoding text extremely laborious, time-consuming, and exhausting for students who are otherwise fully capable of understanding difficult and complex text. Audiobooks and text-to-speech capabilities can make an important difference for students who need to keep up with the quantity and pace of readings in college. In some circumstances, these resources may also positively impact fluency, motivation, vocabulary, and comprehension of written material (Wolfson, 2008; Wood et al., 2018; Park, Takahashi, et al., 2017). Figure 8.2 contains a few examples of the rapidly increasing range of resources available to students (Bouck et al., 2018).

Students use *writing skills* in almost all post-secondary courses, requiring simultaneous use of multiple skill sets at a pace that can be daunting for students with disabilities that impact written expression (Kellogg & Raulserson, 2007). For example, some students may have trouble with the actual act of writing (i.e., handwriting), and other students have trouble with grammar and mechanics. Unless the course is focused on written expression, either of these can provide unnecessary barriers for communication around higher-order skills and deep learning. Figure 8.3 provides examples of technologies that are helpful to some students.

Figure 8.2. Technologies to Support Reading

Name	Description
TTS Accessibility in smartphones/ tablets	Students may change the settings in most smart devices to allow them to use the device to read the contents of the entire screen or read highlighted sections of text. It is a free resource included within most devices.
Rewordify	Rewordify is an app that simplifies difficult words for students who have trouble with reading and comprehension. Freely available online and in app store (www.rewordify.com).
Speechify	Speechify is an app that allows students to take pictures of text and listen to it at up to 2–3x normal reading speed. Freely available online and in app store (www.getspeechify.com).
NaturalReader	NaturalReader is an app that allows students to upload text, images, and documents that can be converted to audio. Students then listen to natural-sounding voices read the text. NaturalReader is a free resource available online and in app store (www.naturalreaders.com).
Read&Write	Read&Write is a toolbar that allows students to hear the text aloud and look up the meanings of words. Individual and campus subscriptions needed (www.texthelp.com/products/read-write).

Figure 8.3. Technologies to Support Written Expression

Name	Description
Ginger	Ginger helps students correct their errors in grammar, punctuation, spelling, and other writing mechanics. In addition to making corrections, it also allows students to listen to what they have written. Ginger is a free resource available online and in the app store (www.gingersoftware.com).
Grammarly	Grammarly improves students' written communication skills by fixing their grammar, spelling, and style errors. It is a free resource available online and in the app store.
Co:Writer	Co:Writer is a tool that predicts phrases and words for students. It also corrects spelling and grammar mistakes. Co:Writer also has a speech-to-text feature and works in different languages such as Spanish, French, German, and English. Monthly subscriptions available online and in the app store (www.learningtools. donjohnston.com/product/cowriter).
Dragon Naturally Speaking	Dragon Naturally Speaking is a speech-to-text software that allows students to dictate and transcribe their writing assignments. Prices vary. Available online and in stores (www.nuance.com/dragon).
Sonocent Audio Notetaker	Sonocent Audio Notetaker is an online system that captures audio, text, and images in a single system. Students can use their smartphone, tablet, or laptop in class to record information lectures. Annual or "life" subscriptions available for download online (www.sonocent.com).
Livescribe Pen	Livescribe pens help students turn their handwritten notes into digital files. While using the pen, students can record their lectures along with taking notes. Students can then listen again to the lecture when reviewing their notes. Prices vary online and in store (www.livescribe.com).

Figure 8.4 provides math-related assistive technology examples. Coaches can be instrumental in ensuring that students follow the proper procedures for determining which resources to use and communicating about these tools with instructors.

Figure 8.4.   Technologies to Support Math

Name	*Description*
MathTalk	MathTalk is a software that allows student speech recognition for math problems. Students who use the program can dictate their math equations and then print, save, and email their work. Available for purchase online (www.mathtalk.com).
Talking Calculators	Talking calculators assist students by orally presenting numbers and calculations in a natural voice. Instead of having to read the numbers from the screen, students are able to listen to the numbers they are inputting, as well as their results. Available for purchase online (www.independentliving.com/category/calculators).
EquatIO	EquatIO is an online software that allows students to digitally write mathematical equations, graphs, and formulas. When using the software, students can dictate, type, or hand-write mathematical expressions. Available for purchase online (www.texthelp.com/en-us/products/equatio).

Sample technology resources that can assist with planning and time management are listed in figure 8.5. As mentioned earlier, the accompanying support and accountability that can be provided by a coach can be essential for enabling a student to fully integrate the resource into daily routines and maximize impact on productivity.

Figure 8.5.   Resources for Planning and Time Management

Name	*Description*
Shovel	Shovel is an online planner that allows students to calculate their class, study, and social time. It allows students to compare the workload they have with the time they have to complete it. Freely available for use online and in the app store (www.shovel.com).
Pomodoro Timers	The Pomodoro technique was designed to help students improve their time management and productivity. Students set the timer for 25 minutes and immerse themselves in their work. Once the 25 minutes are over, students take a short 5-10-minute break. Freely available for use online (www.tomato-timer.com).
WatchMinder	WatchMinder is a vibrating watch that helps students increase their productivity by providing daily incremental reminders. These reminders may help reinforce routine, improve transitions, or enhance time-management habits. Available for purchase online (www.watchminder.com).

INFUSING SUPPORTS FOR ALL STUDENTS

Since the establishment of higher education institutions, developmental strategies have been introduced to help bridge the gap between academics and the milestones of student development that occur during the college years of adolescence into adulthood. To meet the needs of students, campus-wide strategies such as mentoring, coaching, advising, and counseling emerged in an effort to address this timeframe of exploration and identity that students go through (McWilliams & Beam, 2013). As institutions have progressed, more formal programming has been established to help meet students where they are in an effort to infuse support at differing points in a student's academic career (McWilliams & Beam, 2013).

Across the country, colleges and universities are infusing programming on campuses in an effort to support students. For example, at Wake Forest University in North Carolina, a mentoring resource center partners with other offices on campus to implement four strategies; advising, counseling, academic coaching, and mentoring. With this approach they are hoping to create a decentralized network of support where offices across campus share tools, resources, and knowledge (McWilliams & Beam, 2013). Instead of only front-loading support for students who are in their first year of college—such as first-year courses, transition programming, or living-learning communities—institutions are starting to see a more effective benefit from offering personal coaching (Dalton & Crosby, 2014). In fact, research shows that coaching has been found to be a promising service delivery model for students who struggle with the academic demands of college (Richman et al., 2014). Some institutions of higher education who offer tutoring support and learning strategy instruction have found this approach to be helpful for students who have learning disabilities or other academic challenges (Parker et al., 2011).

CONCLUSION

In this chapter, we described the key essential elements of academic coaching. We highlighted the importance of establishing core relationships and developing routines with students and shared several examples of effective approaches. We discussed how to address some challenges neurodiverse students may have such as time management, organization, problem-solving, and self-advocacy. This chapter additionally included resources on learning strategies and assistive technology that can benefit students with learning and attention differences and support academic learning in reading, writing, and math. Whether it is within academic mentoring or an academic coaching format, these examples, strategies, and resources can be bundled in flexible ways to deliver the individual supports needed for neurodiverse learners.

Campus Essentials for High Impact

- *Identify and connect coaching or mentoring programs.* The integration of services on your campus helps neurodiverse students access support needed for success.
- *Explore methods of supporting delivery.* Coaching programs can benefit from utilizing varying methods of content delivery and by tailoring supports to the individual student.
- *Examine ways existing programs can integrate services for student success.* Partnerships on campus play an important role in ensuring students receive the services and supports that are needed to achieve academically.

APPENDIX 1

Sample Interview Questions

1. Walk me through a typical week in your life during the academic year.
2. Paint me a mental picture of you studying and doing homework. For example, tell me:
   a. when and where you study;
   b. how you structure your study time; and
   c. what methods, strategies, and resources you use.
3. Would you say that receiving zeroes on assignments is typical for you?
4. If you find that you are having difficulty with an assignment, what do you do?
5. What kinds of situations or experiences make you feel "stressed out" or overwhelmed? How do you react to those situations? How do you cope with stress? How can other people most effectively help you when you feel stressed or overwhelmed?
6. Describe one aspect of college that is a strength for you.
7. Describe one aspect of college that is a challenge for you.
8. What support resources/offices (e.g., Disability Support Services, Counseling Center) have you used in the past?

APPENDIX 2

Compiled Sample Survey Questions

Sample Check-Box Questions

Which areas of executive functioning are the most challenging for you? Please check all that apply:

- *Inhibit/Shift*—ability to control impulses and appropriately stop behavior at the proper time.
- *Emotional control*—ability to modulate emotional responses
- *Self-monitor*—the extent to which one can keep track of one's own behavior and observe the effect of the behavior on others.
- *Initiate*—ability to begin a task or actively and fluently generate ideas.
- *Working memory*—Capacity to actively hold information in mind for the purpose of completing a task or generating a response.
- *Plan/organize*—ability to manage current and future-oriented task demands within a situational context. This includes setting goals, developing appropriate steps to carry out an associated task, and understanding main ideas.
- *Task monitor*—ability to check work and assess performance during or after finishing a task to ensure the attainment of the goal.
- *Organization of materials*—ability to keep workspace, living areas, and materials in an orderly manner.

Note: Adapted from the Brief A (Roth et al., 2005; Weinstein et al., 1987).

Sample Short-Answer Questions

What are your immediate and long-term goals?

Sample Likert-Scale Questions

The questions below could be framed directions and a scale on which the student can indicate a level of agreement:

- I consider myself a dedicated student.
- I often receive zeroes on assignments.
- I have personal goals related to my academics.
- I need to excel in academics to feel good about myself.

- My academic experiences are important to my overall college experience.
- I receive pressure from others to achieve academically.
- I understand the meaning of a college degree.
- I have goals for myself beyond graduation from college.

APPENDIX 3

Sample Student Learning Profile

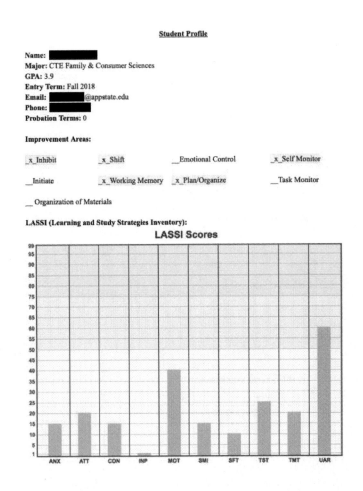

Source: **Student Profile**

Other Unit Involvement:

_x_ SSS   __ ACCESS   _x_ ODR Accommodations

__ Athletics   __ Wilson Scholar

Comments:

███████ is a non-traditional student who has experienced significant academic success, but struggles severely with anxiety. She has extreme test-taking anxiety and does not have a lot of skills to cope with this. She is on the Chancellor's List, but does not feel like this paints an accurate picture of her success. She struggles to articulate what is in her brain and how to get these thoughts onto paper. She lives in ███████ and works with an ADHD Coach when she is off the mountain. She has the capacity to complete assignments, she just struggles to get started, especially if assignments do not have explicit instructions. She does utilizes Google Calendar on her phone and computer and she checks ASULearn regularly. She also uses a smart pen, Dragon Speak, and takes physical notes on slides during lecture. She rarely receives 0's, but will turn assignments in late. She doesn't like to communicate with professors, but will do it if she has to, even though this is extremely stressful for her. When ███████ cannot understand the material, she feels "stupid", and this situation is the most stressful for her. She has a lot of anxiety about becoming a teacher and applying the skills she is learning to her career one day. ███████ called herself a "slow processor" and said that she does not have the skills for "high level thinking." Retaining information is an extreme challenge and classes that require a significant amount of reading are very stressful. In addition to needing academic mentoring from As-U-R, ███████ needs assistance in understanding how to utilize all of the technology that is out there. She knows there are more resources that she could use to be successful, but needs assistance accessing these resources and understanding how to use them.

███ Fall 2018: Is enrolled in graduate 4+1 program which is very very challenging for her. Writing and confidence are very very serious challenges for ███████. She KNOWS what she needs to do, but has LOTS of trouble organizing her thoughts and generalizing new skills from assignment to assignment. Talk to ███ about ███████ if you have additional questions.

Source: **Student Profile**

REFERENCES

Aquino, O. S. (2017). Locus of control, parents' involvement and college disability accommodations. *Theses and Dissertations*, 2378. https://rdw.rowan.edu/etd/2378.

Ashcraft, M. H., & Radvansky, G. A. (2018). *Cognition* (7th ed.). Prentice Hall.

Bellman, S., Burgstahler, S., & Hinke, P. (2015). Academic coaching: Outcomes from a pilot group of post-secondary STEM students with disabilities. *Journal of Postsecondary Education and Disability, 28*(1), 103–108.

Bettinger, E. P., & Baker, R. (2011). *The effects of student coaching in college: An evaluation of a randomized experiment in student mentoring* (Working Paper No. 16881). Center for Education Policy Analysis. Retrieved from http://cepa.stanford.edu/content/effects-studentcoaching-colleqe-evaluation-randomized-experiment-student-mentoring

Bouck, E. C., Working, C., & Bone, E. (2018). Manipulative apps to support students with disabilities in mathematics. *Intervention in School and Clinic, 53*(3), 177–182.

Boyle, J. R. (2001). Enhancing the note taking skills of students with mild disabilities. *Intervention in School and Clinic, 36*(4), 221–224.

Boyle, J. R., Forchelli, G. A., & Cariss, K. (2015). Note-taking interventions to assist students with disabilities in content area classes. *Preventing School Failure, 59*(3), 186–195.

Brown, A. L., Bransford, J. D., Ferrara, R., & Campione, J. (1983). Learning, remembering and understanding. In J. H. Flavell, & E. M. Markman (Eds.), *Handbook of child psychology: Vol. 3: Cognitive development* (4th ed., pp. 77–166). Wiley.

Capstick, M. K., Harrell-Williams, L., Cockrum, C. D., & West, S. L. (2019). Exploring the effectiveness of academic coaching for academically at-risk college students. *Innovative Higher Education, 44*(3), 219–231. doi:10.1007/s10755-019-9459-1

Dalton, J. C., & Crosby, P. C. (2014). The power of personal coaching: Helping first-year students to connect and commit in college. *Journal of College and Character, 15*(2), 59–66. https://doi.org/10.1515/jcc-2014.:.0010

Deiorio, N., & Miller, J. A. (2016). Developing an academic coaching program. *MedEdPublish, 5*(3), 57. https://doi.org/10.15694/mep.2016.000143

Farrell, E. F. (2007). Some colleges provide success coaches for students. *Chronicle of Higher Education.* http://www.chronicle.com/article/some-colleges-provide-success/lO133

Flavell, J. H. (1979). Metacognition and cognitive monitoring: A new area of cognitive developmental inquiry. *American Psychologist, 34*(10), 906–911.

Gan, Y., Hu, Y., & Zhang, Y. (2010). Proactive and preventive coping in adjustment to college. *The Psychological Record, 60*(4), 643–658.

Goudreau, S. B., & Knight, M. (2018). Executive function coaching: Assisting with transitioning from secondary to post-secondary education. *Journal of Attention Disorders, 22*(4), 379–387. https://doi.org/10.1177/1087054715583355

Gurpinar, E., Bati, H., & Tetik, C. (2011). Learning styles of medical students change in relation to time. *Advances in Physiology Education, 35*(3), 307–311. https://doi.org/10.1152/advan.00047.2011

Hofmeister, P., & Vasishth, S. (2014). Distinctiveness and encoding effects in online sentence comprehension. *Front. Psychol., 5,* 1237. doi:10.3389/fpsyg.2014.01237

Homa, D. (2008). *Long-term memory.* In N. J. Salkind (Ed.), *Encyclopedia of educational psychology.* SAGE.

Hoover, E. (2011, March 9). A close-up look at student coaching. *The Chronicle of Higher Education.* http://chronicle.com/blogs/headcount/a-close-up-look-at-student-coaching/27964

Husmann, P. R., & O'Loughlin, V. D. (2019). Another nail in the coffin for learning styles? Disparities among undergraduate anatomy students' study strategies, class performance, and reported VARK learning styles. *Anatomical Sciences Education, 12*(1), 6–19.

Kader, F. A., & Eissa, M. A. (2015). The effectiveness of time management strategies instruction on students' academic time management and academic self-efficacy. *International Journal of Psycho-Educational Sciences, 4*(1), 43–50.

Kellogg, R. T., & Raulerson, B. A. (2007). Improving the writing skills of college students. *Psychonomic Bulletin & Review, 14,* 237–242. https://doi.org/10.3758/BF03194058

Killion, J., Harrison, C., Bryan, C., & Clifton, H. (2014). Teacher-coach relationships. *Tools for Learning Schools, 17*(4), 1–7.

Kreider, C. M., Medina, S., & Slamka, M. R. (2019). Strategies for coping with time-related and productivity challenges of young people with Learning Disabilities and Attention-Deficit/Hyperactivity Disorder. *Children, 6*(2), 28.

KU Center for Research on Learning. (n.d.). *The Strategic Instruction Model (SIM) learning strategies.* https://sim.drupal.ku.edu/learning-strategies

Locke, E. A. (1977). An empirical study of lecture note taking among college students. *The Journal of Educational Research, 71*(2), 93–99. https://doi.org/10.1080/00220671.1977.10885044

McWilliams, A. E., & Beam A. R. (2013). Advising, counseling, coaching, mentoring: Models of developmental relationships in higher education. *The Mentor: Innovative Scholarship on Academic Advising, 15.* https://doi.org/10.26209/MJ1561280.

Meltzer, L. (2018). Creating strategic classrooms and schools: Embedding executive function strategies in the curriculum. In L. Meltzer (Ed.), *Executive function in education: From theory to practice* (2nd ed., pp. 263–299). Guilford Press.

National Academic Advising Association (NACADA). (2017). *Academic coaching.* https://nacada.ksu.edu/Resources/Clearinghouse/Academic-Coaching.aspx

National Center for Learning Disabilities (NCLD). (2017). *Transitioning to life after high school.* National Center for Learning Disabilities.

Nezu, A. M., D'Zurilla, T., & Nezu, C. M. (2012). *Problem-solving therapy: A treatment manual.* Springer.

Park, H. J., Takahashi, K., Roberts, K. D., & Delise, D. (2017). Effects of text-to-speech software use on the reading proficiency of high school struggling readers. *Assistive Technology, 29*(3), 146–152.

Park, J., Lu, F.-C., & Hedgcock, W. M. (2017). Relative effects of forward and backward planning on goal pursuit. *Psychological Science, 28*(11), 1620–1630. https://doi.org/10.1177/0956797617715510

Parker, D. R., & Boutelle, K. (2009). Executive function coaching for college students with learning disabilities and ADHD: A new approach for fostering self-determination. *Learning Disabilities Research & Practice, 24*(4), 204–215.

Parker, D. R., Hoffman S. F., Sawilowsky, S., & Rolands, L. (2011). Self-control in post-secondary settings: Students' perceptions of ADHD college coaching. *Journal of Attention Disorders, 17*(3), 215–232.

Pierceall, E. A., & Keim, M. C. (2007). Stress and coping strategies among community college students. *Community College Journal of Research and Practice, 31*(9), 703–712.

Pinto, J. K., Geiger, M. A., & Boyle, E. J. (1994). A three-year longitudinal study of changes in student learning styles. *Journal of College Student Development, 35,* 113–199.

Powell, W., & Kusuma-Powell, O. (2011). *How to teach now: Five keys to personalized learning in a global classroom.* Association for Supervision and Curriculum Development (ASCD).

Prevatt, F., & Yelland, S. (2015). An empirical evaluation of ADHD coaching in college students. *Journal of Attention Disorders, 19*(8), 666–677.

Price, L. (2004). Individual differences in learning: Cognitive control, cognitive style, and learning style. *Educational Psychology, 24*(5), 681–698. https://search.proquest.com/docview/62123573?accountid=10639

Richman, E., Rademacher, K., & Maitland, T. (2014). Coaching and college success. *Journal of Postsecondary Education and Disability, 27*(1), 33–52.

Riding, R., & Rayner, S. (1998). *Cognitive styles and learning strategies: Understanding style differences in learning and behavior.* David Fulton.

Rimm-Kaufman, S., & Sandilos, L. (2019). *Improving students' relationships with teachers to provide essential supports for learning.* American Psychological Association.

Robinson, C., & Gahagan, J. (2010). Coaching students to academic success and engagement on campus. *About Campus, 15*(4), 26–29.

Roth, R. M., Isquity, P. K., & Gioia, G. A. (2005). *Behavior rating inventory of executive function—adult version (BRIEF-A).* Psychological Assessment Resources.

Rummel, N., Levin, J. R., & Woodward, M. M. (2003). Do pictorial mnemonic text-learning aids give students something worth writing about? *Journal of Educational Psychology, 95*(2), 327.

Santrock, J. W. (2017). *Educational psychology* (6th ed.). McGraw-Hill.

Schneider, W. (2015). *Memory development from early childhood through emerging adulthood.* Springer.

Serry, T., Oates, J., Ennals, P., Venville, A., Williams, A., Fossey, E., & Steel, G. (2018). Managing reading and related literacy difficulties: University students' perspectives, *Australian Journal of Learning Difficulties, 23*(1), 5–30. https://doi.org/10.1080/19404158.2017.1341422

Sfrisi, S. J., Deemer, S., Tamakloe, D., & Herr, O. J. (2017). The investigation of the learning style preferences and academic performance of elementary students with ADHD. *Excellence in Education Journal, 6*(2), 32–49.

Shaywitz, S. E. (2003). *Overcoming dyslexia: A new and complete science-based program for reading problems at any level.* Knopf.

Smoker, T. J., Murphy, C. E., & Rockwell, A. K. (2009). Comparing memory for handwriting versus typing. *Proceedings of the Human Factors and Ergonomics Society Annual Meeting, 53*(22), 1744–1747. https://doi.org/10.1177/154193120905302218

Soemer, A., & Schwan, S. (2012). Visual mnemonics for language learning: Static pictures versus animated morphs. *Journal of Educational Psychology, 104*(3), 565.

Sonocent Ltd. (2019). *Sonocent.* https://sonocent.com

Suritsky, S. K. (1993). Note-taking difficulties and approaches reported by university students with learning disabilities. *Journal on Postsecondary Education and Disability, 10*(1).

Swartz, S. L., Prevatt, F., & Proctor, B. E. (2005). A coaching intervention for college students with attention deficit/hyperactivity disorder. *Psychology in the Schools, 42*(6), 647–656.

Torres, S. M. (2014). The relationship between Latino students' learning styles and their academic performance. *Community College Journal of Research and Practice, 38*(4), 357–369. https://doi.org/10.1080/10668926.2012.761072

Weinstein, C. E., Acee, T. W., & Jung, J. H. (2011). Self-regulation and learning strategies. *New Directions for Teaching & Learning, 2011*(126), 45–53. https://doi.org/10.1002/tl.443

Weinstein, C. E., & Mayer, R. E. (1986). The teaching of learning strategies. In M. C. Wittock (Ed.), *Handbook of research on teaching* (pp. 315–327). Macmillan.

Weinstein, C. E., Palmer, D. R., & Schulte, A. C. (1987). *LASSI: Learning and Study Strategies Inventory.* H&H Publishing.

Weinstein, C. E., Tomberlin, T. L., Julie, A. L., & Kim, J. (2004). Helping students to become strategic learners: The roles of assessment, teachers, instruction, and students. In J. Ee, A. Chang, & O. Tan (Eds.), *Thinking about thinking: What educators need to know* (pp. 282–310). McGraw-Hill.

Wolfson, G. (2008). Using audiobooks to meet the needs of adolescent readers. *American Secondary Education, 36*(2), 105–114. http://search.ebscohost.com/login.aspx?direct=true&AuthType=ip,shib&db=ehh&AN=32143831&site=ehost-live&scope=site

Wood, S. G., Moxley, J. H., Tighe, E. L., & Wagner, R. K. (2018). Does use of text-to-speech and related read-aloud tools improve reading comprehension for students with reading disabilities? A meta-analysis. *Journal of Learning Disabilities, 51*(1), 73–84. https://doi.org/10.1177/0022219416688170

Woolfolk, A. E. (2017). *Educational psychology* (13th ed.). Pearson; Springer.

Chapter 8: Campus Spotlight

STEPP Program, East Carolina University

Morgan James

Source: **ECU STEPP Program**

Our Two-Part Mission: The STEPP Program's mission is to provide access
to a college education for students with learning disabilities who demonstrate
the potential for postsecondary success. By partnering with students, their
families, and a variety of educational communities, STEPP's innovative
model fosters a network of opportunities, resources, and supports designed
to equip and empower students at East Carolina University and across the
nation.

Part 1: The first part of our mission is a commitment to our students! By
considering a wider range of admission criteria and offering a comprehensive
program based on best practices for serving students with learning disabilities, the program provides a unique opportunity to a population that traditionally may not have access to college. The program maintains a consistent 93%
Year 1–Year 2 retention rate, and higher than 80% graduation rate.

I just wanted to share something with you or brag a bit. Sean has made Honor Roll this entire semester and was awarded a $1,000 scholarship this week. I really feel this change has come because he now knows he has a fighting chance in college—thanks to STEPP. Anyway, just wanted to share this and many thanks to you this morning.

—Parent

Part 2: We have a unique opportunity to work and learn alongside our students and share what we learn with our larger educational community. By researching best practices with students and sharing resources that we find effective, STEPP is committed to helping students across our nation. For example, a free transition curriculum on the program website is downloaded thousands of times each year (https://www.ecu.edu/cs-acad/stepp/curriculum.cfm).

About East Carolina University & STEPP: East Carolina University is a public university in eastern North Carolina that enrolls approximately 29,000 students each year. The STEPP Program provides access for participants to a small community within this large university environment. Funded primarily with private gifts, the program is relatively small, serving between 50 and 60 students at a time at no additional cost to participants.

Video: https://news.ecu.edu/2019/10/25/learning-disabilities-awareness-month

STEPP Program Components Include:

- *Admission and College Transition Support*: Students apply to the program during their junior year of high school, enabling the program to help students take one *STEPP* at a time to prepare for the college environment throughout the year before they transition to ECU.
- *Implementing a Daily Structure:* The program superimposes an external structure early in the student experience that fades as students gain confidence, independence, and a personalized support network. For example, required study hall hours for first-year students enable each student to create a weekly schedule with ample time devoted to academics within a resource-rich environment conducive to effective studying.

- **Providing a Parallel Curriculum:** Seminar-style classes are strategically integrated during key transition points in the college experience while students pursue the major of their choice. This curriculum is designed to work in the background to equip students with the skills and habits essential to academic and long-term success.

Source: **Thumbs up**

- **Engagement with Academic Coaching/Mentoring:** Graduate student mentors are available to help students develop effective and efficient academic routines, provide encouragement, and troubleshoot daily college living issues as needed. First-year students are required to meet weekly with an assigned mentor.
- **Access to Tutoring Services:** Students connect with the campus Pirate Academic Success Center (https://pasc.ecu.edu) for most tutoring, but the STEPP program offers peer tutors in high-need areas that are often impacted significantly by learning disabilities (e.g., English and math). Close proximity to this support enables students to include tutoring sessions into weekly planning routines and study hall schedules.

- *Infusing Advising Support:* An advisor in the STEPP Program works closely with advisors in each student's major using a co-advising model that blends understandings about the student's learning disability and the requirements of the specific major.
- *Access to Assistive Technology:* The program maintains a varied inventory of assistive technology resources to enable students to explore emerging tools that can help reduce barriers to accessing, managing, and expressing information.
- *Establishing a Support Network:* The STEPP Program connects students with a network of support professionals across ECU's campus.

Chapter Nine

Library Services

Jamie E. Bloss, Amanda Haberstroh, G. J. Corey Harmon, and Jana Schellinger

The growing number of neurodiverse patrons, students, staff, and faculty on today's college campus challenges the function and organization of the traditional campus library. Increasing the understanding of neurodiverse learning needs and tailoring library resources and space design contributes to the relevancy of the contemporary campus library. This chapter explores the ways campus libraries can transform and become a more welcoming learning environment for their neurodiverse patrons. The authors examine the modern academic library and the integration of Universal Design for Learning (UDL) principles, changes to space design, consider student access, examine assistive technologies, and explore the valuable role campus partnerships can play in developing neurodivergent friendly libraries.

Neurodiversity is diversity in how human brains and minds function (Tumlin, 2019; Armstrong, 2010). The National Institutes of Health now estimate that 39 million Americans (15%) have learning disabilities (ASGCLA, 2019). Students considered to have learning differences are but a fraction of those considered neurodivergent. Neurodiversity includes autistic students, staff, and faculty or anyone with dyslexia, ADD or ADHD, dyspraxia, or Tourette's syndrome. This would also include any of the following neurodiverse variations: Alzheimer's, cerebral palsy, epilepsy, brain injury, stroke, speech and language differences, ALS, Parkinson's, or blindness and deafness caused by brain differences. Tumlin (2019) mentions the learning disabilities hyperlexia, dyscalculia, and dysgraphia as well as people with mental health conditions.

Presenting the library as a kind of "home base" can be helpful for neurodiverse students if some changes are made in terms of available resources. A predictable environment where services and spaces are not always changing can benefit neurodiverse students (Myles, 2005). The library just being what it is, a resource space for students, can serve as that "home base" or "escape place" within the campus environment with design changes such as quiet study areas, white noise machines, Brody WorkLounge seating, and other spatial elements. Students with learning differences may require a quiet space to study and focus on materials or may prefer to work in groups in the study rooms. Although all students use the library and its services in different ways, neurodiverse students should always feel welcome in the library to use it for their purposes and needs including as a place to meet with support staff from the University Writing Center or the Speech Communication Center and their own personal learning assistants.

RAISING AWARENESS OF NEURODIVERSE STUDENTS

The literature shows that faculty members should receive training to accommodate neurodiverse students versus students who receive standard accommodations for documented disabilities (Drake, 2014). Having that extra experience and knowledge of neurodiversity increases the amount of success students can obtain when they feel supported and understood by their professors. Given the diverse population that they serve, librarians should also receive some basic training in how to assist, teach, and work with people who are neurodiverse beyond the typical disability inclusivity training that is offered. As Tumlin states, "Neurodivergent people use every kind of library, which is why it is important for every kind of librarian to be familiar with neurodiversity" (2019, p. 4). At East Carolina University (ECU), training is provided on creating inclusive learning environments, and all staff are encouraged to attend some of these sessions. However, if no specific training on working with neurodiverse patrons is offered explicitly, self-education is also encouraged (Cho, 2018). Librarians working with autistic students specifically should receive training, as there is no one-size-fits-all method of instruction or accommodation to serve patrons with autism.

Students and faculty members need to be aware of the alternative materials and services offered by the campus library. Austin Community College District Library has an excellent webpage with all of their services and accommodations listed for students with disabilities (Austin Community College District Library, n.d.). Accessible web resources that list services, instructional accommodations, circulating materials, and available computer software communicate to neurodiverse library users that their needs are a priority and efforts are made to provide assistance. Michigan State University (MSU) made strides by editing their electronic information technology (EIT) purchasing procedures relating to accessibility of their e-resources. If an item is still inaccessible despite new policies and procedures in place, the libraries offer an online remediation service where users can request accessible versions of documents, e-resources, and other materials when they need it (Schroeder, 2018). MSU also makes sure their accessibility services are apparent on their website.

SPACE AND ACCESS

The modern academic library has largely moved away from the quiet cloister and the "shushing" librarians of the past to become a vibrant part of the academic community. Many have cafés or coffee shops conveniently located within them, robust group study areas or information commons, and even gaming spaces available to users. The core mission of the library, however, remains the same: to provide a place for students and faculty to meet their information needs with the help of professional librarians. The ALA Code of Ethics states that librarians should "provide the highest level of service to all library users through appropriate and usefully organized resources; equitable service policies; equitable access; and accurate, unbiased, and courteous responses to all requests" (American Library Association, 2008). While the Code of Ethics is not a binding document, it is a guiding work that librarians adhere to whenever possible.

Space and access are understandably joined in a library context because of the way libraries are used. While a user could gain access to a library's electronic resources without ever setting foot in the building, they may not understand how to fully utilize them. Such users may also miss out on the print collection, which, depending on the field of study, may be more important than the digital resources. As such, it is important that both space and access be equally open to everyone regardless of neurocognitive or physical ability.

Technology is especially important to provide as an accommodation and the library can be a place where students can come to access a wide variety of technologies to support their learning needs. Computers—both Mac and PC—can be used to compensate for communication difficulties with a wide variety of students. Screen reader and dictation software can assist dyslexic students (Redford, 2017). Similarly, options for autistic students who prefer to communicate through text or email can be provided via accessible places to check email or by reference chat with a librarian (Myles, 2005).

ECU's Laupus Health Sciences Library also offers a virtual reality (VR) lab where students can explore anatomy in a different way. While it might not be recommended for students who experience issues with sensory overstimulation, for others it might be a missing link in connecting them to new explorations to enhance their educational experience. It can assist with students who have had trouble focusing in the traditional classroom setting; using the headset can increase students' concentration on the material or information that is set out in front of them with no distractions from elsewhere in the room (Pan et al., 2006). Users who prefer to learn by visual methods can also access the Ideum Touch Table in the library, which is essentially a large touchscreen that allows students to explore anatomy databases. Anatomical models also provide students with a hands-on learning experience. Audiobooks, which are often already provided by libraries, are an excellent option for dyslexic learners (Redford, 2017). The goal is to deliver learning materials to students in as many ways as possible.

LIBRARY SPACES

The main entry area to many modern libraries can be a loud and chaotic place with people moving about or working together, fluorescent lights buzzing, printers whirring, and a plethora of signs that most people ignore. This type of environment can be distressing for some neurodiverse users. Emily Lawrence (2013), a librarian with autism, suggests that older fluorescent lights can be a nightmare for autistic users, as well as those who are light-sensitive or prone to migraines due to their harsh nature and the low buzz that they emit. As such, they should be avoided whenever possible. Of course, it is unlikely that there is the budget to completely replace all the fluorescent light fixtures within the building, but newer LED lights may provide an acceptable alternative.

As library users move through the library, they may encounter open spaces with large tables for group study and modular furniture. The "learning commons" model, while helpful to some students, can overwhelm a neurodiverse student and discourage them from seeking out the library. Contemporary library environments offer a constant barrage of stimuli such as "flickering lights, background noise and countless other sensory distractions" that can cause autistic people to experience sensory overload (Remy & Seaman, 2014, p. 25). This can be countered by ensuring that there is adequate and well-marked quiet study space within the library, whether that be entire floors, sections of the library that can be closed off, or individual study rooms. Additionally, libraries could offer white noise in these to help minimize distractions. White noise may be pumped through an overhead speaker system or provided individually in the form of circulating white noise machines.

More broadly, private study spaces should be made available as a safe and sensory-friendly option for those who desire them. Ideally, the library can create a sensory room that offers "multi-sensory engagement and exploration using light, textures, colors, and sound" (Sarrett, 2017, p. 689). Realizing that library space is at a premium though, offering any space that could be used as an "escape room" to neurodiverse students would be a boon. These rooms would ideally lack windows (or at least have shades) and should have white noise, as well as non-fluorescent lighting with the ability to adjust brightness. Spaces like these can greatly benefit autistic students because these areas provide students the opportunity to decompress or engage in stimming, or self-stimulatory, behaviors (Sarrett, 2017). If private study rooms are not available, study carrels in quiet areas can also offer positive sensory experiences (Anderson, 2018).

Facilitating the independent use of library resources may encourage neurodiverse users to view the library as a welcome space. Clear signage is extremely beneficial to neurodiverse students because it can help set their expectations and offer direction to the spaces they might find most conducive to their studies. "Libraries should provide very obvious signage alerting students to which sections are quiet and in which sections socialization and communication are allowed"; this signage should be available both online and physically in the library (Anderson, 2018, p. 654). In addition to directional signs, the library should also clearly list policies about food (whether and where it is allowed), fragrances (acknowledging others' potential sensitivity to them), and noise (indicating where to find quiet areas).

As libraries have embraced the "learning commons" model, many libraries prioritize mobile furniture that can be used to create group study spaces or be moved to allow different activities in a space. This is positive for libraries in general as it makes them more agile, but it is important not to privilege collaborative social learning over quiet and solitary study space (Lawrence, 2013). Establishing private study rooms is the primary method by which these quiet spaces are created; however, study carrels and other furniture, such as the Brody WorkLounge (see figure 9.1), can offer alternatives by creating line-of-sight barriers that can ease the anxiety that students are being watched by others (Anderson, 2018). If a library can create a dedicated sensory room, it should include "a variety of seating options, such as armchairs, ball chairs, beanbags, and comfortable floor seating" (Sarrett, 2017, p. 690). Where it is not possible to create permanent private study areas, mobile walls, especially if they are sound absorbing, could prove greatly beneficial.

Access in a library context can be very broad. As has already been discussed, it can focus on the facility itself, but it can also refer to the people and resources within the library. Once the neurodiverse student has moved through the main entrance, they are often met by the formidable wall of the circulation or reference desk. Additionally, they need to determine how to get

A student using the Brody WorkLounge. Photo credit: Michelle Bone.

the resources they require. Library personnel can serve as a bridge between the user and these resources. Libraries are more than just buildings that house books; they also house experts on information retrieval. In addition to their general role of guiding people to the knowledge they seek, librarians often take on the additional roles of teacher, counselor, and friend. This can be a great benefit for neurodiverse students because they often communicate differently from neurotypical students.

Librarians need to educate themselves so that they can better recognize when they might be assisting a neurodiverse user; they are then able to adapt the interaction or methodology they are using to better suit that individual's needs (Remy & Seaman, 2014). There is no lack of training available to librarians, and it is often offered in a variety of formats, including those designed for busy librarians (Anderson, 2018). Indeed, the literature shows that library users generally had positive interactions with library employees, but they are frustrated and dismayed by the lack of awareness and training regarding neurodiversity (Pionke, 2017). Librarians are in a unique position within higher education because they have the greatest opportunity to interact with every student on campus in some way. This makes them ideal candidates to take the lead on increasing awareness of and championing the needs of neurodiverse students.

In recent years, many libraries have implemented a personal librarian model. The library at the United States Military Academy at West Point divided its entire freshman class (approximately 1,200 students) among 12 librarians in preparation for the 2016–2017 academic year. This involved the librarian sending direct communications to each of the approximately 100 students introducing themselves and explaining how the librarian could help the student. Librarians also made sure to include information about personal librarians when providing instruction to freshmen. While most students never responded, some did, and personal relationships formed as a result. A system like this could be implemented specifically to assist neurodiverse students as well, though it would require self-identification on the part of the students. James Cho (2018) discusses the way that librarians at Aldephi University implemented this type of program for students with autism. To begin, librarians at Adelphi University received training on autism. Librarians then conducted outreach, taught information literacy based on Universal Design for Learning (UDL), provided individual consultations, and helped students learn how to evaluate information as well as how to cite and understand plagiarism. This process was made easier at Adelphi University because an existing program (Bridges to Adelphi) could be leveraged to funnel neurodiverse students toward the personal librarian program (Cho, 2018). In this way, partnerships between this library and other departments on campus proved mutually beneficial.

Neurodiverse students often report having difficulty navigating social situations (Sarrett 2017). Libraries can do much to assist with this, but perhaps the simplest option is to offer an online reference service since "research has found autistic students prefer online interactions with campus staff, peers, and each other" over face-to-face interactions (Sarrett, 2017, p. 690). The implementation of an online help system can remove the social anxiety and allow the student to more easily explain what they need than might happen in a face-to-face encounter. Online services can also expand to include other library functions such as requesting items from other libraries through interlibrary loan or even having a one-on-one consultation via a video chat service. While these types of services can be incredibly helpful, they do need to be clearly marked on the library's website; additionally, if these services are only staffed during certain times, those times need to be clearly listed in an obvious location online and in the physical library.

The main purpose of any library is to provide access to resources, typically information. While the provision of books and databases should remain the primary focus of libraries, it is beneficial to consider lending items outside of these expected resources to support a broader segment of the student population, including the neurodiverse. This expanded lending collection can include such varied items as noise-cancelling headphones, white noise machines, lightweight standing desks, bookstands, or even anatomical models. Each of these types of items can benefit any student, but the noise-cancelling headphones and the white noise machines may have the greatest benefit for Autistic students because they can help with sensory overload or be used to create a makeshift sensory room in a standard study room.

LEARNING AND INSTRUCTIONAL SUPPORT

Traditional library instruction methods often include one-shot orientation sessions during which librarians are asked to guide students through a thorough but brief tour of the library's resources (usually either as a quick dive into the library's website, or a physical walkthrough of the library's space, or perhaps a combination of both). In addition to these tours, faculty often request that the librarian provide demonstrations of selected library resources, usually to include a discussion on how to perform adequate searches within those resources. Depending upon the needs of the instructor and type of the program the students are in, these demonstrations can vary from basic searching techniques to more advanced techniques, such as properly applying Boolean operators and learning the differences between controlled vocabulary and keywords as they work within a search structure. Often, instruction sessions are limited to a single class time within the semester and vary depending on the length of the class itself but typically runs from half an hour to over an hour. Librarian instructors, knowing they will likely not encounter this group of students in a classroom setting in the future, may feel internal and external pressure to teach the students everything they will need to know to successfully utilize library resources. Instruction can take the form of traditional methods (including lecture and PowerPoint), despite the librarian instructor's own awareness of more accessible methods. For the sake of time, these more experimental methods may not be explored.

Compounding this issue further is the reality that many librarian instructors will not be able to discern whether a student has a disability or is neurodiverse; students are not required to report their disabilities, and "many students choose not to self-identify, possibly for fear of being stigmatized" (Chodock & Dolinger, 2009, p. 24). Unless the disability is obvious (such as a disabled student who has a visible mobility limitation and is therefore unable to participate in activities requiring movement), the librarian instructor may never receive feedback to indicate that the material is not engaging the neurodiverse or invisibly disabled student (Remy & Seaman, 2014).

The current traditional model of library instruction is neither sustainable nor reasonable when held against accepted standards of accessibility in instruction; however, acceptance of this model is rampant across institutions of higher education. Evidence supports incorporating new, more accessible methods of instruction to facilitate student engagement and information retention. Both concepts necessarily inform one another—without student engagement, the retention of information is far less likely to occur. Librarian instructors are often aware of this relationship between engagement and retention, but many are not properly educated on various forms of teaching pedagogy, as it is not a common element in curricula across Master of Library Science programs (Cho, 2018). Librarian instructors can and do learn teaching methods, however, often through observation, webinars, and trial-and-error (Cho, 2018).

UDL INFUSED SERVICES

In the 1870s, almost a century before Universal Design (UD) was developed and well before educators applied UD principles to education as Universal Design for Learning (UDL), the American Library Association (ALA) was founded. Its mission is to "provide leadership for the development, promotion, and improvement of library and information services and the profession of librarianship in order to enhance learning and ensure access to information for all" (American Library Association, 2019). This mission, specifically the principle of access, has permeated and guided the field of librarianship. As awareness of the unique needs of library patrons has grown, librarians have worked to accommodate these needs, including the needs of a neurodiverse population; however, our understanding of these needs and how we can develop programming with this population in mind is growing.

Within the ALA are many divisions, including the Association of College and Research Libraries (ACRL). The ACRL is the largest division of the ALA and represents academic and research librarians. The ACRL's core commitment includes valuing "different ways of knowing" and identifying and working to "eliminate barriers to equitable services, spaces, research, and scholarship" (Association of College & Research Libraries, 2019). This commitment is a guiding principle for all sections of the ACRL and guides academic librarians' interactions with all populations, including neurodiverse people. One of the ACRL's most important contributions to academic librarianship is the development of standards, guidelines, and frameworks to guide academic librarians.

The ACRL's Standards for Libraries in Higher Education (2018) include:

1. institutional effectiveness;
2. professional values;
3. educational role;
4. discovery;
5. collections;
6. space;
7. management/administration/leadership;
8. personnel;
9. external relations.

The guidelines of UDL provide the means to achieve the ACRL Standards. Institutional effectiveness can be tied to the UDL principle of providing multiple means of action and expression when the library solicits feedback about programs or services, or when a librarian evaluates how well students understand the content of an educational experience. The educational role can be tied to all three UDL principles. Librarians who teach may provide multiple means of representation of their instructional materials, from PowerPoint slides to audio recordings to graphical representations of material. They provide multiple means of action and expression by providing different ways for students to demonstrate what they have learned, from presenting before the class to providing pre- and post-surveys. The librarian may also provide different means of engagement through group work, a flipped classroom where students complete pre-reading and come to class for a project, or independent learning options. UDL principles dictate that collections are accessible, discoverable, and usable.

Librarians can apply the UDL guidelines, providing multiple means of representation, action and expression, and engagement, to each of these areas within the academic library to better assist neurodiverse populations. A central theme of the UDL guidelines is the idea that library spaces, services, and experiences should be designed with all patrons in mind and not simply adapted as the need arises (CAST, 2018). Many neurodiverse patrons are not outwardly identifiable; however, their unique needs can affect how they engage the library. Librarians who are invited as guest speakers in a course may not be able to identify neurodiverse students and will not receive paperwork from the university accommodations office to identify these students. In this case, it is even more crucial that the librarian develop these educational experiences with neurodiverse students in mind. In a distance consultation with a librarian, a student with dyslexia may not be comfortable with real-time chat because of the rapid reading and response pace. In a library classroom, an individual with ADHD may not sit through a lengthy lecture without a change of activity. Flashy videos might trigger adverse reactions in those with epilepsy. Many approaches for assisting neurodiverse library patrons follow, but they all tie back to the principle of UDL. These principles improve library experiences for all patrons, as well as improve the experiences of neurodiverse patrons (Burgstahler, 2002).

The UDL model offers librarians the opportunity to enact best pedagogical practices without formal, didactic training and is compatible with methods librarian instructors already employ. The guidelines for UDL are published online (http://udlguidelines.cast.org) and comprise three principles, nine guidelines, and 31 checkpoints (CAST, 2018). Within each checkpoint are several recommendations for actions that educators can put into practice. The three overarching principles for UDL and their affiliated guidelines and checkpoints are summarized in table 9.1.

Because these principles and guidelines were written with a broad audience in mind, they are similarly broad and flexible, allowing librarian instructors the opportunity to apply their own interpretation and knowledge of best practices for teaching their material to their students. The UDL principles are also compatible with the ACRL Framework; both systems encourage freedom of creative practices while providing structure for proactive and intentional instructional design. In fact, upon reviewing the UDL principles, many librarian instructors may find that they have already begun incorporating these concepts into their own teaching methods (Nall, 2015).

While the principles and guidelines of UDL may appeal to librarian instructors in theory, the practice of implementing the recommendations may be daunting to many. UDL takes an active approach to instruction design and may require that librarians intentionally engage in pedagogy rather than acquire pedagogical skills passively through experience alone (Chodock & Dolinger, 2009; Catalano, 2014). Employing UDL in library instruction may also require experienced librarian instructors to consider multiple teaching methods with which they themselves may not already be familiar or comfortable. Intentionally designing one's library instruction, however, not only may prove to be valuable in engaging students with their information literacy skills, but also may serve as a building block to strong rapport between individual students and their librarians.

PROVIDE MULTIPLE MEANS OF ENGAGEMENT: GUIDELINES 7, 8, AND 9

The first principle of UDL explores the need to develop varied ways of engaging with students and of encouraging students' engagement with the material

Table 9.1. Universal Design for Learning Guidelines (CAST, 2018)

Principles	Provide multiple means of engagement (Principle 1)	Provide multiple means of representation (Principle 2)	Provide multiple means of action and expression (Principle 3)
Access	Provide options for recruiting interest (Guideline 7): Optimize individual choice and autonomy (Checkpoint 7.1) Optimize relevance, value, and authenticity (Checkpoint 7.2) Minimize threats and distractions (Checkpoint 7.3)	Provide options for perception (Guideline 1): Offer ways of customizing the display of information (Checkpoint 1.1) Offer alternatives for auditory information (Checkpoint 1.2) Offer alternatives for visual information (Checkpoint 1.3)	Provide options for physical action (Guideline 4): Vary the methods for response and navigation (Checkpoint 4.1) Optimize access to tools and assistive technologies (Checkpoint 4.2)
Build	Provide options for sustaining effort and persistence (Guideline 8): Heighten salience of goals and objectives (Checkpoint 8.1) Vary demands and resources to optimize challenge (Checkpoint 8.2) Foster collaboration and community (Checkpoint 8.3) Increase mastery-oriented feedback (Checkpoint 8.4)	Provide options for language and symbols (Guideline 2): Clarify vocabulary and symbols (Checkpoint 2.1) Clarify syntax and structure (Checkpoint 2.2) Support decoding of text, mathematical notation, and symbols (Checkpoint 2.3) Promote understanding across languages (Checkpoint 2.4) Illustrate through multiple media (Checkpoint 2.5)	Provide options for expression and communication (Guideline 5): Use multiple media for communication (Checkpoint 5.1) Use multiple tools for construction and composition (Checkpoint 5.2) Build fluencies with graduated levels of support for practice and performance (Checkpoint 5.3)

(continued)

Table 9.1. (continued)

Principles	Provide multiple means of engagement (Principle 1)	Provide multiple means of representation (Principle 2)	Provide multiple means of action and expression (Principle 3)
Internalize	Provide options for self-regulation (Guideline 9):	Provide options for comprehension (Guideline 3):	Provide options for executive functions (Guideline 6):
	Promote expectations and beliefs that optimize motivation (Checkpoint 9.1)	Activate or supply background knowledge (Checkpoint 3.1)	Guide appropriate goal-setting (Checkpoint 6.1)
	Facilitate personal coping skills and strategies (Checkpoint 9.2)	Highlight patterns, critical features, big ideas, and relationships (Checkpoint 3.2)	Support planning and strategy development (Checkpoint 6.2)
	Develop self-assessment and reflection (Checkpoint 9.3)	Guide information processing and visualization (Checkpoint 3.3)	Facilitate managing information and resources (Checkpoint 6.3)
		Maximize transfer and generalization (Checkpoint 3.4)	Enhance capacity for monitoring progress (Checkpoint 6.4) (CAST, 2018)
Goal: expert learners who are . . .	Purposeful and motivated	Resourceful and knowledgeable	Strategic and goal-directed

they are learning. According to the UDL guidelines, "Learners differ markedly in the ways in which they can be engaged or motivated to learn" (CAST, 2018). In other words, students, regardless of neurodiversity or ability, will find didactic material engaging for various reasons; when an instructor intentionally chooses a variety of engagement methods, there is an increased likelihood that the material will engage a wider range of students. In fact, as Chodock and Dolinger (2009) discuss, "This spectrum of students challenges academic librarians to develop new approaches to delivering information literacy instruction" (p. 24). Guidelines 7, 8, and 9 reinforce the concept of using multiple approaches to ensure engagement as they describe how instructors can recruit interest (Guideline 7), sustain effort and persistence (Guideline 8), and promote self-regulation in learners (Guideline 9) (CAST, 2018).

The concept of "engagement" itself presents a philosophical conundrum, as "students may, in fact, measure engagement differently than instructors and librarians do" (Lantz et al., 2017, p. 189). While instructors may measure engagement in terms of how the students respond to the lesson itself, students turn inwardly and consider how the material may appeal to them, showing preference to ease of use (Lantz et al., 2017). Students must understand the value of didactic material to find it engaging and to desire to engage with it (Checkpoint 7.2); therefore, librarian instructors who, for instance, describe learning objectives for library instruction have an opportunity to engage students by showing them the value of the material. Effort and persistence can be sustained through group activities, allowing students to demonstrate learning as well as to facilitate collaboration (Checkpoint 8.3). Library instruction that incorporates self-assessment in the form of surveys (such as pre- and post-tests) promote self-regulation among learners, demonstrating to them areas that have been strengthened after the didactic demonstration (Checkpoint 9.3). In a 2009 study at California State University, Bakersfield, students who were exposed to a variety of engaging library instruction methodologies indicated in a survey that the incorporation of UDL positively affected their overall engagement with library instruction (Zhong, 2012). Librarian instructors particularly incorporated hands-on learning exercises and group work as their keystone UDL methodologies. By varying their teaching methods, librarians promoted community learning, reinforced self-regulation, and increased overall engagement with their learners.

PROVIDE MULTIPLE MEANS
OF REPRESENTATION: GUIDELINES 1, 2, AND 3

Representation in the second UDL principle refers to the specific ways that learners are presented with didactic information (CAST, 2018). In many classroom settings, the goal to have multiple means of representation suggests that instructors should consider the manner in which their didactic lessons are physically displayed (Guideline 1), as well as to carefully rephrase complicated concepts, taking great care to repeatedly define any jargon or symbols that are used (Guidelines 2 and 3). In library instruction, presenting the material often relies on the use of library and information science specific jargon, terminology that many librarians may not have been familiar with themselves until they were library and information science students. New and seasoned instructors alike must bear in mind that terminology like *controlled vocabulary*, *Boolean operators*, and *keywords* may have little to no meaning to learners, regardless of neurodiversity or ability (Zhong, 2012). For the neurodiverse or disabled student in particular, these jargon-laden instruction sessions can impose additional barriers to learning that may ultimately discourage the learner from utilizing library resources altogether. To the "outsider," industry-specific jargon serves as a gatekeeper, reifying a specific acquisition of knowledge as superior to not acquiring that knowledge.

Librarian instructors who actively include UDL in their lessons intentionally incorporate multiple means of representation to reinforce and support learning. Zhong (2012) argues that "Boolean logic should be introduced by different methods, such as using diagrams (graphically), oral explanations (aurally), and psychomotor activities" (p. 37). Carefully planning one's lessons is, simply put, unavoidable when the librarian instructor utilizes UDL; however, this preparation and planning, although potentially more time-consuming than traditional methods of enacting a live demonstration, enables students of all abilities to succeed and engage with the didactic material (Chodock & Dolinger, 2009).

In fact, librarian instructors may already be considering ways to reach out to students to improve engagement, even if the instructor is not aware of UDL as a pedagogical approach (Nall, 2015). For instance, librarians who pair traditional lecture with handouts, captioned videos, or online material (such as LibGuides or other tailored online reference guide) support many learners by allowing for repetition of material as well as self-pacing for the student who may need to learn on a different timetable from neurotypical peers (Nall, 2015; Catalano, 2014). A 2013 assessment of two cohort groups (2011 and 2012) at ECU indicates that "students with undisclosed or undiagnosed learning disabilities in the classroom benefit from techniques gleaned from working with Cohorts 2011 and 2012" (Hoover et al., 2013, p. 30). These techniques include "repetition, slower pace, multimedia presentations (video and online tutorials), active learning, and individual follow-ups" (Hoover et al., 2013, p. 27). These chosen methods follow Checkpoints 1.2, 1.3, and 2.5

by offering alternatives to auditory and visual information, as well as utilizing multiple media to illustrate concepts (CAST, 2018).

Librarian instructors limited to one-shot instruction may find these UDL principles particularly appealing because the reinforcement of multiple modes of representation allow students to access information at a later date when they may have difficulty recalling detailed instructions. The repetition of information (e.g., through traditional lecture, handout, and online tutorial) ultimately maximizes transfer and generalization (Checkpoint 3.4) by allowing learners to apply methods to multiple scenarios (Catalano, 2014). Librarian instructors understand that the transferability and generalizability of their didactic lessons is key—in a traditional undergraduate setting, many students will only receive library instruction a few times throughout the entire course of their academic program. Demonstration of didactic material must reinforce to learners that the material can be applied beyond the single example provided by the instructor.

PROVIDE MULTIPLE MEANS OF ACTION AND EXPRESSION: GUIDELINES 4, 5, AND 6

The final principle of UDL invokes the "how" of learning (CAST, 2018). Instructors are encouraged to facilitate active learning through multiple means of action and expression; in other words, the ways students are meant to "do" something with the material presented to them (CAST, 2018). For traditional classrooms, this particular principle may seem more feasible than in the library instruction setting; however, with some creativity and active lesson planning, the librarian instructor may find this principle to be quite simple to fulfill. In a traditional library instruction session, the librarian instructor may stand at the front of the classroom, pointing to a projected image on the screen and either offer a live demonstration or a slideshow with screenshots of how a search may be completed. Students are expected to sit quietly and absorb the material, raising hands to ask questions for clarity when necessary.

Under this third principle of UDL, however, librarian instructors are encouraged to consider ways that students may become actively involved (Guideline 4), express themselves (Guideline 5), and demonstrate comprehension (Guideline 6). Because the instructor will not necessarily be informed of a learner's neurodiversity or disability, regardless if the student has formally disclosed elsewhere on campus, it is necessary for librarian instructors to appeal to as wide a range of neurodiversity and abilities as possible (Remy & Seaman, 2014; Shea & Derry, 2019).

When librarian instructors use diverse teaching pedagogies, "neurotypical students, ASD [autism spectrum disorder] students, and librarians alike can benefit from each other's unique learning styles and embrace the diversity of the inclusive classroom and reference transaction" (Remy & Seaman, 2014, p. 27). For instance, while some movement activities (such as moving across the room to sit with assigned groups) can exclude physically disabled students, librarian instructors may still utilize physical activities to facilitate learning without requiring physically disabled students to call attention to their disability by not participating. Instructors can put students into groups where they currently sit, and pepper instruction with questions where students call out answers after conferring with their group members (Checkpoint 4.1). To incorporate a more diverse approach for communication, librarian instructors may utilize technology—while this may be a barrier to some, requiring that only one student use the technology in any given group may allow other group members to participate regardless of ability to utilize technology (such as asking the group to respond to an audience polling site using one group member's smartphone) (Checkpoint 5.2). Finally, it is key that librarian instructors encourage appropriate goal-setting (Checkpoint 6.1); in other words, instructors must help students set their pace, manage expectations for learning, and demonstrate means for improvement that may be pursued outside of the classroom (such as online tutorials or one-on-one reference sessions).

CAMPUS PARTNERSHIPS

Campus partnerships can benefit the library and neurodiverse users by leveraging partner assets while limiting costs. The key is to keep an open mind toward collaborations that can assist neurodiverse patrons. Many of these partnerships are beneficial to all patrons, not only to those who are neurodiverse. Strong partnerships between libraries and campus departments are overall beneficial to students and faculty. In addition to the support these partnerships facilitate, libraries can also assist campus partners in research efforts that can ultimately lead to improved outreach to neurodiverse individuals.

The library can partner with the campus disability office. This is a great opportunity for library staff to learn about the different neurodiverse students and faculty they may encounter and their unique needs. Because neurodiversity includes a variety of people with a variety of needs that may not be obvious to faculty and staff, education is essential. As library staff become more knowledgeable about the needs of their patrons, they are better able to make suggestions for building alterations, tech purchases, and circulation needs. Educated library staff can provide suggestions to all patrons as needs are communicated.

A library that collaborates with the campus wellness organization or gym can provide unique opportunities for students and faculty. If the library can circulate, or otherwise make available, wellness equipment, such as yoga mats, exercise balls, or desk bikes, they can provide opportunities for those with ADHD to release some pent-up energy while remaining in the library to work. If the library can offer a space for the wellness organization to provide classes or keep equipment, this can be a safe place for neurodiverse students and faculty to take a break and do something physical. This type of partnership can also improve the health of the entire campus.

From an academic standpoint, partnerships with the campus tutoring center, writing center, public speaking center, or peer study groups can be beneficial. Some libraries open study rooms for these groups to meet. If a neurodiverse student is already comfortable in the library, the availability of these services within the library is beneficial. The library commons area is a great place for students to meet and study collaboratively. This allows students who do not take notes well or those who do not read well to join a study group with those who are stronger in those areas for collaborative study. This type of group learning and study reinforces the class lessons and can benefit all in the group. These types of partnerships also cause the library to be a learning hub where student needs are easily met.

If a library can partner with college or university facilities services, there are several benefits. They can work together to choose color schemes for study rooms that are less distracting to those with visual sensory needs. They can install blinds to block distractions from the outside world. They can replace buzzing fluorescent lights with quiet alternatives, including LED tube bulbs. They can also install white-noise speakers to limit distracting sounds. This partnership can be tremendously beneficial to neurodiverse students but can also benefit all students by limiting sensory overload and excess library noise.

If a library has or can partner with an information technology (IT) department, there are several options to increase accessibility for all, including neurodiverse students. Library websites and databases can be optimized for screen readers and mobile devices. The IT department can also provide software suggestions and support for production and captioning of instructional videos. These videos not only benefit those who may have difficulty seeing PowerPoint slides or keeping up with notes during a presentation. They also assist those who are auditory learners, those who become distracted during a class, or those who are studying late at night and are attempting to not distract others in the vicinity. The IT department can suggest technologies for the library to purchase that will increase accessibility, but only if the library develops those relationships and communicates their priorities and needs.

Finally, librarians are often called on to instruct students in the classroom or use distance education techniques like videos; however, few librarians have knowledge of educational techniques for neurodiverse students. The library can partner with the education department or faculty development team to learn about techniques to make their instruction more accessible to neurodiverse students. From creating PowerPoint slides with high contrast text, to including interactive activities in learning experiences, to limiting classroom distractions, librarians can learn and implement educational techniques that will benefit all classroom learners and optimize the experience of neurodiverse students.

Librarians are skilled at collaborating across disciplines. Intentional collaborations with different departments within the college or university setting for the purpose of increasing accessibility for neurodiverse students should be a priority. From collaborations that make the physical environment more comfortable to collaborations that improve the learning environment, these efforts can improve the experience of all library patrons and can especially improve the experiences of those who are neurodiverse. Keep an open mind to possible collaborations and build relationships. Ideas for collaborations can come from many areas of campus.

CONCLUSION

Libraries have come a long way in becoming more user-friendly and accessible over the years, but providing further resources to neurodiverse patrons will certainly benefit all library user groups. Newly published research articles acknowledge that more research on providing helpful resources and accommodations to neurodiverse user groups needs to be conducted to further implement changes in libraries. Libraries have always provided access to accessible spaces and technologies, yet still more can be accomplished to accommodate all users and make the library space a more welcoming place for everyone regardless of ability, learning differences, and preferences.

Campus Essentials for High Impact

- *Evaluate and redesign teaching tools.* Make an effort to incorporate UDL guidelines into your existing teaching strategies. Investigate effective teaching strategies and methods and designing new interactive activities such as videos or "Guide on the Side" instruction.
- *Offer inclusivity training for all campus library staff.* Increase staff knowledge of neurodiversity and supporting student, faculty, and staff learning needs.
- *Consider methods of incorporating UDL principles in circulation resources.* Investigate the addition of models, e-books, and other helpful resources for student use.

- *Establish teams to investigate and implement technology tools.* Explore tool options that widen services for neurodiverse learners. Consider screen reader software, dictation software, and other apps; offer access to noise-cancelling headphones and touch table computers. Consider the role a VR technology lab and app license purchases can play in supporting neurodiverse patrons.
- *Redesign services to welcome neurodiverse students.* Add a page to the library website about specific services and accessibility accommodations. Offer individualized appointments for students with the librarians. Provide multiple ways to connect with reference staff. Consider the implementation of a personal librarian program for students.
- *Explore campus partnerships to better support neurodiverse students.* Investigate potential campus partnerships with other departments and programs.
- *Redesign library spaces to welcome neurodiverse students.* Provide quiet spaces and group activity areas for collaboration; modify an existing room that can be used as an "escape place," such as through clear signage and advertisements to users. Consider replacing fluorescent light tubes with LED tubes.

REFERENCES

American Library Association. (2008). *Code of ethics.* http://www.ala.org/advocacy/sites/ala.org.advocacy/files/content/proethics/codeofethics/Code%20of%20Eth-ics%20of%20the%20American%20Library%20Association.pdf

American Library Association. (2019). *Mission & history.* http://www.ala.org/aboutala/mission-history

Anderson, A. (2018). Autism and the academic library: A study of online communication. *College & Research Libraries, 79*(5), 645–658. doi:10.5860/crl.79.5.645

Armstrong, T. (2010). *Neurodiversity: Discovering the extraordinary gifts of autism, ADHD, dyslexia, and other brain differences.* Da Capo Press. https://ebookcentral.proquest.com/lib/eastcarolina/detail.action?docID=537922

ASGCLA. (2019). Library services for people with disabilities policy. http://www.ala.org/asgcla/resources/libraryservices

Association of College & Research Libraries. (2018). *Standards for Libraries in Higher Education.* http://www.ala.org/acrl/standards/standardslibraries

Association of College & Research Libraries. (2019). *ACRL equity, diversity and inclusion.* http://www.ala.org/acrl/aboutacrl/directoryofleadership/committees/racialethnic

Austin Community College District Library. (n.d.). *Library services for students with disabilities.* https://library.austincc.edu/gen-info/Services/disability-about.php

Burgstahler, S. (2002). Distance learning: Universal design, universal access. *AACE Journal, 10*(1), 32–61.

CAST. (2018). *The UDL guidelines.* http://udlguidelines.cast.org/

Catalano, A. (2014). Improving distance education for students with special needs: A qualitative study of students' experiences with an online library research course. *Journal of Library & Information Services in Distance Learning, 8*(1–2), 17–31. doi:10.1080/1533290X.2014.902416

Cho, J. (2018). Building bridges: Librarians and autism spectrum disorder. *Reference Services Review, 46*(3), 325–359. https://doi.org/10.1108/RSR-04-2018-0045

Chodock, T., & Dolinger, E. (2009). Applying universal design to information literacy: Teaching students who learn differently at Landmark College. *Reference & User Services Quarterly, 49*(1), 24–32. doi:10.5860/rusq.49n1.24

Drake, S. M. (2014). *Academic success experiences of individuals with autism spectrum disorder* (1525824453) [Doctoral dissertation]. ProQuest Central, ProQuest Dissertations & Theses Global. http://search.proquest.com.jproxy.lib.ecu.edu/docview/1525824453?accountid=10639

Hoover, J. K., Nall, H. C., & Willis, C. (2013). Designing library instruction for students with learning disabilities. *North Carolina Libraries (Online), 71*(2), 27–31.

Lantz, C., Insua, G. M., Armstrong, A., Dror, D., & Wood, T. (2017). "I'm a visual learner so I like this": Investigating student and faculty tutorial preferences. *Internet Reference Services Quarterly, 22*(4), 181–192. doi:10.1080/10875301.2018.1427171

Lawrence, E. (2013). Loud hands in the library: Neurodiversity in LIS theory & practice. *Progressive Librarian, 41*, 98–109.

Myles, B. S. (2005). *Children and youth with Asperger syndrome: Strategies for success in inclusive settings.* Corwin Press.

Nall, C. (2015). Academic libraries and the principles of Universal Design for Learning: Representation beyond courses. *College & Research Libraries News, 76*(7), 374–375. doi:10.5860/crln.76.7.9345

Pan, Z., Cheok, A. D., Yang, H., Zhu, J., & Shi, J. (2006). Virtual reality and mixed reality for virtual learning environments. *Computers & Graphics, 30*(1), 20–28. https://doi.org/10.1016/j.cag.2005.10.004

Pionke, J. J. (2017). Toward holistic accessibility: Narratives from functionally diverse patrons. *Reference & User Services Quarterly, 57*(1), 48–56. doi:10.5860/rusq.57.1.6442

Redford, K. (2017). Dyslexia: Disability or difference? *Educational Leadership, 74*(7), 64–67. https://eric.ed.gov/?id=EJ1138107

Remy, C., & Seaman, P. (2014). Evolving from disability to diversity: How to better serve high-functioning autistic students. *Reference and User Services Quarterly, 54*(1), 24–28.

Sarrett, J. C. (2018). Autism and accommodations in higher education: Insights from the Autism community. *Journal of Autism and Developmental Disorders, 48*(3), 679–693. https://doi.org/10.1007/s10803-017-3353-4

Schroeder, H. M. (2018). Implementing accessibility initiatives at the Michigan State University Libraries. *Reference Services Review, 46*(3), 399–413. https://doi.org/10.1108/RSR-04-2018-0043

Shea, G., & Derry, S. (2019). Academic libraries and Autism Spectrum Disorder: What do we know? *The Journal of Academic Librarianship, 45,* 326–331. https://doi.org/10.1016/j.acalib.2019.04.007

Tumlin, Z. (2019). "This is a quiet library, except when it's not." On the lack of neurodiversity awareness in librarianship. *Music Reference Services Quarterly, 22*(1–2), 3–17. doi://dx.doi.org/10.1080/10588167.2019.1575017

Zhong, Y. (2012). Universal Design for Learning (UDL) in library instruction. *College & Undergraduate Libraries, 19*(1), 33–45. doi:10.1080/10691316.2012.652549

Chapter 9: Campus Spotlight

Hands-On Learning in the Library: Anatomical Models at Laupus Health Sciences Library, East Carolina University

G. J. Corey Harmon

Our Mission: Laupus Health Sciences Library at East Carolina University (ECU) began making anatomical models available for students pursuing degrees in health-related fields in 1980. Assisting students in learning anatomy and physiology concepts through hands-on models, the collection has grown to 236 models ranging from single organs to entire bodies.

Student Usage: As evidenced by the high level of use, ECU students appreciate the models, which comprise about 40% of the library's annual circulation. The top five most-used models include a disarticulated half skeleton, a muscular leg, a muscular arm, a skull, and a model of the ear. As of December 1, 2019, the circulation count for the models was 20,799 (since 2011).

UDL in Action: Studies have shown that students who use physical models have higher learning outcomes than students who use two-dimensional photographs of plastic models or 3D computer-based renderings (Pawlina & Drake, 2013). The students specifically like that the 3D nature of the models allow them to touch the physical aspects of the anatomy, which enhances their learning. In keeping with UDL principles, anatomical models may be helpful for any kind of student as a visual and tactile learning aid.

Challenges of High Student Usage: Maintenance is a major concern with the model collection. During the 2018–2019 academic year, library personnel observed that several of the models had become too damaged to continue circulating and evaluated whether to replace them or slowly discontinue the service. Based on circulation numbers, as well as anecdotal evidence such as the results of an informal survey of model requests from students, Laupus personnel chose to replace the damaged models and expand the collection further.

While they are typically heavy-duty plastic, most have several parts that must be maintained. Laupus personnel have begun physically inspecting every model at least once a semester, and damaged models are pulled from circulation when they are returned. This helps library staff to keep up with repairs and identify items that may need to be replaced. In order to ensure that as many people can use the models as possible, ECU students are limited to two models at a time for three hours.

Making Learning Accessible: All models include paper guides that are helpful resources for students learning anatomy concepts. Very popular in student usage, the paper guides often are separated from their respective models. To mitigate the loss of those paper guides, Laupus personnel utilize unique QR codes as a link to individual model guides. Recognizing the need for alternative methods of engagement with course materials, traditional paper guides will continue to be available upon request for those users who prefer them.

Model Collections Are a Costly Resource: While Laupus Health Sciences Library has chosen to support an expansive model collection, it is not a service that is feasible for every library. High-quality anatomical models are expensive to purchase, and they are not designed to be handled to the degree that the students use them. That said, Laupus has received a positive return on investment over the past 30-plus years. The cost-per-use for the entire collection is $9.94, with some individual models being as low as a few cents per use and others being much higher.

REFERENCE

Pawlina, W., & Drake. R. L. (2013). Anatomical models: Don't banish them from the anatomy laboratory yet. *Anat Sci Educ., 6*(4), 209–210. doi:10.1002/ase.1380

Chapter 9: Campus Spotlight

Partnering with the STEPP Program, Joyner Library, East Carolina University

Jamie E. Bloss and Amanda Haberstroh with Jeanne Hoover, Clark Nall, and Carolyn Willis

Background on the Partnership: The partnership between Joyner Library at East Carolina University (ECU) and the Supporting Transition and Education through Planning and Partnerships (STEPP) Program began in 2011. The STEPP Program is a comprehensive support program that serves college students with documented learning disabilities. In 2010, the STEPP Program moved into a space in Joyner Library, and a natural collaboration formed. Carolyn Willis, a librarian at Joyner Library led the effort to bring together a team of librarians to work with the STEPP Program's students.

Source: ECU Joyner Library

Programmatic Supports: The library team had many ideas when they started working with the STEPP Program students in 2011, including classes, individual research consultations, and additional orientation sessions about the library. Today, the STEPP Program–library partnership includes two approaches: (1) Fall semester library boot camp led by Joyner Library staff, and (2) one-on-one research consultations and connectivity with individual librarians that are sustained throughout a student's ECU college years.

Using UDL to Plan Teaching Strategies: Whether among the STEPP Program cohort or other information literacy classes they teach, the librarians at Joyner Library can never visually identify which students might be neurodiverse and which are neurotypical. Although the specific group they worked

206

with was diagnosed with learning disabilities, the librarians were not told which student had which condition.

The partnership between the STEPP Program and Joyner librarians has influenced the methods and approaches employed at the reference desk. Because of this uncertainty of individual abilities, all library instruction must be designed with UDL in mind so that anyone may benefit. In research consultations, librarians offer a quiet space to work with fewer distractions, which can be beneficial to any type of learner.

Out of all their teaching strategies, the librarian instructors found repetition and pacing the most helpful in the sessions. For example, when training students to recognize and find call numbers on the shelf (often a stressful and daunting activity), students completed two different interactive activities, demonstrating a similar learning outcome through multiple modes.

In the beginning, librarians brought the STEPP Program students into the library for three classes so as not to overwhelm them in a single session. The sessions were divided among three topics: first, librarians provided an overview of services and the homepage of the library; second, librarians introduced the One Search bar (ECU's discovery tool) on the website for searching activities; and third, librarians focused on subject-specific databases. Since the partnership's inception, librarians scaled down to provide only one or two class sessions. This decision was prudent for both the librarians and the students because STEPP Program students come to the library with their other classes as well. Providing these students with some instruction before they come with their classes, however, gives them a head start while also building the students' confidence and the librarians' rapport. The librarians also practice peer-teaching, or team-teaching, and work together. Rapport among the STEPP Program students is likewise significant. Because there are only 10 students in each new STEPP Program cohort, the librarians have integrated icebreakers into the lesson. Icebreakers include asking students "Where are you from?" or "What fun thing did you do this summer?" Icebreaker activities work especially well for smaller groups, but they can be cumbersome in larger groups.

Group Activities and the Use of Multimedia: Teamwork and group activities can bolster confidence and a sense of overall independence for all students. For example, among the activities the Joyner librarians planned for the STEPP Program students is a group activity focused on call numbers. Session facilitators provide books on a cart, and the students are asked to arrange the books in order by call number as a group. Librarians assign the groups a specific call number and have them locate a book on the shelf together. For students who might still feel stressed about finding a book on the shelf, librarians emphasize the "pull and hold" service (in which library personnel will locate the book, remove it from the shelf, and hold it at the circulation desk until the student retrieves it), eliminating the barrier of reading call numbers for worried students.

In an effort to employ UDL principles, video tutorials are provided by the department before they send students out to do the activity. Videos are shared with the students, including a video about evaluating resources and an overview titled "The Research Process." Interjecting videos into their teaching helps to break up instruction time and to ease student understanding by delivering the material in multiple modes.

Another interactive group activity for library orientation sessions involves the use of the Pic6 app, which allows students to walk through the library taking pictures on an iPad. The students use the app and iPad to take pictures of important service points, a book on the shelf, and something they find confusing. David Hisle and Matthew Whaley in Joyner Library set up this app and planned the activity for students.

Integrating New Resources: Joyner Library's partnership with Project STEPP has been the impetus for additional resources design to better assist neurodivergent students. One example is the inclusion of databases with articles that can be read aloud to users, and the IBISWorld database, which has a video included with each section. Joyner librarian Katy Webb worked to add the "Guide on the Side" learning tool to the library's website, which provides a guide that directs a user through a database; this is an open-source, freely downloadable resource from the University of Arizona Libraries.

Program Assessment: In terms of assessing the students' information literacy skills after they complete the program, the facilitators conducted pre- and post-tests with the STEPP Program students. Over several years, the results shown were on par with the regular instruction sessions with neurotypical students.

For more information regarding the library-program partnership summarized above, see Willis and colleagues' (2013) article "Designing Library Instruction for Students with Learning Disabilities."

REFERENCE

Willis, C., Nall, C., & Hoover, J. (2013). Designing library instruction for students with learning disabilities. *North Carolina Libraries*, *71*(2).

Chapter Ten

Campus Living/Residence Hall Services

Angela Holleman, Jeffrey G. Coghill, and Elizabeth M. H. Coghill

The residence hall systems on college campuses began when Harvard University established housing for its students. As time has progressed, the needs of students have changed to provide equity in housing for diverse groups of students. At first, housing was established for practical purposes and aided in the building of a community of scholars, many of whom had traveled great distances from home to attend school (Blimling, n.d.). It wasn't until fall 2017 that the Office of the Provost at Harvard assembled the first meeting of the University Accessibility Committee to promote campus accessibility, and that included an initiative called the House Renewal Project to redesign interior and exterior spaces to meet the varying needs of today's students.

Community is just as important today as it was when Harvard established housing communities for students in 1636. Colleges are continuing to admit more students, many of them neurodiverse, who see and experience the world in different ways. Spaces where neurodiverse students gather should be thoughtfully designed. Physical accessibility is important, but so is social and intellectual accessibility (Dolmage, 2017).

Dorms are more than just warehouses for on-campus students. The quest for campus space, even in a perfect world, can have both positive and negative consequences on a campus. Administrators grapple daily with the needs of campus users. On some campuses, lounge spaces where students used to gather for social activities, relaxation, or study have been converted to dorm spaces to add beds for students (Hankerson, 2019). It is important to think about how this change in communal space impacts our campus communities. The conundrum of where to house students is perplexing and can have short-term or long-term effects for dorm populations. Add to the mix students with neurodiverse needs, and traditional solutions to everyday dorm space issues are no longer the best options.

NEURODIVERSE STUDENTS'
SUCCESS IN COLLEGE LIVING SPACES

Residence hall environments can be challenging for neurodiverse students in many ways. Brown and Poore-Pariseau (n.d.) highlight three areas that pose difficulties: (1) increased anxiety levels resulting from space design, (2) challenges with maintaining social interactions, and (3) trouble with mastering college success skills such as time management and organization. Jennifer Sarrett (2018) notes in her article "Autism and Accommodations in Higher Education: Insights from the Autism Community" that autistic students need special assistance to make their college experience a success. She recommends the following considerations with respect to communal working and living spaces: (1) social accommodations, (2) neurodiverse-friendly spaces, and (3) stakeholder awareness.

SOCIAL ACCOMMODATIONS

Social accommodations for neurodiverse students can positively impact their ability to support meaningful peer engagement in college. Langlois (2018) highlights the importance of sense of community facilitated by living in the residence hall and its connections to sense of belonging. Peer engagement can be supported through mentoring, mediation assistance, and the establishment of student-led disability support groups. On some campuses, peer engagement is supported through housing-based peer mentoring services. Peer mentors trained in neurodiversity issues can encourage interactions and attend social events with students, maintain regular check-in sessions, and answer questions about interactions with peers. Neurodivergent students are also challenged when communicating with faculty and staff. Mediators trained in neurodiversity, challenges surrounding autism, and mediation management can help students establish successful interactions with staff and faculty. Students could benefit from campus housing staff establishing formal and informal support groups for neurodiverse residents (Sarrett, 2018). Sarrett recommends establishing a disability support group that includes low-impact, sensory-friendly events organized around the interests of the individuals in the group. It is important to note that some neurodiverse students may or may not participate in activities or remain in the room participating in direct contact with groups (Sarrett, 2018).

NEURODIVERSE-FRIENDLY SPACES

Chapter 4, "Welcoming Spaces for Learning," introduces the concept of welcoming and neurodiverse-friendly spaces on campus, which are especially needed in campus residence halls. Establishing a space dedicated for social gatherings can assist with peer engagement activities. Some institutions are incorporating sensory rooms that provide neurodiverse students a place to escape to with low lighting, low noise levels, and a policy that prohibits strong smells. It is also helpful to provide noise-cancelling headphones in common spaces and allow students the ability for periods of time as determined by the student. Sensory spaces allow students with high stimuli sensitivities to have a place to retreat and recharge on campus. Brown and Poore-Pariseau (n.d.) suggest residence hall spaces include a meditation room that serves to help students with sensory needs find a much-needed location to de-stress.

Dolmage (2017) encourages us to view Universal Design (UD) as a process that encourages opportunities for learning and growth. Brown and Poore-Pariseau (n.d.) underscore UD as a design process that anticipates and plans for diverse users in the design process. Anticipating needs allows for spaces to function in supportive ways for neurodiverse and neurotypical students. In creating spaces that are universally designed, we often think about the space itself and not what students are bringing into that space and how the space evolves as we evolve with use. Robsham (2016) highlights the impact constant change on both personal and environmental levels makes on mental and emotional health.

STAKEHOLDER AWARENESS

Awareness and training sessions are needed in many areas on campus, and residence halls are no exception. Staff, faculty, and administration require training on autism, neurodiversity, and accommodations for both in and out of the classroom. Awareness programming for peers has been found to assist in furthering the understanding of the challenges and strengths of neurodivergent students. Sarrett (2018) also recommends the inclusion of autistic and neurodivergent student feedback on program development and extending training and awareness sessions to peers as well as campus staff. Robertson and Ne'eman (2008) note that the university community should extend awareness outside of the neurodiverse community to the general campus community to let others know about neurodivergent students.

PREPARING NEURODIVERSE
STUDENTS FOR RESIDENCE HALL EXPERIENCES

Pre-exposure to Campus Life

Pre-exposure to campus can be very effective for a neurodiverse student who is preparing to live on campus. They may want to research and contemplate their move to campus in advance to reduce any anxiety about changes that are new and unfamiliar. Prior to arrival on campus, students can be encouraged to use email or social media to connect with future roommates. Students might also ask the housing staff questions about housing accessibility and want to arrange a tour, look at pictures of housing options, and read about what life is like on campus. Social media is a perfect way for students to research campus life at different schools. In addition, campuses are taking advantage of using platforms like Instagram for highlighting welcome week, providing a detailed look at residence halls or move-in day with their Instagram stories. For neuro-diverse students who like to do research, social media is a tool that can help with making better decisions about what school is the best fit (Tran, 2019).

Campuses have started to offer specific programming during orientation or prior to fall classes that provides freshman and transfer students the opportu-nity to get adjusted to campus life early and meet other neurodiverse students. This can be beneficial for some students who require an environment that is less stimulating with reduced distractions. Students benefit from structured activities that can assist them in transitioning to the unstructured college en-vironment, especially residence hall living (Francis et al., 2018).

The College of William and Mary sponsors a summer orientation experi-ence for neurodiverse students. The program is designed to introduce and prepare students for their new college environment and provide structured activities that foster peer engagement. As a part of the program, students are encouraged to make choices in the extent to which they participate in events or they can choose to participate in alternative ways. Alanna Van Valken-burgh, of William and Mary, notes that "William and Mary orientation is very extensive, very loud and pretty difficult for most neurodivergent students," but headway has been made at William and Mary to make the introduction to campus life more inclusive of a wider variety of students with social and cognitive differences (Koenig, 2019).

Early Move-In

Campuses often allow new students to move in early prior to the first day of classes. Organizers of welcome week social activities can make these events inclusive for people who struggle with social settings, by keeping these possibilities in mind:

- Allow students to opt out of events, and provide quiet spaces and frequent breaks for students challenged by sensory stimuli.
- Make engagement activities less stressful by assigning groups versus having students pick partners. The group process can be a high anxiety trigger for a neurodiverse student.
- Plan for allowing food preferences to be shared when arranging food-related events.
- Consider the signage and directions provided for student events. Do they address the needs of all learners?
- Assist residents in establishing relationships through activities and events by providing social engagement tips for students before and during activities.

Sarrett (2018) shares an interesting model proposed by a survey participant: Offer sessions wherein group members can indicate an interest they have or would like to learn about, perhaps with a visual indicator (i.e., a picture of a board game, TV show, or restaurant), and have them stand by their indicated topic. Other students can then approach the student who is hosting that interest and decide on shared activities to participate in or simply have a conversation about that interest. In this way, small groups or pairs of students can find others with common interests (Sarrett, 2018).

Social group meetings that keep a consistent agenda or regular schedule prove to be beneficial for neurodiverse students (Sarrett, 2018). Students have indicated that they would like a space of their own, away from neurotypical students, with interest groups that cater to the needs of the neurodiverse (Sarrett, 2018). They also desire student-run community service organizations that go outside the bounds of typical on-campus activities (Robertson & Ne'eman, 2008).

As Burgstahler notes, allowing students the choice to take breaks can be very important for neurodivergent participants (Burgstahler & Russo-Gleicher, 2015).

Supporting Residence Hall Success

Campus housing can provide a supportive living community for all students, but the added options for single-room accommodations can be particularly helpful. For example, a student on the autism spectrum may require specific accommodations in order to manage the demands of the communal model of campus residence halls. Residence halls should offer a single housing option to neurodivergent students. Single-room options allow for the student to meet their sensory needs while still being included in the residence hall experience.

When engaging in group topic discussions and activities, it is recommended to use small groups to facilitate interest in a particular topic. Participating neurodiverse students can be assisted by hosting smaller group meetings versus a larger-scale floor meeting, encouraging opportunities for structured social activities like game nights and hosting screen-free events, and allow students to opt out of the larger venues that can cause high anxiety for some students (Brown & Poore-Pariseau, n.d.). Programming needs to ensure a basic understanding of the needs and special considerations of their residents. The nature of resident assistant (RA) role as mentor and peer can help neurodivergent students navigate hall-based relationships. Training sessions should include topics covering the needs of various student populations, in order to create a welcoming and inclusive space within the residence halls. Professional staff should take the lead on designing social programming to include life skills, such as doing laundry, cooking on campus, and managing personal finances. Include topics that benefit all student residents but would have particular appeal and value for neurodiverse students (Cox et al., 2017).

Living with Roommates

Although some neurodivergent students will choose to request single rooms, others prefer to experience the resident hall system by having a roommate. Rooming with another student can be challenging for any student. The Organization for Autism Research (2017) has a sample roommate agreement form to use as a guide for helping students define and communicate their expectations with roommates about sharing a living space. This type of agreement could be very helpful for neurodiverse students as a guideline for defining their specific needs with roommates in housing.

Managing Life Skills

For many neurodiverse students moving out from the support systems in place in the family home can be challenging. Removal from regular routines impact their transition to the residence halls and can negatively affect their mental well-being. Living for the first time outside of the family home, students must independently handle personal hygiene care, consider their safety on campus, manage finances, maintain a proper sleep schedule, and manage their nutrition and medication needs (Francis et al., 2018). Many new college students experience difficulty balancing these new demands, especially those who have never lived outside the home, experienced high parental involvement in their basic care, and are lacking in the self-advocacy skills needed to request help.

Rules and Conduct

As mentioned earlier in this chapter, neurodiverse students may have trouble navigating the "social roadmap" of the campus residence hall. Some neurodiverse college students may affiliate with the disability services office on campus for support with academic and housing accommodations when they arrive on campus. Others may not seek accommodations if they thrive academically and want to try living with roommates in their first year. If a student with autism came from a home where there was an established roadmap of routines and rules, they may have come to rely on this as a roadmap to keep their environment predictable and safe. Once the student moves on campus, the drive to follow established routines and rules can cause problems with communication and social interactions when unexpected changes in housing happen, as they could easily with a new roommate or social situation.

Consistent rules and structure are a good universal model for all students. Training for housing staff working with neurodiverse learners should highlight the importance of rules and routines and ways to apply them in housing settings to reduce the incidence of stress and problem behavior. Rules should be concise and observable and posted visually and other formats to be inclusive for all types of learners (University of Nebraska–Lincoln, 2020).

Neurodiverse students with autism can have social and communication challenges that impact interactions with others on campus. This often occurs in housing. In an effort to make social connections, a student may not realize the fine line between wanted and unwanted attention. Complaints about a student's behavior that end up escalating to the Conduct Office or Title IX can be avoided if the student understood expectations and the unspoken social rules in dorms and living spaces. In an article about the nexus between autism and Title IX, author Lee Burdette Williams (2018) notes the importance of helping students better understand social cues and communication expectations. Where it was once a student's parent or guardian providing social interpretation for a student, it may now be the Disability Services Office who is asked to step in to meet with a student to explain the social rules in housing and the intention versus the impact of the student's behavior, or with housing staff seeking support with the student (Williams, 2018).

SUPPORTING THE ROLE OF RESIDENT ASSISTANTS (RAS)

A fundamental role for RAs is to create a welcoming environment (Fisher, 2015). Neurodiverse students benefit from having resident hall assistants who have a better understanding of their needs and are equipped to assist them in their transition to the college campus. "RAs are those individuals who have the most direct contact with students, therefore, they are able to build relationships with them, understand issues the residents might struggle with and find ways to encourage that resident to seek the resources they may need" (Fisher, 2015). Training programs for RAs are essential for working effectively with their residents (Robertson & Ne'eman, 2008). The role of the RA in dorm living is crucial. RAs are on the front lines of student interactions, often before a student begins his or her first day of class. They are peers to the neurodiverse student and serve as representatives of the university with a myriad of responsibilities and little training to work with neurodiverse students. Thus, it is the responsibility of campus stakeholders such as Disability Support Services professionals to be sure that RAs are equipped with the necessary training to make the success of neurodiverse students likely. If RAs are trained to work with neurodiverse students, they can "help with the creation and implementation of a successful community" (Fisher, 2015).

There is a debate as to whether to inform RAs when neurodiverse students are a part of the group on their floor. Some neurodiverse students may not need specific services and may feel uncomfortable revealing their status to their RA. The RA may not need to be notified depending on student strengths and challenges (Fisher, 2015). On the other hand, RAs will benefit from a greater understanding of neurodivergent residents and with this knowledge can better assist in providing low-sensory environments, access to support with social interactions, and support in building rapport with their RA (Fisher, 2015).

To create a sense of belonging for all students and to foster a welcoming campus environment, RAs can help bring awareness of support services and the needs of neurodiverse residents (Fisher, 2015). At the University of Tennessee–Chattanooga (UTC), resident assistants in the dorms participate in a special training program they call Mosaic. Mosaic staff will sit in on meetings between Mosaic students and their roommates when necessary. In addition, UTC has added sensory rooms across campus, which provide quiet spaces to decompress. The rooms are equipped with weighted blankets, textured pillows, and moldable kinetic sand, which can be soothing when students are experiencing sensory overload (West, 2019).

ADDRESSING THE CHALLENGE OF SENSORY OVERLOAD

While housing accommodations may be beneficial, some neurodivergent students experience overload from their sensory systems. RAs and other housing personnel can provide these students with the option of leaving hall programs and events for a short or extended break to decompress when a period of sensory overload occurs. Residence hall staff can also work with students to develop other options for sensory accommodations. For example, sensory-processing differences can lead neurodiverse college students to feel overwhelmed or overloaded in specific settings at college campuses. They may require adjustments to be made to the physical environment, such as modification of overhead lighting (e.g., dimming or removing fluorescent lights) and room alterations that reduce distracting background noise. Some autistic college students may require compensatory sensory-assistive tools, such as sunglasses to reduce visual glare indoors and headphones that filter out background noise while still permitting the student to listen to conversations (Robertson and Ne'eman, 2008). This can be especially true in housing when students are living in dorm room environments with other students.

HOUSING SPACE AND FURNITURE NEEDS

We know that furniture choice and space design influence the adaptability and effectiveness of campus environments including residence halls. Multiple studies provide Universal Design recommendations for campus living professionals in designing spaces in residence halls for neurodiverse residents. Recommendations include room size, table design, choice of chairs, adaptability of furniture, and lighting.

Social Space and Room Size

According to Wexler and Luethi-Garrecht (2015), a "room's size and dimensions have a direct connection to how students receive information. Ideal room space and audibility of sound depend on volume, pitch, and duration—components that must function equally well in order to convey the message successfully" (p. 17). Rooms that are too small or too large can have detrimental effects on group activities depending on the types of neurodiverse students who engage in them.

Tables and Chairs

Choices in table design and workspace arrangement matter for supporting learning within a classroom or social space on campus. An inclusive space might have a table and workspace that is adjustable in height and allows for expanding surfaces that can permit for more bodily freedom and variation of bodies. Adaptability in grouping tables in different configurations creates options for collaboration and engagement and expands possibilities for neurodiverse students (Wexler & Luethi-Garrecht, 2015). Ergonomically styled chairs have built-in mechanisms that allow for swiveling, height adjustment, and the ability to roll. This makes the natural body movement of students more kinetic, allows for more changes in posture, and enhances concentration (Wexler & Luethi-Garrecht, 2015).

Adaptability of Furniture

Spaces that are designed to be adaptable to the varied ways they are used fosters inclusion. Consider college classrooms that are defined by stationary desks with attached chairs. The use of these rooms is limited by room configuration and fixed furniture. Portability and the ease of moving furniture to meet the needs of activities is paramount to making any space more accessible. "The movable workspace also allows for autists to engage and disengage from the community of their peers when needed" (Wexler & Luethi-Garrecht, 2015, p. 17).

Lighting

Addressed more fully in chapter 4, "Welcoming Spaces for Learning," lighting choices matter in the spaces we design. Some neurodiverse students may be sensitive to different types of lighting used in campus spaces. For example, when designing living spaces for students, it is worth considering the roles "the quality of light distribution and lighting color [play] in both the overall and specific spaces" (Wexler & Luethi-Garrecht, 2015, p. 18). Some students prefer natural lighting and find that "ideal rooms have windows for integration of natural daylight, which has a direct impact on the emotional and physical wellness of students" (Wexler & Luethi-Garrecht, 2015, p. 18). Fluorescent lights have a light cycle of 60 times per second that is offending to people with visual hyperactivity. The humming sound of these lights can also be intrusive (Shore, 2003).

NEURODIVERSE STUDENT PERSPECTIVES

In a video project titled *Designing Inclusive Dorm Communities*, at Stanford University (2020), two neurodiverse students were interviewed about their experiences living in a dorm community. The video discussed Universal Design principles as they pertaind to campus housing and incorporated the nine suggestions for dorm staff who want to learn more about how to support and include neurodiverse residents:

1. Provide multiple modes of communication (e.g., emails, online forums, group chats) to lessen social and sensory barriers for students who struggle with in-person dialogue but still want to participate.
2. Ask the student what is and is not helpful. Don't make assumptions regarding student needs.
3. Engage the student. Resident advisors should not wait for a neurodiverse student to initiate communications.
4. Welcome residents to discuss any challenges they have; normalize and talk openly about their experiences (e.g., discussion about mental health and counseling, exploring pre-planning like interactions with housing staff, roommates, professors).
5. RAs should design social activities and events with neurodiverse students in mind by providing choices for alternatives to group activities and captioning for videos. Students do not always disclose they have a disability, nor should they have to in order to have access that is equal to other students.
6. Explore alternative methods for conducting and communicating information from mandatory meetings.
7. Make meetings as universally accessible as possible. Provide options for participation. Does the meeting need to be in person, or is there another way to participate? When planning an event or activity, look for a room environment with limited auditory and sensory distractions. Have an alternative space available if the event is overwhelming.
8. When planning regular dorm activities, RAs should consider the space, provide structure and intention, and allow residents to interact in ways most comfortable for them.
9. Establish dorm norms that are universally inclusive for every resident. Consider engaging students in discussions about sensory sensitivities, and discuss ways to reduce sensory barriers like creating a sensory room/space to benefit all residents.

Dr. Kerry Magro (n.d.), who is neurodiverse and has earned a doctorate in educational technology leadership, reminds neurodiverse students in dorms,

"Firstly, strongly consider requesting a single room. Secondly, make sure you get yourself out there. Take some time to meet with the director of your dorm. You will need to force yourself out of your comfort zone because that's where the most progress can be made." He considers being a dorm resident, and former resident advisor (RA), part of the college experience and a part of "a process" to learning independence by becoming self-sufficient (Magro, n.d.)

ONE ADMINISTRATOR'S EXPERIENCE: ANGELA HOLLEMAN

Disability Support Services staff can play an important role in the success of neurodivergent students as residents in campus housing. In my experience as a disability services provider on a college campus, I have received calls and emails from housing staff asking for suggestions to help students who are struggling with relationships with roommates or in other social settings. In my direct work with students, my focus is to help students understand behavior that is inconsistent with their values. For example, we talk about how their behavior and actions do/do not align with their goals. Like all students, neurodiverse students who identify as autistic have a desire to fit in and want to seek friendships but may not understand how to go about it. If I am working with a student to identify ways to establish friendships, I identify the steps that will lead them closest to this goal and map out the different options to get there.

Brown and colleagues (2018) point out that some students with autism "lack nuance around social norms and dating behaviors can unknowingly violate the statutes," and this could lead to complaints from other students that escalates to reports to Title IX or Student Conduct. As a representative of the Disability Services Office, and to support a student, I have been asked to attend meetings with Title IX and Student Conduct. When a student expresses they are a visual learner, I am able to help them navigate the conduct or Title IX process by advocating for a visual to explain where they are in the process. The next step might be to answer what the student can anticipate will happen next, so they understand information that is both implicit and explicit and how to complete any follow-up items they need to do.

CONCLUSION

This chapter provides specific recommendations on ways housing leadership can better address the needs of neurodivergent students. Having trouble coping with many facets of residence hall life, campuses can provide structured environments and activities that form a bridge from home and high school to new college environments. Living away from family for the first time, students are challenged to manage changes in their routines, social interactions, and balance the new demands of college life. There are ways we can assist them in making a successful transition to dorm life and provide environments where they feel welcomed and understood.

Campus Essentials for High Impact

- *Raise awareness of neurodiversity among housing staff.* Providing resources and training for residence hall staff can help improve the housing experience for neurodivergent students.
- *Incorporate principles of universal design in residence hall spaces.* Consider the addition of sensory spaces that allow students a place to decompress and retreat. Review space design to identify potential areas for improvement like lighting, furniture, and space configuration.
- *Preparing neurodiverse students for residence hall experiences prior to enrollment.* Add events and programming experiences specifically for neurodiverse students to better assist them in transitioning to campus.
- *Revamp programming to foster peer engagement.* Support neurodivergent students with smaller meetings and events, as well as structured social activities, and collaborate with campus offices to design activities that build social and communication skills.

APPENDIX 1

Support Model Planning Worksheet

Rochester Institute of Technology (RIT)

- Campus Profile
  - What is the size of your campus (total enrollment)?
  - What is the estimated size of your population of students with ASD?
    - Identified
    - Not-Identified (best estimate)
  - Are there a growing number of students with ASD on your campus? What is the rate of growth?
  - What is the distribution of graduate versus undergraduate students with ASD?

- Existing Services
  - ○ What services currently exist on your campus to support *all* students in the transition to college (e.g., orientation, first year programs)?
  - ○ What services currently exist on your campus to support *all* students in persistence to college (e.g., academically, socially, residentially)?
  - ○ What services currently exist on your campus to support *all* students in the transition to the workforce (e.g., internships, career preparation, job placement)?
  - ○ What services currently exist on your campus that serve students with ASD in an indirect manner (e.g., professional development/training, awareness programming, campus experts)?
  - ○ What services currently exist on your campus that serve students with ASD in a direct/targeted manner (e.g., coaching/mentoring, social skills groups in counseling services, disability services)?
  - ○ What is the current level of experience among your professional staff in supporting students with ASD (e.g., academic advisors, residential staff, counseling center staff)?
  - ○ How prepared are your faculty to support students with ASD in the classroom?
  - ○ How strong is the support from the general campus community regarding the need for targeted supports for students with ASD? How might additional support be garnered prior to advancing programmatic initiatives?
  - ○ How strong is the potential buy-in from decision-makers regarding targeted supports for students with ASD? How might additional support be garnered prior to advancing programmatic initiatives?
- Prevailing Challenges
  - ○ Considering the prevailing challenges or issues currently being experienced with or around students with ASD, what skillsets (or domains) are presenting the greatest challenge for students with ASD on your campus?
    - ■ executive functioning
    - ■ academic skills
    - ■ self-care
    - ■ social competence
    - ■ self-advocacy
    - ■ career preparation
    - ■ other
- Considering a Campus Response
  - ○ What level of response are you seeking to achieve at this time?
    - ■ Awareness and acceptance programming
    - ■ Faculty/staff professional development specific to students with ASD

- Extending existing services to meet a more specialized need
- Developing targeted services for students with ASD
- Developing a comprehensive program service model for students with ASD Action Planning

Regardless of institutional goals, it is strongly recommended that planning begin with the establishment of a task force. Once formed, this work group may draw upon the campus profile, existing services, and prevailing challenges sections in the bulleted list above to determine short- and long-term goals for your campus. Based on these goals, the sections below will help guide the work group in decision-making related to priorities and implementation plans. These sections map to the earlier resource guide materials (as indicated). It may be helpful for the task force to review this material as they consider campus responses.

- Task force development
  o Who are the potential change agents on your campus?
  o Who could be involved in an initial and ongoing task force?
  o What department(s) or personnel might take a leadership role?
- Issues related to disclosure
  o How will your campus handle issues of disclosure related to campus professionals?
  o How will your campus handle issues of disclosure related to students?
- Opportunities for indirect impact
  o What steps could your campus take to increase awareness and acceptance?
  o What steps could your campus take in training the campus community?
  o What steps could your campus take to develop campus expertise?
  o What steps could your campus take to enhance existing programs and services?
- Opportunities for direct impact
  o Based on the challenges presented by the population of students with ASD on your campus, would coaching and mentoring services be a priority? If so, what resources are available or would be required?
  o Based on the challenges presented by the population of students with ASD on your campus, would targeted skill development services be a priority? If so, what resources are available or would be required?
  o Based on the challenges presented by the population of students with ASD on your campus, would summer transition programming services be a priority? If so, what resources are available or would be required?

○ Based on the challenges presented by the population of students with ASD on your campus, would supportive living services be a priority? If so, what resources are available or would be required?

○ Based on the challenges presented by the population of students with ASD on your campus, would student empowerment efforts be a priority? If so, what resources are available or would be required?

○ Based on the challenges presented by the population of students with ASD on your campus, would social programming services be a priority? If so, what resources are available or would be required?

Further Considerations for the Development of a Comprehensive Program

If the needs and resources identified merit consideration of a comprehensive support program, the following areas will require serious discussion and development.

- Based on the size and scope of the program you are considering and the resource availability, what policies and procedures might you consider for an admission criteria and intake process?
- Based on the size and scope of the program you are considering, what resources can you utilize for program staffing, and what training and supervision will be required to support this model?
- Based on the size and scope of the program you are considering, what program funding source can you pursue to support the initiative?
- What external resources (e.g., funding agencies) might be available to support a program or its participants?
- Based on the model you develop and the stakeholders in your program, how will you evaluate program success? (Rochester Institute of Technology, 2014)

REFERENCES

Blimling, G. S. (n.d.). *College and university residence halls*. https://education.stateuniversity.com/pages/1845/College-University-Residence-Halls.html

Brown, J., & Poore-Pariseau, C. (n.d.). Universal design and students with autism: Best practices that may benefit all students. https://collegeautismspectrum.com/downloads/2017-NASPA_JaneBrown-CindyPoorePariseau.pdf

Brown, J. T., Wolf, L. E., & Sullivan, L. (2018). Students with autism: Challenges with conduct and Title IX. *Disability Compliance for Higher Education, 23*(7), 1–5. doi:10.1002/dhe.30386

Burgstahler, S., & Russo-Gleicher, R. J. (2015). Applying universal design to address the needs of postsecondary students on the autism spectrum. *Journal of Postsec-*

ondary Education and Disability, 28(2), 199–212. https://files.eric.ed.gov/fulltext/EJ1074670.pdf

Cox, B. E., Thompson, K., Anderson, A., Mintz, A., Locks, T., Morgan, L., Edelstein, J., & Wolz, A. (2017). College experiences for students with autism spectrum disorder: Personal identity, public disclosure, and institutional support. *Journal of College Student Development, 58*(1), 71–87. https://doi.org/10.1353/csd.2017.0004

Dolmage, J. (2017). *Academic ableism: Disability and higher education.* University of Michigan Press.

Fisher, T. (2015). *Resident assistant training and students with high functioning autism* [Unpublished master's thesis]. Eastern Illinois University. https://thekeep.eiu.edu/cgi/viewcontent.cgi?article=2964&context=theses

Francis, G. L., Gordon, S., Kliethermes, A. J., Regester, A., Baldini, D., & Grant, A. (2018). Developing and implementing a postsecondary education program for young adults with intellectual and developmental disabilities: Processes and procedure. *Teacher Educators' Journal, 11*, 134–156.

Hankerson, M. (2019, August 13). VCU converts student lounges into temporary dorm rooms in newest residence hall. *Virginia Mercury.* https://www.virginiamercury.com/blog-va/vcu-converts-student-lounges-into-temporary-dorms-in-newest-building/

Koenig, R. (2019). Colleges enlist peer mentors to make campuses more welcoming to neurodivergent students. *EdSurge News.* https://www.edsurge.com/news/2019-08-08-colleges-enlist-peer-mentors-to-make-campuses-more-welcoming-to-neuro-divergent-students

Langlois, M. K. (2018, September 20). The stresses of dorm life. *Reporter.* https://reporter.rit.edu/features/stresses-dorm-life

Magro, K. (2019). *Living in a college dorm with autism.* http://kerrymagro.com/living-in-a-college-dorm-with-autism

Organization for Autism Research. (2017, July 25). *Roommate agreements.* https://researchautism.org/roommate-agreements

Robertson, S. M., & Ne'eman, A. D. (2008). Autistic acceptance, the college campus, and technology: Growth of neurodiversity in society and academia. *Disability Studies Quarterly, 28*(4), 14. doi:10.18061/dsq.v28i4.146

Robsham, K. (2016, February 1). *How to create a welcoming environment in student affairs.* https://www.presence.io/blog/how-to-create-a-welcoming-environment-in-student-affairs

Rochester Institute of Technology. (2014). *Emerging practices for supporting students.* Rochester Institute of Technology. https://www.rit.edu/studentaffairs/ssp/sites/rit.edu.studentaffairs.ssp/files/docs/ASDinHigherEdGuide.pdf

Sarrett, J. C. (2018). Autism and accommodations in higher education: Insights from the autism community. *Journal of Autism & Developmental Disorders, 48*(3), 679–693. doi:10.1007/s10803-017-3353-4

Shore, S. (2003). *Beyond the wall: Personal experiences with autism and Asperger Syndrome.* Autism Asperger Pub.

Stanford University Medicine. (2020). *Designing inclusive dorm communities.* https://med.stanford.edu/neurodiversity/education.html

Tran, T. (2019). *Social media in higher education: 8 essential tips.* https://blog.hoot-suite.com/social-media-in-higher-education/

University of Nebraska–Lincoln. (2020). *Rules and routines.* Nebraska Autism Spectrum Disorders Network. https://www.unl.edu/asdnetwork/virtual-strategies/rules-and-routines

West, C. (2019, November 26). On the dean's list, with autism: Colleges add autism support services, but they're pricey. *USA Today.* https://www.usatoday.com/story/news/education/2019/11/26/autism-autistic-spectrum-asd-college-student-services-awareness-university-tennessee/4303692002

Wexler, A., & Luethi-Garrecht, A. (2015). Beyond accommodations: Designing for nonverbal/nonauditory learners in the inclusive art room. *Art Education, 68*(2), 14–21. doi:10.1080/00043125.2015.11519309

Williams, L. B. (2018). Colleges should understand the special issues related to autism and Title IX. *Inside Higher Ed.* https://www.insidehighered.com/views/2018/02/08/colleges-should-understand-special-Issues-related-autism-and-title-ix-opinion

Chapter 10: Campus Spotlight

Boxes and Walls, University of Wisconsin–Whitewater

Terry Tumbarello

Our Mission: Boxes and Walls is an interactive diversity experience created for our students and the entire University of Wisconsin–Whitewater (UWW) community. It is an oppression experience highlighting social justice awareness. The program is designed to let the partici-

UNIVERSITY OF WISCONSIN
WHITEWATER

Source: University of Wisconsin–Whitewater

pant experience a few different social justice issues and put them in the shoes of students on our campus who identify with those experiences on a daily basis.

The planners of the program decided that UWW students would benefit from receiving more information on what it was like to live on campus as an autistic student. The purpose of this activity was to provide participants with a sample perspective of what an individual with Autism Spectrum Disorder (ASD) may feel when entering an environment/situation that can trigger sensory overload.

Total attendance in 2018 was *1,237* people, including students and college staff.

Program Inception: In August 1998, Residence Life at the University of Wisconsin–Whitewater created an experiential diversity education program for RA (resident assistant) training. The goal was to create an experience similar to the popular Behind Closed Doors training that many campuses do during RA training. Thus, Boxes and Walls: The Oppression Experience was created. For the first few years of the program, each room allowed the participants to experience a historical glimpse into that room's represented identity and the oppression those identities experienced through the years. In 2004, the program evolved to focus more on the oppression experiences that current UWW students were facing.

Adding Disability Awareness: In 2018 and again in 2019 Boxes and Walls featured a nonvisible disability room for the first time. The room featured an autism-focused scenario as well as a scenario centered on depression, anxiety, and suicide ideation. This room was created to be more inclusive of all of our students with disabilities, not just those with visible disabilities. UWW was seeing an increase of incidents that involved students on the autism spectrum and their peers who were not. At the core of these incidents seemed to be a lack of understanding of the disability and a lack of knowing how to best communicate with students on the spectrum.

Processing Room: The last room of the program is a processing room in which participants meet with a facilitator and a counselor. The facilitator describes what they just experienced, encouraging them to share what they were feeling and thinking immediately after experiencing Boxes and Walls. The counselor also assists in processing those feelings. The decision was made in 2019 to have the nonvisible disability room just prior to the processing room in case the room's content was triggering.

Program Assessment: Each year, the program averages between 1,200 and 1,250 students who complete the program. In 2019, the program featured the following experiences: physical ability, Latinx, gender identity, African American, LGBTQ+, and nonvisible disabilities. As Boxes and Walls has evolved, it has remained true to its core, to provide UWW students the opportunity to immerse themselves in an experience that depicts what it is like to be a UWW student from an underrepresented identity. The program's power and impact to student learning is best demonstrated when participants personally feel even a small percentage of the oppression that many of our students live with on a daily basis; they have the desire to impact change in themselves and others.

To watch Boxes and Walls in action, visit https://www.youtube.com/watch?v=zpBHY-gQPYg and https://www.youtube.com/watch?v=dZiFv2S6OZs.

Chapter Eleven

Campus Health and Wellness

Shawnté Elbert, Ta-Kisha Jones, and Elizabeth M. H. Coghill

The transition from high school to college is challenging for any student, but those who are neurodiverse have additional obstacles that impact their ability to engage and thrive. The campus environment requires neurodiverse students, both directly and indirectly, to conform to campus "norms" that are set by those who are neurotypical. The lack of training for neurotypical faculty, staff, and students puts pressure on neurodiverse students to respond to challenging social cues or unclear communication in a way that doesn't make others feel uncomfortable. Bias, perceptions, and stereotypes shape how many people engage with those who are different from them.

Higher education expectations are placed on students and staff alike to succeed. Whether a student survives or thrives in this process can be contingent on many factors. Health and wellness promotion teaches a holistic integration of student well-being. This approach to wellness supports campus communities and helps them succeed. The neurodivergent community is no exception and can be positively impacted when we teach from a holistic wellness perspective. This chapter explores the relationship between neurodiverse students and campus wellness, college health promotion and services, recreation, case management, and health literacy. This chapter provides suggestions for helping neurodiverse students achieve campus wellness. Chapter authors will focus on campus wellness from a public health approach, which is holistic and includes all aspects of a person that influences their well-being.

CAMPUS WELLNESS AND WELL-BEING

The mission of campus health and wellness is to establish a culture of health and wellness within the campus community so that students can live and

229

thrive. Well-being connects elements of campus life: social, community, career, financial, physical, and emotional well-being in order to achieve and maintain balance. Well-being supports a student's ability to be resilient, and to achieve their full potential. By being mindful and aware of life balance, students are able to manage aspects of campus life in a holistic way, supporting the achievement of personal and career success.

In each aspect of well-being, getting basic needs met at the individual level creates an opportunity for all students to develop, thrive, and succeed personally and academically. At the campus community level, the campus environment benefits when students are happy with their lives and feel safe. Wellness can be viewed and assessed via nine dimensions of well-being. These dimensions include: financial (short and long term), cultural (diversity, equity, inclusion, social justice), physical (body), intellectual (mind), emotional (feelings), social (family, friends, relationship), occupational (career, skills), environmental (air, water, food, safety), and spiritual (values, purpose, intuition, vitality) (Stoewen, 2015; Kitko, 2001; Roscoe, 2009; Spurr et al., 2012; Miller & Foster, 2010). Wellness is the ability to live life in its entirety and to make the most of one's personal abilities. Wellness imposes personal accountability through self-evaluation. It involves life-long learning and evolving to enhance personal well-being. The process of achieving well-being is continuous and dynamic and requires individuals to (1) be *aware* by seeking more information about how they can improve, (2) make *choices* by considering a variety of options and selecting those that seem to be in your best interests, and (3) attain *success*, which is determined by each individual, based on their personal goals and achievements (Cloninger et al., 2012; Smith et al., 2006).

Campus health and wellness transcends any one program, departmental effort, or service. No one department can own an institution's health and wellness efforts; every department has a responsibility to support stakeholders, and the ability to do so can make a considerable difference in improving campus wellness. Many colleges and universities are moving toward implementing a public health approach on how they serve students, with an emphasis on prevention. These departments "play a critical role in the retention, progression, and graduation of students by providing access to and/or coordination of quality, affordable, convenient health and wellness services and programs delivered by professionals who are attuned to the unique stressors and needs of college students" (American College Health Association, 2016).

By approaching campus wellness from an integrated perspective, campuses can capitalize on synergies from all campus health and wellness departments and strengthen to efforts toward positively impacting student well-being.

Integrating efforts allows staff to reach broader audiences through cross-marketing initiatives, presents a unified voice on well-being, and increases the exposure of departments to stakeholders. An integrative wellness approach removes barriers and departmental silos and combines staff expertise to enable students to fully engage in their higher education experience. In addition, integrative approaches around student health and wellness assist in preparing graduates for life beyond campus.

UNDERSTANDING THE ROLE
OF COLLEGE HEALTH AND PROMOTION

The Carnegie Foundation's College Health defines *college health* as "the cautious convergence of health and education. It is a campus community with a common purpose and a shared vision. College well-being cannot be isolated from social, physical, mental, financial, political or cultural factors, nor can it be separated from a sense of belonging and meaning. College health is developmentally appropriate, educationally effective, accessible, and convenient" (Swinford, 2002; American College Health Association, 2016). For higher education, the educational and outreach component of college health is often referred to as health promotion (Eddy & Eifert, 2017; Eifert et al., 2017; Ferreira et al., 2018). *Health promotion* can be defined as enabling people to take control over their health and its social determinants, and thereby improve their overall health (Kumar & Preetha, 2012). It includes interventions at the individual (knowledge, skills, attitude), interpersonal (social network), organizational (environment), community (cultural values, norms), and public policy levels to facilitate adaptations conducive to improving or protecting health.

College health promotion is an aspect of medicine that focuses on college-aged students' clinical and preventative care. Often ranging from 17 to 28 years of age, college health promotion has expanded to include nontraditional students (Turner & Hurley, 2015). Often an unrecognized or unknown specialty of our health care system, college health practice presents challenges because of the forms of clinical care that often require coordination with campus and community resources. A multidisciplinary approach by health and wellness practitioners is part of the complex nature of college health and wellness. Turner and Hurley (2015) share key guiding principles for college health professionals, including patient sensitivity, service quality and economy, ethical decision-making, continuous evaluation and improvement, and enabling student personal growth and development.

CAMPUS HEALTH LITERACY

Students experience significant growth and development of adult emotional, social, and cognitive skills and progress toward taking accountability for health decision-making during their college years (Havinghurst, 1972). Campuses support student development through health literacy programming. Health literacy is "the degree to which individuals have the capacity to obtain, process, understand, communicate and utilize basic health information and services needed to make appropriate health decisions to prevent or treat illness" (Epperson, 2012; Institute of Medicine [US] Committee on Health Literacy et al., 2004). A student's level of health literacy informs professionals of their limits to search for and use health information, adopt healthier behaviors, and adhere to prescribed treatment plans. Limited health literacy is associated with unhealthier health outcomes and higher medical costs (Epperson, 2012; Institute of Medicine [US] Committee on Health Literacy et al., 2004). Research indicates that within the university population, low or no health literacy can also decrease a student's academic success.

Health literacy not only focuses on an individual's skills and abilities but also reflects the efforts of healthcare systems and practitioners to make health information and services understandable. Campus health and wellness professionals must concentrate on improving individual skills and making direct services, education, and information systems more health literate. Health literacy also includes staff helping students learn how to advocate for themselves. Examples include teaching students how to say "no" to treatment approaches, how to request more time in decision-making, and providing meaningful educational opportunities to engage neurodiverse students from a consent perspective.

A key component of student health literacy is to make their support system partners in their success. Parents/guardians, friends, and partners can often provide resources and possess better ways to communicate with their student. As a student transitions to higher education it is imperative that the student's support system is not shut out completely. For a neurodiverse student who may be balancing medical care and learning differences, health literacy becomes a lynchpin in their ability to self-advocate and fully understand their own medical needs.

POST-SECONDARY STUDENT HEALTH CENTERS

Higher education institutions have created different models of student health centers, each with varying types of services and resources afforded to campus constituents. Most health centers for students are not facilities connected to academic departments. Some of the student health centers are run as a first-aid clinic, while some are run by a nurse, or with multidisciplinary staff employed. Student health services vary from campus to campus, depending on the campus's size, student enrollment, scope of practice, and whether care is expanded to faculty, staff, dependents, partners, and the public.

College health staff can include doctors, physician assistants, administrators, psychologists, nurses, mental health professionals, health educators, athletic trainers, nutritionists, and pharmacists (Eddy & Eifert, 2017; Eifert et al., 2017). Some college health programs include experts in tobacco cessation, health and wellness coaches, massage or physical therapists, and other holistic health providers (Eddy & Eifert, 2017; Eifert et al., 2017). College health practitioners are often members of a national organization, such as the American College Health Association (ACHA) or the National Association of Student Personnel Administrators (NASPA) (Eddy & Eifert, 2017; Eifert et al., 2017).

Student health departments have transitioned from a clinic with a primary role to treat students who are sick or injured to expanding their services to meet the significant health needs of today's student demographic. The mission of student health centers has been redefined and expanded. Administrators work to remove barriers to access and treatment for students in relation to cost, location, off-campus referrals, facilities, scope of care, and the hours of operation. In addition, expanding from reaching primarily medical problems and extending to also controlling chronic conditions, preventative care, and supporting healthier habits.

Campus student health centers can create welcoming environments for neurodiverse students—for example, providing quiet waiting spaces or noise-reduction headphones to navigate loud lobbies. In a recent article from *Nursing Times*, a student nurse suggests the following adjustments designed to support neurodiverse staff and patients alike. Aaron Hobin, a neurodiverse nursing student, suggests health centers should designate resources to assist people in reading documents. Adding assisted technologies to help staff and patients review health education materials can be beneficial as well. Small changes to health center environments can significantly support neurodiverse students (Ford, 2020).

TRANSITION TO CAMPUS HEALTH SERVICES

Today's student transitions to college with preexisting illnesses and disorders that require higher levels of assistance. Their needs require trained professionals to assist in maintaining medication compliance and diagnoses. College-aged students are at a critical stage in their development, and many are just learning to manage their own health and health care with less parental/guardian oversight. Some university student health centers are actively engaged in educating students on the impact of using tobacco, alcohol, and other drugs, while promoting primary prevention strategies around healthier nutrition, sleeping, and physical activity strategies. The long-term effects of student health centers actively supporting wellness is a vital influencer of college student abilities to modify their behavior post-college.

Neurodiverse students are challenged by the transition from the high school environment and the new demands of the college campus. Parents/guardians can play a vital role in helping students successfully transition to higher education. Parents/guardians should begin conversations with their student on how to and when to utilize student health and access wellness support services. Ongoing conversations that encourage students to utilize student health and wellness services assist neurodiverse students in successfully managing college life. Closely aligned with supporting the development of student advocacy skills, there are key suggestions for parents and educators to employ prior to college transition. Parents/guardians can help their student build health advocacy skills by allowing them to take the lead on their health and wellness during their senior year of high school. Tasking students with calling and scheduling appointments, picking up medications, and leading update discussions with their medical providers develops important health literacy and advocacy skills. Parents/guardians should provide access to health insurance cards before students arrive on campus. Modeling health communication skills, such as listing health concerns to discuss with their provider, also helps students learn to successfully manage their health care. Assisting students in maintaining a list of medications and increasing their health knowledge of medication use leads to successful decision-making and overall health.

CAMPUS HEALTH PROMOTION PROGRAMS

Higher education institutions have addressed national health priorities through education and access to preventative care (Turner & Hurley, 2015). Well-being is supported by developing healthy learning environments for students (Turner & Hurley, 2015). To incorporate well-being into campus culture, university health professionals should identify stakeholder concerns and risks. Health educators can focus their energy on prevention in order to increase protective factors and reduce the risks to personal and community health (Turner & Hurley, 2015; American College Health Association, 2012). Utilizing the public health/population health model can help college health professionals accomplish these efforts (American College Health Association, 2012).

The American College Health Association (ACHA) documents that health promotion services and programs focus on primary and secondary prevention on campus, operating as a functional area of college health or student affairs/ life (American College Health Association, 2012; Eddy & Eifert, 2017). Professionals use a public health/population health model to achieve these efforts (American College Management Association, 2012). Practitioners train campus and community stakeholders on alcohol, tobacco, and other drugs, sexual health, consent, mental health, first aid, nutrition, stress and time management, healthy lifestyles, peer education, and the prevention of chronic diseases (American College Health Association, 2012; Eddy & Eifert, 2017).

CAMPUS RECREATION

Campus recreation encompasses behaviors and events that create a sense of pleasure and satisfaction. For neurodiverse students exercise can be particularly important in building opportunities to develop social skills, physical fitness, and motivation. Recreational activities can be the basis for students to have greater self-confidence. Participation in campus recreation and leisure activities helps neurodiverse students learn skills unique to specific sports and activities. Student participation in recreational programs helps to improve life skills that can be applied to outside campus life.

The field of campus recreation has emphasized the advantages of engaging in campus recreation events, facilities, programs, and services. There is substantial evidence documenting the importance of recreational engagement on college and university campuses. Students taking part in recreational activities have improved health and wellness and higher retention rates. Students who participate frequently in a range of campus recreational opportunities benefit even more. In addition, campus recreation facilities and programs continue to be a factor for students when deciding what college/university to attend.

Campus recreation programs can serve neurodiverse students as part of a comprehensive treatment plan and can impact physical, social, and spiritual wellness dimensions. Due to the potential for sensory overload, some activities may need to be tailored for campus neurodiverse students. Campus recreation programs can market times when the facility is less busy, adjusting lights, e-sports events, creating an individualized fitness program that includes teaching safe exercise practices, peer support or smaller group fitness classes where sound is adjusted, and providing earplugs/headphones.

CAMPUS CASE MANAGEMENT

Following the 2007 Virginia Tech mass shooting, case management has risen in importance within higher education (Adams et al., 2014). Providing support to students at varying degrees of distress is not new in higher education. Campus case managers commonly work within counseling centers, serve on deans of students' staff, or work in campus advocacy offices tasked with supporting the entire campus community (Adams et al., 2014). Campus case management involves representing the student in interactions with the university.

Case management in higher education can be defined as "a student-centered, goal-oriented process for assessing the particular needs and services of a student and assisting them to access and utilize those services" (Adams et al., 2014, p.448). Many student affairs staff operate as case managers in the scope of their job duties on campus. Adams et al. (2014) outline four case management stages essential to a student affairs case management model. Case managers must determine the needs of the student and collect information regarding the student's situation (Adams et al., 2014). Case managers serve as advocates and are often responsible for speaking and/or acting on behalf of a student. Through advocacy, case managers are called on to coordinate campus services, assist students in managing the higher education system, work to empower students in decision-making and taking responsibility for actions, and negotiate the campus system (Adams et al., 2014).

Case managers advocate, refer, and form collaborative relationships with on- and off-campus resources. Commonly, case managers refer students to: on-campus counseling services and off-campus counseling resources, victim advocates, substance abuse treatment services, dietitian services, student health, liaison between parents/guardian/support systems, disability support services, and the student ombudsman. Due to their ongoing interactions with these departments, case managers often work with neurodiverse students by serving as an advocate, resource generator, and accountability professional to ensure their success on campus. Finally, case managers seek to meet student needs and resolve the situation at hand (Adams et al., 2014).

STUDENT HEALTH AND WELLNESS

Wellness is an active process of becoming aware of and making choices toward a healthy and fulfilling life. Wellness is more than being free from illness; it is an energetic process of change and growth. The World Health Organization (n.d.) defines *wellness* as "a state of complete physical, mental, and social well-being, and not merely the absence of disease or infirmity" (Sartorius, 2006). In order to adopt an approach where the whole student is served, campuses should focus on serving neurodiverse and neurotypical students from a holistic wellness framework. Serving the whole student's health and wellness is not just the responsibility of health and wellness departments but must engage all sectors of campus. Beyond assistance from disability support services, neurodiverse students can benefit from clinical, prevention, and socially focused education and outreach. The Comprehensive Transition Education Model (CTEM) and Comprehensive Transition Services Model in table 11.1 encourages support teams to make nine domains the focus of transition planning, education, and services, which fall within all of the nine dimensions of wellness (Myles et al., 2005).

For campuses that offer counseling, the counseling center offers a range of mental health services to students desiring help with personal or professional concerns. Some counseling centers specialize in developmental issues and clinical apprehensions common to college students. These include identity development, personal growth, relationship and familial problems, and academic and personal stress. Services provided by counseling staff incorporate outreach activities and educational presentations; individual, couples, and group therapy; as well as consultations with friends, faculty/staff, and parents/guardians concerned about a student in distress. During crisis situations on and off campus, counseling staff are called on to respond by providing immediate intervention, stabilization, and support to the campus community.

PEER HEALTH EDUCATION

College peer relationships are influential on the development of students (Astin, 1993). The success of peer health education resides in the power of the peer relationships built from peer interactions. *Peer educators* can be defined as peers who utilize their skills and knowledge to assist their peers in making health-related decisions (National Association of Student Personnel Administration, 2019). Peer educators can positively influence and educate those around them and have the importance to be the most impactful to one another on campus Astin (1993).

Peer health education services can play a role in cultivating safe spaces. The positive influence of peer education is significant. With peer health education, students have the opportunity to gain health literacy, awareness, and positive self-advocacy for relevant campus wellness topics. When it

Figure 11.1. Comprehensive Transition Education Model (CTEM) and Comprehensive Transition Services Model (CTSM) Domains (based on Sitlington et al., 2000)

Domain	Brief Description	Dimension(s) of Wellness Connection
Communication and Academic Performance	Expressive and receptive communication skills Academic skills	Intellectual, Social
Self-Determination	Making one's own decisions and acting on them, as well as participating in more self-directed learning	Intellectual, Emotional, Social
Interpersonal Relationships	Social skills such as those related to communicating with others (e.g., initiating, maintaining, and ending conversations) and understanding and managing emotions (e.g., conflict resolution)	Emotional, Social, Cultural
Integrated Community Participation	Participating in one's community, such as restaurants, stores, parks, libraries, places of worship, events, government, and volunteering	Social, Spiritual, Environmental
Health and Fitness	Monitoring one's health, including scheduling/attending check-ups, and recognizing symptoms and determining how to respond to them Understanding and applying the principles of nutrition and exercise Understanding sexuality Being prepared to handle medical emergencies	Physical, Emotional
Independent/Interdependent Living	Adaptive behaviors, such as personal hygiene, cleaning, cooking, and managing one's finances	Physical, Emotional, Financial
Leisure and Recreation	Activities that are relaxing and enjoyable in one's down time, such as those related to sports, arts and crafts, and music	Physical, Social, Cultural
Employment	General skills related to working, such as following instructions, being punctual and responsible, and taking criticism Occupational skills (i.e., searching and applying for jobs, integrating self into a new work environment), and basic job skills (i.e., working well independently or part of a team, communicating well, reading, and math)	Social, Occupational, Emotional, Intellectual, Financial
Further Education and Training	Ability to seek out, apply, and succeed at postsecondary educational opportunities	Spiritual, Intellectual, Occupational, Financial

comes to high-risk behaviors like smoking, drinking, and sex, it's important that everyone is knowledgeable and comfortable to make the best choice for themselves. With sensitive topics, trusting, friendly, and educated peers help to create a positive environment to learn.

The needs of neurodiverse students can be addressed in peer education programs. For example, the Peer Health Education program at Indiana University–Purdue University Indianapolis adopted the use of adult sensory toys and fidget spinners during trainings and for general student office use. The use of sensory items not only supports peer educators but also provides support when the students are training their peers in health and wellness topics. These tools not only function as stress relievers but also support neurodiverse peers. Several relaxing and stimulus-based activities were placed throughout the open space, affording students with various needs to take part and increase social connectedness and a sense of belonging.

EDUCATING CAMPUS PERSONNEL

Personnel within higher education must be comfortable engaging with diverse communities and respecting the differences unique individuals bring to the campus. *Health education* focuses on building stakeholders' abilities through educational, motivational, skill-building, and consciousness-enhancing practices for behavior change. By influencing stakeholders' capacities and offering environmental encouragement, meaningful and lasting change in the health of individuals and communities can occur (McQueen & de Salazar, 2011). Many professional organizations require ongoing professional development, and in order to serve today's students, administrators must commit to the training and education of all staff to ensure cultural competence.

Continuous professional development allows professionals to be aware of the unique stressors, communication difficulties, cultural beliefs, and expectations that can impact a student's experience. Best practice for health and wellness professionals requires they maintain professional competencies, work within their scope of practice, adhere to codes of professional practice, and adopt ethical principles including dignity, respect, student confidentiality, privacy, and informed consent (American College Health Association, 2016). Sara Gardner, program director at Bellevue College, shares her perspective and suggestions for six best practices for health and wellness professionals when engaging with neurodiverse students.

1. Participate in bias training regarding neurodiverse students.
2. Be aware of language choices when communicating with students.

3. Support open communication by asking for clarity when needed.
4. Evaluate and create a welcoming environment for neurodiverse students in rooms, lounges, offices, and campus open spaces. Consider offering adjustable lighting for students sensitive to high levels of stimuli and provide relaxing activities in office waiting areas (i.e., coloring, fidget spinners).
5. Offer multiple formats for information on department websites.
6. Support student advocacy skills by offering treatment as optional, versus mandated.

COORDINATING CAMPUS CARE AND SUPPORT

The transition to college requires neurodiverse students to seek out and initiate accommodations, resources, and support. This process can be challenging for any student, but some neurodiverse students decide not to disclose needs and register through the Disability Services office. Neurodiverse students commonly struggle to be understood by peers, faculty, and staff, who then refer them to various resources on campus. At Central Washington University, Wendy Holden, director of Disability Services, shares how working with her colleagues has allowed her to holistically support students who are struggling. Holden serves on the Coordinated Assistance & Resource Education (CARE) Team, which is a multidisciplinary team of professionals dedicated to a proactive and collaborative approach to the prevention, identification, assessment, and management of challenges impacting student success. The CARE Team provides coordinated support and resources to identified individual students, as well as to others impacted (living community, classmates, clubs/organizations, faculty, family, partners, etc.). Additionally, the CARE Team aims to identify campus-wide trends and determine plans for interventions designed to embrace holistic wellness. Her expertise provides needed feedback and suggestions on how to support the student and educate the faculty, staff, or peers who reported any behaviors of concern about the student.

Campus CARE/assessment teams work hard to counter the misconception that reporting someone to the team will result in unfavorable consequences such as expulsions or going through the conduct process (The Jed Foundation, 2016). To address misconceptions, campus teams should conduct specific and ongoing outreach communicating the purpose and benefits of the team. Reporting a student or peer who is experiencing difficulties can assist in creating a healthier campus culture, one that emphasizes ensuring the student gets the support that is needed. "The need goes beyond just offering help for troubled students" (The Jed Foundation, 2016). Furthermore, "when people care about each other and feel their institution cares about them, the odds of detecting someone who is struggling before it becomes a crisis" (The Jed Foundation, 2016).

CONCLUSION

College students are at a significant time in their development to adulthood. As they identify and discern their own health and wellness without the management of parents/guardians, students shape the way they view and incorporate wellness into life beyond campus. For neurodiverse students, the steps to personal responsibility for health and wellness can be difficult. The active involvement of parents/guardians guiding advocacy for assistance, communicating medical needs, and managing life skills negatively influences the ability for students with learning differences to adopt the primary responsibility for their wellness needs.

Extending health education and wellness beyond the provision of mental and medical health services, college wellness programming influences and affects the well-being of the campus community. Dedication to campus-wide holistic health prevention and education programming benefits the overall success of all students and influences their ability to maintain health into their adult years.

Campus Essentials for High Impact

- *Embed health* into all aspects of campus culture, across administration, operations, and academic mandates.
- *Include health themes in campus policies.* Evaluate, create, and coordinate campus policies and practices with attention to health, well-being, and sustainability.
- *Create supportive campus environments.* Enhance the campus environment as a living laboratory, identifying opportunities to study and support health and well-being, as well as sustainability and resilience in the built, natural, social, economic, cultural, academic, organizational, and learning environments.
- *Generate thriving communities and a culture of well-being.* Be proactive and intentional in creating empowered, connected, and resilient campus communities that foster an ethic of care, compassion, collaboration, and community action.
- *Support personal development.* Develop and create opportunities to build student, staff, and faculty resilience, competence, personal capacity, and life-enhancing skills—and so support them to thrive and achieve their full

potential and become engaged local and global citizens while respecting the environment.

- *Create or re-orient campus services.* Coordinate and design campus services to support equitable access, enhance health and well-being, optimize human and ecosystem potential, and promote a supportive organizational culture (Okanagan Charter, 2015).

REFERENCES

Adams, S. D., Hazelwood, S., & Hayden, B. (2014). Student affairs case management: Merging social work theory with student affairs practice. *Journal of Student Affairs Research and Practice, 51*(4), 446–458. doi:10.1515/jsarp-2014-0044

American College Health Association. (2016). Framework for a comprehensive college health program. https://www.acha.org/documents/Programs_Services/web-handouts_2016/FR1-168_Chin.pdf

Astin, A. W. (1993). *What matters in college?: Four critical years revisited* (1st ed.). Jossey-Bass.

Cloninger, C. R., Salloum, I. M., & Mezzich, J. E. (2012). The dynamic origins of positive health and wellbeing. *International Journal of Person Centered Medicine, 2*(2), 179–187. doi:10.5750/ijpcm.v2i2.213 [doi]

Eddy, J. M., & Eifert, E. K. (2017). Introduction to special issue on health education and health promotion in college settings. *American Journal of Health Education, 48*(4), 212–214. doi:10.1080/19325037.2017.1329579

Eifert, E. K., Hall, M. E., Gropper, S. S., & Kondor, M. (2017). Health promotion and institutions of higher education: One university's experience. *American Journal of Health Education, 48*(4), 219–221. doi:10.1080/19325037.2017.1316691

Epperson, A. B. (2012). *The capacity of a southern university to promote and support health literacy among college students: A case study approach* [Unpublished doctoral dissertation]. Southern Illinois University Carbondale. https://opensiuc.lib.siu.edu/dissertations/615

Ferreira, F. M. P. B., Brito, I. D. S., & Santos, M. R. (2018). Health promotion programs in higher education: Integrative review of the literature. *Revista Brasileira De Enfermagem, 71*(suppl 4), 1714–1723. doi:S0034-71672018001001714

Ford, M. (2020, January 10). Student nurse urges NHS to make adjustments for neurodiverse staff. https://www.nursingtimes.net/news/education/student-nurse-urges-nhs-to-make-adjustments-for-neurodiverse-staff-10-01-2020

Havighurst, R. J. (1972). *Developmental tasks and education.* McKay.

Institute of Medicine (US) Committee on Health Literacy, Nielsen-Bohlman, L., Panzer, A. M., & Kindig, D. A. (2004). Health literacy: A prescription to end confusion. doi:NBK216032 [bookaccession]

Kitko, C. T. (2001). Dimensions of wellness and the health matters program at Penn State. *Home Health Care Management & Practice, 13*(4), 308–311. doi:10.1177/108482230101300416

Kumar, S., & Preetha, G. (2012). Health promotion: An effective tool for global health. *Indian Journal of Community Medicine: Official Publication of Indian Association of Preventive & Social Medicine, 37*(1), 5–12. doi:10.4103/0970-0218.94009

McQueen, D. V., & de Salazar, L. (2011). Health promotion, the Ottawa charter and "developing personal skills": A compact history of 25 years. *Health Promotion International, 26 Suppl 2*, ii194–201. doi:10.1093/heapro/dar063

Miller, G., & Foster, L. T. (2010). *Critical synthesis of wellness literature.* University of Victoria, Faculty of Human and Social Development & Department of Geography.

Myles, B. S., Hagen, K., Holverstott, J., Hubbard, A., Adreon, D., & Trautman, M. (2005). Life journey through autism: An educator's guide to Asperger Syndrome. Organization for Autism Research. https://files.eric.ed.gov/fulltext/ED508621.pdf

National Association of Student Personnel Administrators. (2019). Certified peer educator (CPE) training kit. https://www.naspa.org/project/certified-peer-educator-cpe-training

Okanagan charter: An international charter for health promoting universities and colleges. (2015). Paper presented at the *International Conference on Health Promoting Universities and Colleges.* https://www.acha.org/documents/general/Okanagan_Charter_Oct_6_2015.pdf

Roscoe, L. J. (2009). Wellness: A review of theory and measurement for counselors. *Journal of Counseling & Development, 87*(2), 216–226. doi:10.1002/j.1556-6678.2009.tb00570.x

Sartorius, N. (2006). The meanings of health and its promotion. *Croatian Medical Journal, 47*(4), 662–664.

Sitlington, P. L., Clark, G. M., & Kolstoe, O. P. (2000). *Transition education and services for adolescents with disabilities.* Allyn and Bacon.

Smith, B. J., Tang, K. C., & Nutbeam, D. (2006). WHO health promotion glossary: New terms. *Health Promotion International, 21*(4), 340–345.

Spurr, S., Bally, J., Ogenchuk, M., & Walker, K. (2012). A framework for exploring adolescent wellness. *Pediatric Nursing, 38*(6), 320–326.

Stoewen, D. L. (2015). Health and wellness. *The Canadian Veterinary Journal = La Revue Veterinaire Canadienne, 56*(9), 983–984.

Swinford, P. L. (2002). Advancing the health of students: A rationale for college health programs. *Journal of American College Health, 50*(6), 309–312. doi:10.1080/07448480209603450

The Jed Foundation. (2016). *Balancing safety and support on campus: A guide for campus teams.* Higher Education Mental Health Alliance (HEMHA).

Turner, H. S., & Hurley, J. L. (2002). *The history and practice of college health.* University Press of Kentucky.

World Health Organization. (n.d.). *Constitution.* https://www.who.int/about/who-we-are/constitution

Chapter 11: Campus Spotlight

Neurodiversity Navigators, Bellevue College, Washington

Sara Gardner

Our Mission: The Neurodiversity Navigators is an educational support program for neurodivergent students enrolled at Bellevue College in Washington State. Built on principles of the social justice and neurodiversity models of disability, the program seeks to highlight the value neurodiverse students bring to the campus community as unique, diverse individuals. The program philosophy is to provide advocacy, access support, and educational programming for neurodivergent students, and support them in learning to embrace their own singular selves.

Source: **Autism Spectrum Navigators**

Bellevue College: Located in Bellevue, Washington, Bellevue College is a 4-year post-secondary institution with an undergraduate enrollment of 14,891students in fall 2018.

Neurodiversity Navigators: Under the leadership of Sara Gardner, the program started in 2011 with 18 students and has grown to currently serving 130 students within the full program and over 300 more students with peripheral services.

I want to thank you for being there for me and for what I learned in the ASN program.

The classes on self-awareness and career development have been the reason I have decided on pursuing a career in urban agriculture.

—Neurodiversity Navigators student

Program Components: In the first year of the program, students meet one-on-one with a trained peer mentor once a week, and in groups the second year. The program offers a dedicated study hall for all neurodivergent students, regardless if they are enrolled in the program. Each quarter the program hosts parent meetings, where the staff assist parents in developing an adult relationship with their student. Two other unique components of the program for students include staff facilitating communication with their instructors and offering campus awareness and training.

The Neurodiversity Navigators program focuses on four skill-building areas:

1. executive functioning;
2. social interaction;
3. self-advocacy; and
4. self-regulation.

Program Outcomes: The Neurodiversity Navigators program's retention rate for students enrolled has reached 95%, higher than Bellevue College's neurotypical student population. Student participants have completed 85% of their classes as compared to a completion rate of 69% for satisfactory academic progress. Bellevue College's autism program is one of the most highly rated when researching schools with programs for neurodiverse students and the needed supports for success.

Chapter Twelve

Disability Support Services

Clarissa Barnes, Jennifer Williams,
and Tamara Mancini

Approximately 60% of students with disabilities enroll in some type of post-secondary education within 8 years of leaving high school (Newman et al., 2011). However, only 40% of students with disabilities who received special education services in secondary school self-disclose in the college setting (Cole & Cawthon, 2015; Newman, 2005). As post-secondary institutions have increased enrollments of neurodiverse students (Raue & Lewis, 2011), it is important that Disability Support Services/Student Accessibility Services (DSS/SAS) use effective methods to facilitate transition, retention, and success for our students as they navigate the college environment (Daviso et al., 2011; Horowitz et al., 2017). Additionally, with the recent ADA Amendments Act (Pub. L. 110-325, 2008) and the Higher Education Opportunity Act (PL 110-315, 2008), there is a strong emphasis in identifying how our post-secondary campuses can support neurodiverse students.

This chapter will explore the important role DSS/SAS offices play in supporting students with physical and learning disabilities on the college campus. Authors will examine the accommodations process, review models for support offices, and present current support services trending in post-secondary environments. In addition, the chapter will provide key recommendations for campus stakeholders who support neurodivergent student success.

EXPECTATIONS AND TRANSITIONS

Before we outline the traditional roles and definition of DSS/SAS on post-secondary campuses, we need to recognize that the transition to post-secondary education marks a significant shift in the framework in how we support neurodiverse students. Figure 12.1 provides a summary of the major differ-

Figure 12.1. Differences in Serving Neurodiverse Learners Between K–12 and Institutions of Higher Education

K–12	Higher Education
Governed by the Individuals With Disabilities Education Act (IDEA).	Governed by Section 504 of the Rehabilitation Act and the Americans With Disabilities Act (ADA).
Requires parent/guardian participation.	Parent/guardian participation is prohibited without documented permission from the student.
Services are initiated and directed by others (e.g., parents and teachers).	Services are initiated and directed by the student.
Both academic accommodations and modifications are permissible.	Academic accommodations are permissible.
Services are designed to support the student in making *progress*.	Services are designed to support the student in having *access*.

ences between the educational contexts in secondary environments and those in post-secondary environments.

Most notably, we see the transition from the public-school system to higher education in the shift from entitlement to access. Federal legislation, particularly IDEA, requires that K–12 schools meet the needs of learners with documented disabilities who qualify for special education services. This mandate to provide a free and appropriate public education (FAPE) includes the provision of providing related services (e.g., speech therapy, occupational therapy) and including the student's guardians as part of the team. Under IDEA, the responsibility of identifying students, selecting services, and providing services falls on the school district. As such, the process is heavily adult driven, and students generally participate in the process as recipients of services rather than as involved team members. Once students leave the K–12 system and enter the post-secondary setting, IDEA no longer applies. The protections for college students with disabilities are mandated by Section 504 of the Rehabilitation Act and ADA. These requirements prevent discrimination and ensure our campuses provide equitable access to the learning environment. There are no provisions to provide additional services or involve families, and FERPA does not allow us to contact guardians without specific permission from students. This process requires our college students to self-advocate and lead the charge related to identification, selection of services, and implementation of those services.

Special education services in the K–12 environment allow both modifications and accommodations to be used to meet the needs of a particular student. Modifications are changes made to the instructional environment or materials that change the nature of the academic task—for example, offering only two answer options on a multiple-choice exam instead of four. Accommodations are changes made to the instructional environment or materials that increase the accessibility of the instruction or materials to a particular student but do not change the nature of the academic task. A common example of an accommodation in post-secondary education is allowing a student to take a multiple-choice exam in a distraction-free environment and with additional testing time. Accessibility services offered in higher education settings only allow for the use of accommodations. The use of modifications, for students who are degree-seeking, is not permissible. The accommodations offered in college are often focused on physical access and access to instruction in academic contexts.

ROLE AND DEFINITION OF
SERVICES OF POST-SECONDARY CAMPUSES

Institutional Role

Accommodations remove barriers. That is an easy statement to agree with and one that most DSS/SAS specialists view as their mantra. An institution of higher education has a duty to comply with federal law: the Americans with Disabilities Act (ADA). The responsibility to provide reasonable accommodation is a fundamental statutory requirement because of the nature of discrimination faced by individuals with disabilities. Although students with disabilities can apply to schools and perform essential functions of a curriculum without any reasonable accommodations, there are often barriers that keep them from performing as they could with some form of accommodation. These barriers may be physical obstacles (such as inaccessible facilities or equipment), or they may be procedures or rules (when or how assignments are due, length of exam times, or how lecture notes are provided). Reasonable accommodations remove these educational barriers for individuals with disabilities. As part of the charge as a DSS/SAS provider, one role may include the day-to-day operations of the office with responsibilities that include ensuring the institution's compliance with federal regulations that protect the rights of individuals with disabilities as they align with the vision, mission, and strategic plan of the institution.

The DSS/SAS specialist traditionally participates in an interactive process with any student who provides an application and disability-related documentation. Initially a tool used in employment accommodations, the *interactive process* refers to the collaborative, good-faith effort in determining ADA accommodations. It is widely used among DSS/SAS specialists in higher education, and often discussed among colleagues at national conferences or on disability education listservs. This interactive process involves the DSS/SAS of the higher education institution and a qualified student. The purpose of the interactive process is to allow DSS/SAS, as an unbiased communicator, an opportunity to streamline the reasonable accommodation process and ensure that effective accommodations are provided. The interactive process includes two components: analysis and communication.

Analysis: The DSS/SAS specialist and student with a disability work together to identify barriers within an academic program. This may also include further discussion with faculty or curriculum directors as needed in various higher education programs. Analysis should include documentation to be reviewed, identification of abilities and limitations, as well as accommodations used by the student in previous settings. The student is then provided with a range of possible accommodation options, and the best options are discussed pertaining to the student's current academic situation.

Communication: The provider/student team discusses the accommodation process and accommodation needs in order to specify implementation in the class setting. At this time, faculty can clarify the "how to" of the accommodation with student and DSS/SAS. In this model, the interactive process is viewed as a circle that starts and ends with DSS/SAS offices.

Disability support specialists also work with faculty/staff/departments to provide necessary accommodations in all aspects of the student's academic plan. No matter what process is used to provide the accommodation, communicating that information to the faculty and the school stakeholders is a key component that also often entails training for faculty and staff, and students. It is also vital to encourage communication between the students and faculty allowing for students to self-advocate and to take ownership of their educational rights. To continue with this collaborative spirit, it is essential that DSS/SAS professionals connect with their institutional educational and instructional technology (EIT) team, or their informational technology (IT) team. EIT or IT support is a must when organizing accessibility within postsecondary education. Our technology offices can assist in maintaining accessibility features within course content and across websites. Furthermore, their support can offer maintenance of accessible content within learning management systems (LMS) and keeping all accessibility software up to date and ready to use in libraries or testing facilities. Beyond the various collaborations that a DSS/SAS professional can establish, it is important to remember that the institution, as a whole, shoulders the responsibility for providing an accessible education to all students.

Determining Campus Accommodations

Many disability rights scholars will say the standard in the law is "reasonable-ness," but what is reasonable? Merriam-Webster's definition of *reasonable* includes: "being in accordance with reason"; "not extreme or excessive" (Merriam-Webster, n.d.). Is it reasonable if it is fair? We would argue that *reasonable* and *fair* are not the same animal. A reasonable accommodation is assistance or a change that will enable an individual with a disability to have access to the educational program. Under the ADA, educational institutions are required to provide reasonable accommodations to qualified individuals with disabilities, unless doing so would pose an undue hardship. Examples include: (a) It is reasonable to give a student extra time on a 2-hour exam, but it is unreasonable to give a student an extra day for a 2-day take-home exam; (b) Spell-check might not be appropriate or reasonable on a medical termi-nology exam, but extended time may be. The most common types of accom-modations include extra time on exams, utilizing class note-takers, receiving assignments or notes given by faculty, assistance with implementing learning strategies, alternative exam formats, and access to adaptive equipment and technology (Abreu et al., 2016).

A qualified individual is one who meets the necessary requirements and can perform the essential functions with or without an accommodation. At this point, we get into the specific details in the federal law. Section 504 of the Rehabilitation Act of 1973 was the first disability civil rights law in the United States. Under the 504 regulations, (34 C.F.R. §104.43[a]), "no quali-fied individual with a disability shall, on the basis of disability, be excluded from participation in, be denied the benefits of, or be otherwise subjected to discrimination under any post-secondary education program of a recipi-ent of federal funds." Recipient colleges and universities were required "to take steps to ensure that no student with a disability be denied the benefits of, excluded from participation in, or otherwise subjected to discrimination because of the absence of auxiliary aids for students with impaired sensory, manual, or speaking skills." When Congress enacted the Americans with Disabilities Act of 1990 (ADA), their objective was to provide "a clear and comprehensive national mandate for the elimination of discrimination" and "clear, strong, consistent, enforceable standards addressing discrimination." This "broad scope of protection" was amended in 2008, and is published in the U.S. Code, under the chapter heading "Equal Opportunity for Individuals with Disabilities."

Institutions of higher education often focus on Title II, which specifies that public entities "make reasonable modifications in policies, practices, or pro-cedures when the modifications are necessary to avoid discrimination on the basis of disability, unless the public entity can demonstrate that making the modifications would fundamentally alter the nature of the service, program, or activity." In the application of both laws, students with disabilities must be qualified to participate in post-secondary education activities. A qualified student with a disability is one who meets the admission and essential eligibility requirements of a program or service, with or without: modifications of rules, policies, or procedures; removal of architectural, communication, or transportation barriers; provision of auxiliary aids and services.

Title II (Part 35, Subpart A—35.107) of the ADA notes the designation of a responsible employee to coordinate university efforts to comply with and carry out responsibilities under the law. This employee is your DSS/SAS professional. The law does not require special treatment of students with disabilities but does require that students be given the opportunity for equal participation in post-secondary programs. By providing appropriate academic adjustments and auxiliary aids necessary for eligible and qualified students, we can facilitate the students' fullest possible participation in the college academic programs. For documented students, the institution *must* provide auxiliary aids to ensure their participation in college classes and activities and is required to accommodate the academic participation of qualified students with disabilities.

DSS/SAS offices across the country support their students, faculty, and staff to make decisions regarding whether an accommodation is appropriate through an individualized, interactive process and an understanding of the context. Reasonable accommodations are just one piece of the puzzle. Typical services for students include a wide range of classroom accommodations dependent on information provided by the student and their documentation (see table 12.2). In addition, partnering with EIT/IT, identifying campus resources, and working with other administration to ensure access is key—especially in a world where programs are increasingly offered online. Providing

Table 12.2. Post-secondary Accommodations Organized by UDL Principles

Multiple Means of Engagement	Multiple Means of Representation	Multiple Means of Action and Expression
Removing physical barriers	Language interpreters	Text-to-speech access
Changing environments	Auxiliary aids	Recording devices
Accessible seating	Policies/procedures in multiple formats	Use of laptops on exams
Extended time on tests	Alternative exam formats	Use of calculators
Course substitution waivers	Copies of notes	Voice-recognition software
Reduced course load	Audio recordings/smart pens	Assistive technology training
Help with study skills/time management	Audio or electronic textbooks	Alternative exam formats

student training and development, as well as faculty/staff training, are also important components within a DSS/SAS office to foster campus-wide collaboration to support neurodiverse students.

CURRENT PRACTICES
FOR SERVING NEURODIVERSE STUDENTS

In order to ensure that neurodiverse students truly have access to college as a transformative experience, institutions of higher education need to move away from the model that is primarily focused on providing academic/classroom accommodations and move into a model influenced by social disability theory and universal design, one that focuses on supporting the whole student in all of the contexts that he or she should have access to on a college campus. The social model requires institutions to be reflective regarding the barriers to learning that may form for neurodiverse learners and how those barriers might be removed or lessened. As such, the social model calls for Universal Design for Learning (UDL) to be applied across the campus environment to allow not only access to but also true participation in the college community (Leake & Stodden, 2014).

Though access to academics is a critical part of the college experience, it should be noted that higher education is more than a series of courses designed to teach specific skills and knowledge. Rather, college can be conceptualized as an *experience*. In addition to coursework, the college experience includes residence life, student organizations, athletics, and the development and maintenance of social and professional networks. Many neurodiverse learners may experience social and communication difficulties as well as deficits in executive function that affect their participation in the college experience both in and out of the classroom (Grieve et al., 2014).

When moving beyond classroom accommodations to support neurodiverse learners, it is necessary to address their feelings of anxiety, depression, and isolation/marginalization (Gelbar et al., 2014). Reports of isolation may be indicative of a service need that is not being met (Leake & Stodden, 2014). Failure to support neurodiverse students in connecting socially is especially problematic because students who do not identify with an affinity group may not persist (Leake & Stodden, 2014). Gelbar and colleagues (2014) highlight research regarding the efficacy of different services or service delivery options, but the current literature provides only insights regarding current practices and not specific evidence regarding which practices are best and the conditions under which they should be implemented.

Sarrett (2018) sought to expand the literature by seeking feedback directly from students who identify as autistic. Sarrett's work supports the results reported by Gelbar and colleagues (2014), as most of the accommodations received were academic in nature. Of the 31% of students who reported that the accommodations did not meet their expectations, many felt that the accommodations were limited in scope and that they did not meet their mental health, social, and sensory needs. In addition, both students who did and did not feel their accommodations met their needs expressed that accessing accommodations was often difficult. The inconsistency with which the accommodations were provided in practice is problematic and potentially representative of an issue related to the students' need to self-advocate.

Summers and colleagues (2014) identify consistent themes related to working with neurodiverse students: students' lack of knowledge regarding their rights and responsibilities related to accommodations; students' lack of self-awareness resulting in students not identifying the need for accommodations; and deficient self-advocacy and self-determination skills. Thus, the following recommendations may be appropriate: college faculty and administrators need to develop mechanisms for supporting students in identifying the need for and gaining access to accommodations, training for faculty and staff, training for peers, and neurodiverse spaces on campus (Sarrett, 2018). Furthermore, programs designed to support neurodiverse students should solicit feedback from the population being served and conduct programmatic assessments designed to assess the effectiveness of the programs in meeting their goals (e.g., of supporting neurodiverse learners).

In addition to the needs identified by evaluating lived experiences with neurodiverse students, we should evaluate variables linked to student persistence when changing or creating support programs. Kutscher and Tuckwiller (2019) identify student and institutional variables that influence persistence and graduation rates for neurodiverse students. These include personal characteristics, academic and social engagement, use of accommodations, and campus climate concerns.

Personal Characteristics

Students who reported higher levels of perceived control were more likely to persist to graduation. Linked with this perception of control over their outcome were skillsets such as self-awareness, self-efficacy/confidence, autonomy and goal setting (including self-determination), empowerment and perseverance. Kutscher and Tuckwiller (2019) note that several studies suggest self-efficacy and self-confidence are developed in part through positive social experiences while simultaneously contacting academic success. Further, students seemed to develop self-advocacy skills during their post-secondary experiences. While no data directly links self-advocacy to persistence or graduation, one may assume that students who cannot self-advocate are less likely to be academically successful and therefore less likely to persist and graduate.

Academic and Social Engagement

The relationships between faculty and students are undoubtedly significant to the experiences that students have on campus. Kutscher and Tuckwiller (2019) report the interactions that students have with faculty influenced their willingness to have future interactions and whether students had confidence in advocating for themselves when requesting use of their accommodations. Students who expressed feelings of social alienation were less likely to graduate, suggesting that peer interaction is also a critical factor to success throughout the college experience (Kutscher & Tuckwiller, 2019). Additional research related to campus involvement and persistence suggests that interventions should expand beyond individual intervention for neurodiverse students and should include interventions that address campus climate (Koch et al., 2017).

Use of Disability Services and Accommodations

Students may not be aware of which services are available to them (Kutscher & Tuckwiller, 2019). Understanding what they have access to in terms of accommodations and support is an important first step to students being able to advocate for the use of those accommodations and services. Unsurprisingly, the use of accommodations and services is related to persistence. While there are no data on the effects of poor-quality accommodations, participants in the research have frequently commented on the quality, particularly as it relates to training (e.g., poorly trained tutors) or inconsistency (e.g., note-takers who are unreliable) of those individuals who are providing the accommodations.

Campus Climate: Preparing Campuses to Serve Neurodiverse Students

The current conceptualization of accommodations in higher education applies to the use of accommodations to prevent discrimination in the instructional settings (Kim & Lee, 2016). However, neurodiverse students may experience multiple risk factors, related to their membership in a protected group, that are correlated with decreased persistence. Therefore, accommodations must expand beyond instructional and testing contexts and be applied throughout the campus experience. Just as the needs of students can be complex, so are the variables that influence the way institutions of higher education meet those needs. As such, we will discuss two plausible models for service delivery and the variables that should be considered under either delivery model. When determining how to best adjust campus structure, policies, and processes, institutions of higher education are encouraged to analyze and reflect on institutional data and feedback from neurodiverse students on their respective campuses to determine which changes should be made.

Exploring Service Delivery Models

Though there are a variety of ways to organize the management and delivery of accommodations, the two most prevalent options are through the DSS/SAS office and through stand-alone, often disability-specific, support programs. Services organized through the DSS/SAS office are primarily related to academics, though some social or residential services may be included and offered at no cost to students. Services offered through stand-alone support programs often work in conjunction with DSS/SAS offices, expand beyond the academic environment to provide more intensive "wrap-around" services, and have additional associated service delivery costs.

Collaborative Model

The use of existing support services and offices allows campuses to support neurodiverse students using the resources already earmarked for serving all enrolled students. As such, this method can be cost-effective for the institution and may create a context in which the students are able to access services without any additional financial burden. The primary resource needed for this model of service delivery is staff time, as this model requires improved communication and collaboration across offices on campus. As the number of students served by each office increases, it may also be necessary for an institution to invest in additional faculty and staff to meet the demands of the student population. Longtin (2014) identified the following offices, which exist on most campuses, as exemplars for services that may be included when using the existing framework: disability services, counseling, health clinic, learning center, career development, student center, library, academic departments and programs, residence hall life, and centers for teaching and learning.

Under this model, campus offices work collaboratively to meet the needs of students in their areas of expertise. Faculty who have expertise with neurodiverse students may provide professional development or provide specific services as part of an academic program. For example, if a campus has a graduate speech-language therapy program, faculty and students in that program may provide social skills training to other students on campus. Career development and the campus learning center may work collaboratively to support students in selecting majors and identifying co-curricular activities that will support students in developing the necessary skill sets, both career-specific and generalizable soft-skills. A critical consideration when using this model is the need for coordination, communication, and collaboration across offices. For many campuses, a collaborative model may require a culture shift as all faculty and staff are required to contribute to supporting students in ways that they may find "nontraditional" for their roles.

Stand-Alone Programs

Stand-alone programs shift the responsibility of coordinating services from the DSS office to a specific program. These programs traditionally work with offices across campus (e.g., DSS, residence life), serving as advisors and conduits to connect the student with the resources needed on campus. Such programs can also provide intensive instruction to teach a student skills he or she may need to be successful on campus. Examples of such skills are assertiveness, conflict resolution, use of time-management and organization systems, and study skills. Many stand-alone programs are specific to one or more categories of disability with professional staff who have expertise in meeting the needs of the target population. These staff may also provide professional development for faculty and staff on campus. Additional features of stand-alone programs may include communication with parents/families (with student permission), college transition support, and specialized residence halls designed to meet the specific needs of neurodivergent students such as sensory-friendly residence halls.

PROVIDING EFFECTIVE SUPPORT NETWORKS

With rising numbers of neurodivergent students enrolling in college, DSS/SAS offices cannot be the only source of educational assistance. The following recommendations are applicable to both the collaborative and stand-alone program models. In addition, campus leaders can implement recommendations regardless of their specific campus support model. It is important to note that the implementation of some recommendations may require additional resources and costs on the part of the institution.

Case Management

Students who transition to higher education are faced with the responsibility of identifying their strengths and challenges, advocating for supports that address their challenges, using the supports, and evaluating whether or not those supports are effective at meeting their needs. These responsibilities require self-awareness and executive functioning skills that may be difficult or not yet learned by some neurodiverse students (Grieve et al., 2014). As such, it is critical that support programs have designated individuals who can work with each student to assist them in meeting these demands. The case manager's role should be one that includes instruction, as he or she will be responsible for teaching the student to manage his or her own services.

Over time, the role of case manager can be systematically transferred from the professional to the student as the student learns the necessary organization, advocacy, and self-awareness skills to take on the role. It is worth noting that the case manager is not a "one-stop shop" for the student's needs. Rather, the case manager functions to connect the student to services and support them in recognizing when needs or problems arise and problem-solving those issues with the campus resources available. For example, if a student is in need of a tutor for a specific course, (s)he may communicate that need to a case manager who could help the student navigate the process of requesting a tutor from an academic success center.

Counseling/Mental Health Support

Many neurodiverse students benefit from counseling or mental health support. Sarrett (2018) found that students with Autism Spectrum Disorder (ASD) felt that their mental health needs were not considered or taken into account when accommodations were granted. This perception may be due to the absence of a cohesive network of support. While DSS/SAS offices and stand-alone programs do not need to serve as mental health centers, such offices or programs should work in conjunction with counseling centers and health centers on campus to ensure that the student is receiving the support needed. In this role, the job of the DSS/SAS office and support program is to refer students as needed, facilitate communication, and provide information, when appropriate.

Academic Accommodations and Supports

Accommodations should be handled through the DSS/SAS office in accordance with federal guidelines (e.g., ADA and Section 504). However, many students will need support beyond the accommodations being provided.

Additional supports should be focused on helping students learn the necessary systems for requesting use of the accommodations and advocating for the accommodations with faculty and staff. For example, a student may need to be trained on an online system for scheduling exams with extended time. That same student may also need to be trained to advocate for use of the extended time accommodation in a course where the instructor assesses students using "pop" or unplanned quizzes. The need for such advocacy skills is highlighted by student reports of difficulty related to the processes of securing accommodations and faculty compliance related to ensuring the student can use the accommodation (Sarrett, 2018).

Students can benefit from working with faculty and staff to develop self-awareness. Self-awareness is critical for the student determining what their needs are so that they can appropriately advocate for the necessary accommodations (Morningstar & Shoemaker, 2018). Similarly, students should learn to evaluate the accommodations they are receiving and to provide feedback or advocate if modifications of the accommodations are needed. For example, a student may initially receive a note-taker as an accommodation. However, students may find that it is difficult to reliably get notes from another student in the class. Once that issue is identified, the student can advocate for another accommodation that meets their needs—such as the use of a Smartpen.

Social Accommodations and Supports

In college settings, opportunities for growth and development expand beyond the classroom environment. Similarly, much of the learning in the classroom requires collaboration with instructors or peers and for students to be active, rather than passive, participants. The social difficulties experienced by neurodiverse learners are well documented throughout the literature. Despite the obvious need, many neurodivergent students experience little to no social support when attending institutions of higher education. Sarrett (2018) and Gelbar and colleagues (2014) highlight the specific challenges faced commonly by students with ASD, including feelings of loneliness, isolation, depression, and anxiety. There are campus services to provide social supports, including disability-specific student support groups, engagement with peer mentors, and social skills instruction. However, the model that is most appropriate depends on the goals of the social supports and the resources available.

Residential Accommodations and Supports

As outlined in chapter 10, neurodiverse students may need support in the residence halls. This support may range from building skills related to independent living and developing daily schedules to managing conflicts with room-mates. Programming related to building these skills could be implemented in groups, such as a cooking demonstration involving an entire residence hall floor or provided individually. Campuses should consider student partici-pants and decide between making instructional programming available only to residential students or expanding participants to include students who live off-campus. Specialized physical environments may also be appropriate for neurodivergent students. Necessary changes are student specific and include specialized lighting, posting of visual cues of rules and expectations of the residence halls, decreasing the number of students housed in a particular area, and providing options for single or private rooms.

As suggested in chapter 10, much of the necessary residential support may be in the form of more adequately training residence hall staff in strategies to best support neurodiverse students. This training is critical not only for full-time staff but also for student resident assistants (RAs), who are often the first contact for students who are experiencing an issue in the residence halls. Campus security and other offices that frequently interface with the residence halls on campus should also be included in such training.

TRANSITION SUPPORT

College transition support is necessary when students begin and complete their college experience. DSS/SAS professionals play an important role as neurodivergent students transition into the college campus. Beginning stu-dents benefit from assistance as they transition into a new campus culture. This transition includes a variety of considerations that vary by student and include understanding and coping with the expectations of higher education and transitioning to careers beyond college life.

Transitioning to Higher Education

Acclimating to a new campus is challenging for all students, especially those who are neurodivergent. While transitioning to campus, students can benefit from being oriented to the physical environment of campus. This may include support finding classes, key resource offices, and student spaces. Students should also be given an orientation to the campus culture, including the social expectations of faculty, staff, and students. Making such social expectations explicit is critical for students who, for various reasons, may be unaware of how the expectations of the campus environment differ from the expectations of their high school environment. Once the expectations have been made clear, students who require support to meet those expectations can participate in the necessary instructional opportunities to build those repertoires (e.g., written communication, self-advocacy, conflict resolution).

Several resource tools supporting students to meet these expectations are already available on most campuses, but explicit instruction on how and when to use those tools may be necessary. For example, a student who has difficulty with time management may need to be taught to use Google Calendar to create visual schedules and to set text reminders. Once he or she learns to use Google Calendar, the expectation can be set that he or she enters all appointments into the calendar to increase the probability that he or she will attend the appointment. Another example pertains to self-disclosure and self-advocacy. Students may need to learn how to disclose learning preferences and access accommodations through specific instructions, tutorials, videos, or role play.

Transitioning to Career

As students prepare to transition from the institution of higher education to their career, the focus shifts from acclimating to the college environment to acclimating to the professional environment. During this transition, students should work closely with the appropriate offices on campus (e.g., career development). The role of the DSS/SAS office or stand-alone program would be to facilitate the connection between the student and career development office and to provide necessary accommodations to the student. For example, as the student begins to explore career experiences, he or she will need to work collaboratively with the career development office and the DSS/SAS office or stand-alone program to determine whether or not the student wishes to disclose his/her disability to an employer or colleagues.

Madaus (2006) conducted research on the career transition process and collected the observations of neurodivergent college graduates regarding their career transition experiences. DSS/SAS professionals can play a vital role in implementing recommendations from Madaus's study.

1. Develop opportunities for neurodivergent students to complete internships and field work experiences.
2. Establish career-focused mentoring programs matching students with neurodivergent alumni.
3. Educate students and campus stakeholders regarding neurodiversity and the workplace.
4. Expand training to include self-advocacy and increase student understanding of accommodation laws in the workplace.

5. Continue supports post-graduation and continue alumni connections to campus.

Many of the skillsets needed during this transition may already be a part of the student's repertoire, but he/she may need support in generalizing those skills. Figure 12.3 highlights some helpful transition resources.

Figure 12.3. Highlights of Campus Transition Sources

Transition to Postsecondary	
Oregon GEAR UP *The Transition to College Toolkit*	https://oregongearup.org/
DO-IT *College Transition Help and Finding the Right Campus*	https://www.washington.edu/doit/college-transition-help-and-finding-right-campus
Going to College *My Place, My Learning Style, My Advocacy Plan*	http://www.going-to-college.org/
Washington Association on Postsecondary Education and Disability *Preparing Students with Disabilities for Postsecondary Education Resource Guide*	https://gearup.wa.gov/file/preparing-students-disabilities-postsecondary-education-resource-guide-use-gear-school-staff
National Center on Safe Supporting Environments *Set to Go: Your Guide to the Transition from High School to College and Adulthood*	https://safesupportivelearning.ed.gov/resources/set-go-your-guide-transition-high-school-college-and-adulthood
Office for Civil Rights *Students with Disabilities Preparing for Postsecondary Education: Know Your Rights and Responsibilities* *Transition of Students with Disabilities to Postsecondary Education: A Guide for High School Educators*	https://www2.ed.gov/about/offices/list/ocr/transition.html
PACER National Parent Center on Transition *College Planning*	https://www.pacer.org/transition/learning-center/planning/college-planning.asp
STEPP Program *High School Transition Curriculum*	https://www.ecu.edu/cs-acad/stepp/high-school-transition-curriculum.cfm
LD Online *College and College Prep*	http://www.ldonline.org/indepth/college
Landmark College *Summer College Readiness Program*	https://www.landmark.edu/summer/summer-college-readiness-program

Professional Development for Faculty and Staff

DAA/SAS campus professionals can play an important role in educating campus stakeholders on the needs of neurodivergent students on campus. Professional development for faculty and staff is a necessary component for any program that seeks to increase awareness and eliminate barriers for neurodiverse students. This particular recommendation is aligned with the need for increased awareness on campuses identified by Sarrett (2018). More specifically, college students with ASD identified that all stakeholders, including their peers, needed training to know how to better communicate and interact with similar students. Such training should be designed to educate all members of the community on inclusive and nondiscriminatory practices. For example, the training may include the acceptance of behaviors viewed as different, but not harmful (e.g., repetitive behavior); the use of non-ableist language; and the use of universal design for creating physical and social spaces on campus (Sarrett, 2018; Gelbar et al., 2014). Such professional development may also address issues related to faculty and staff noncompliance in relation to the use of accommodations.

Professional development should be an ongoing process that evolves as the needs of faculty and staff change. The specific goals of campus-wide professional development could be determined by soliciting feedback from the students being served and by assessing the effectiveness of the campus in meeting its goals for supporting neurodiverse students. Some post-secondary campuses are requesting student feedback through electronic surveys (not to be confused with student opinion surveys) or interviews that highlight strategies and teaching techniques perceived as helpful by students.

CONCLUSION

Neurodivergent students experience challenges when utilizing campus support services, including the office dedicated to their success: the campus DSS/SAS office. Campuses are met with a service-and-demand dilemma, leaving stakeholders frustrated with present services. DSS/SAS staff report difficulty in meeting expectations for serving growing student enrollments, and the students they serve share dissatisfaction with the availability of services, experience low rates of campus disclosure, express a lack of self-advocacy education, and convey feelings of social isolation (Abreu et al., 2016). Yet, when students employ accommodations and choose to frequently utilize campus DSS/SAS supports, their grade point averages are positively impacted and academic success is realized (Abreu et al., 2016).

DSS/SAS offices cannot serve neurodiverse students alone. Campuses must move away from a single academic/classroom accommodation model to collaborative approaches that foster a Universal Design for Learning framework that focuses on empowering and supporting the whole student within all college campus contexts. When DSS/SAS offices collaborate actively with campus stakeholders and facilitate and implement essential campus supports, barriers are reduced and even removed as neurodivergent students are empowered to academically achieve.

Campus Essentials for High Impact

- *Provide students with a variety of accommodations.* By collaboratively working with faculty and staff across campus classrooms and offices, a variety of accommodations allowing for multiple means of engagement, representation, and action and expression can be jointly constructed to support neurodiverse students.
- *Collaborate with other campus offices.* Campus offices such as disability services, counseling, health clinic, learning centers, career development, student center, library, academic departments and programs, residence life, and centers for teaching and learning can network to identify campus resources, address student persistence variables, and provide supports for neurodiverse learners.
- *Recognize that support goes beyond academics.* Neurodiverse students need academic, residential, social, and mental health accommodations and supports to experience success in the campus community and persist to graduation.
- *Identify transition supports needed.* Transition supports are instrumental for students. Neurodiverse students need support and resources for transitioning from secondary to post-secondary education. In addition, post-institution supports are needed to facilitate transition to the workforce.
- *Engage faculty and staff across campus in professional development.* To help eliminate barriers for neurodiverse students, DSS/SAS specialists can work with faculty and staff through professional development to increase awareness of neurodiversity, share strategies to help with student communication and behaviors, and provide insights on compliance in using accommodations.

REFERENCES

Abreu, M., Hillier, A., Frye, A., & Goldstein, J. (2016). Student experiences utilizing disability support services in a university setting. *College Student Journal, 50*(3), 323–328.

Americans with Disabilities Act Amendments Act, Pub. L. 110-325, (2008).

Cole, E., & Cawthon, S. (2015). Self-disclosure decisions of university students with learning disabilities, *Journal of Postsecondary Education and Disability, 28*(2), 163–179.

Daviso, A. W., Denny, S. C., Baer, R. M., & Flexer, R. (2011). Postschool goals and transition services for students with learning disabilities. *American Secondary Education, 39*(2), 77–93.

Gelbar, N. W., Smith, I., & Reichow, B. (2014). Systematic review of articles describing experience and supports of individuals with autism enrolled in college and university programs. *Journal of Autism and Developmental Disorders, 44,* 2593–2601. http://doi.org/10.1007/s10803-014-2135-5

Grieve, A., Webne-Behrman, L., Couillou, R., & Sieben-Schneider, J. (2014). Self-report assessment of executive functioning in college students with disabilities. *Journal of Postsecondary Education & Disability, 27*(1), 19–32. http://search. ebscohost.com/login.aspx?direct=true&AuthType=ip,shib&db=ehh&AN=100338 094&site=ehost-live&scope=site

Horowitz, S. H., Rawe, J., & Whittaker, M. C. (2017). *The state of learning disabilities: Understanding the 1 in 5.* National Center for Learning Disabilities. http:// www.ncld.org/transitioning-to-life-after-high-school

Individuals with Disabilities Education Improvement Act, Pub. L. 108-446. (2004).

Kim, W. H., & Lee, J. (2016). The effect of accommodation on academic performance of college students with disabilities. *Rehabilitation Counseling Bulletin, 60*(1), 40–50. http://doi.org/10.1177/0034355215605259

Koch, L. C., Mamiseishvili, K., & Wilkins, M. (2017). Integrated post-secondary services and supports of college students with psychiatric disabilities. *Journal of Applied Rehabilitation Counseling, 48*(1), 16–24.

Kutscher, E. L., & Tuckwiller, E. D. (2019). Persistence in higher education for students with disabilities: A mixed systematic review. *Journal of Diversity in Higher Education, 12*(2), 136–155. https://doi.org/10.1037/dhe0000088

Leake, D. W., & Stodden, R. A. (2014). Higher education and disability: Past and future of underrepresented populations. *Journal of Postsecondary Education and Disability, 27*(4), 399–408.

Longtin, S. E. (2014). Using the college infrastructure to support students on the spectrum. *Journal of Postsecondary Education and Disability, 27*(1), 63–72.

Madaus, J. W. (2006). Improving the transition to career for college students with learning disabilities: Suggestions from graduates. *Journal of Postsecondary Education and Disability, 19*(1), 85–93.

Merriam-Webster. (n.d.). *Reasonable.* https://www.merriam-webster.com/dictionary/ reasonable

Morningstar, M. E., & Shoemaker, A. (2018). Options and skills necessary for navigating a successful transition to post-secondary education. *New Directions for Adult and Continuing Education, 160,* 39–51. https://doi.org/10.1002/ace.20298

Newman, L. (2005). Post-secondary education participation of youth with disabilities. In M. Wagner, L. Newman, R. Cameto, N. Garza, & P. Levine (Eds.), *After high school: A first look at the postschool experiences of youth with disabilities. A re-*

port from the national longitudinal transition study-2 (NLTS2)*. SRI International. http://www.nlts2.org/reports/2005_04/nlts2_report_2005_04_complete.pdf.

Newman, L., Wagner, M., Knokey, A.-M., Marder, C., Nagle, K., Shaver, D., & Wei, X., with Cameto, R., Contreras, E., Ferguson, K., Greene, S., & Schwarting, M. (2011). *The post-high school outcomes of young adults with disabilities up to 8 years after high school: A report from the National Longitudinal Transition Study-2 (NLTS2)*. NCSER 2011-3005. SRI International. https://ies.ed.gov/ncser/pubs/20113005/pdf/20113005.pdf

Raue, K., & Lewis, L. (2011). *Students with Disabilities at Degree-Granting Postsecondary Institutions (NCES 2011–018)*. U.S. Department of Education, National Center for Education Statistics. U.S. Government Printing Office. https://nces.ed.gov/pubs2011/2011018.pdf

Rehabilitation Act of 1973. Section 504. Pub. L. No. 93-112, 87 Stat. 394. (1973).

Sarrett, J. C. (2018). Autism and accommodations in higher education: Insights from the autism community. *Journal of Autism and Developmental Disorders, 48*, 679–693. https://doi.org/10.1007/s10803-017-3353-4

Summers, J. A., White, G. W., Zhang, E., & Gordon, J. M. (2014). Providing support to post-secondary students with disabilities to request accommodations: A framework for intervention. *Journal of Postsecondary Education and Disability, 37*(3), 245–260.

Chapter 12: Campus Spotlight

TECHniques Center, Texas Tech University

Jennifer Williams, Tamara Mancini, and Clarissa Barnes

Our Mission: The TECHniques Center is a fee-for-service program within the Disability Support Services office at Texas Tech University. The only tutoring program of its kind in Texas, the TECHniques Center provides supplemental academic support services

Source: **Texas Tech TECHniques Center**

to meet the needs and to promote the retention of undergraduate students with documented evidence of learning disabilities, Attention Deficit/Hyperactivity Disorder (ADD or ADHD), and/or Autism Spectrum Disorder. Our goal is to support students in becoming independent self-advocates, accomplishing their educational goals, and making education accessible to those who learn differently.

> I can only give my highest praises to the TECHniques Center at Texas Tech University. My success as an undergraduate student is directly correlated with the support provided by the staff in TECHniques Center.
>
> —Texas Tech student

A resource for Texas Tech University students for 20 years, the TECHniques Center began in 1999 with only 20 students and one full-time director and has expanded to include 175 student participants each semester with 60–75 peer tutors, and eight full-time staff members. We are proud to be a nationally recognized program for neurodivergent students.

The TECHniques Center provides a variety of supports and resources, including:

* Tutoring services:
  * The center offers one-on-one tutoring throughout the week with assigned tutors and weekly sessions with an academic counselor. Our program is certified through the College Reading and Learning Association (CRLA), and each semester tutors earn a tutor certification level in order to best assist our students. Tutors at the TECHniques Center represent the peak of tutoring training and performance. The tutoring position at the TECHniques Center is unique because of the peer-to-peer tutoring that allows our tutors to build relationships not otherwise possible in traditional, drop-in tutoring. Our tutors are matched with students based on course choices and are paired for the entire semester. This promotes the consistency and structure that have been proven to benefit our student population. While the emphasis of the job is on helping and cultivating student growth, we are committed to the growth and development of our tutors, as well. Our tutors are specifically trained to work with students with learning disabilities, ADHD, or Autism Spectrum Disorder and continually receive feedback on how to better themselves as tutors and professionals. We love hearing about all the amazing things our tutors do, both in and outside the TECHniques Center, and they are constantly moving on to bright futures after graduation.
  * Find tutor resources at http://www.depts.ttu.edu/techniques/tutors/TutorResources.php.

What the TECHniques Center offered our daughter was a continuation of support for her learning needs and an important reinforcement that she was not "different" or in any way less capable than other students at Tech. I am personally amazed at the way the TECHniques Center made her feel valued, and almost the center of attention, among a student population of 30,000.

—Parents of Texas Tech student

* Academic counseling services:
  * individualized support from academic counselors designed to build academic and self-advocacy skills;
  * supplemental assistance with academic major and career exploration, problem-solving, and course schedule registration (note: academic counselors do not provide major advising); and

- o referrals to various academic support services and co-curricular involvement opportunities on campus and within the community.
- Center resources:
  - o access to Mac and PC computer labs, as well as tutoring resources and study spaces; and
  - o printing is currently available for course-specific needs.

Over 4 years I have received one of the best educations in the State of Texas and numerous hours of help from tutors, peers, and counselors at Student Disability Services' TECHniques Center. I know that my history degree and Spanish minor would never have been possible without the help of all involved. The TECHniques Center was really able to grasp on to who I was during my first semester and use that as a cornerstone to help build me and allow me to grow in my education.

—Texas Tech student

- Transition resources:
  - o TECHniques provides transition from high school to college resources.
  - o Find resources at http://www.depts.ttu.edu/techniques/transition.php.
- New student orientation:
  - o New students must attend a mandatory TECHniques Center new student orientation before receiving tutoring services.
  - o Orientation reviews policies of the TECHniques Center, the roles of tutors and academic counselors, self-advocacy tips, learning styles, and other helpful information.
  - o Students meet their academic counselor and tour the TECHniques Center.
  - o After this orientation, students are contacted by their tutor.
- Scholarship opportunities:
  - o Numerous scholarship opportunities are available for our students.
  - o Find scholarship information at https://www.depts.ttu.edu/sds/scholarships.php.
- Multiple means of engagement:
  - o The TECHniques Center uses multiple social media options to engage students in the program, such as an electronic newsletter, TECHniques Center Blog, Twitter, Facebook, and Instagram.
  - o Visit the program website at http://www.depts.ttu.edu/techniques.

Source: **Texas Tech Crew**

Chapter 12: Campus Spotlight

Student Accessibility Services, Tufts University

Jennifer Williams and Kirsten Behling

Our Mission: Tufts University recently united Student Accessibility Services (SAS) with the Academic Resource Center (ARC) in an effort to provide inclusive resources to all Tufts students, including those with diverse learning needs or styles. Tufts recognizes the multiplicity of our students' abilities and needs as they navigate the

Source: **Tufts SAS**

collegiate environment, supporting students through a multi-model resource-centric approach.

Individually:

- SAS promotes an accessible college experience for students with disabilities, through individual accommodations, the development of self-advocacy skills, and appreciating the value of disability as a form of diversity.
- The ARC enhances this effort through individualized and group-based academic resource supports designed to meet the student where they are and help them succeed in their college experience.

> Listening to questions my peers had in our study groups helped to refresh my memory about what was covered in lecture and further consolidate my learning of topics. Activities done in the study group helped me understand materials. Thank you so much! The tutoring session is truly helpful.
>
> —Tufts student

Together, the SAS and ARC offices offer a wide range of specific supports for students, including:

- *Individualized accommodations for students with disabilities:* These accommodations are determined based on the student's documentation and their individual experience with their disability. Accommodations may include academic, housing, meal plan, parking, and others as needed. SAS works with students at any point during their Tufts career. SAS also works with students who have temporary disabilities.
- *Time management and learning strategies:* Both SAS and the ARC offer support to students looking for help managing their class assignments, studying for an exam, or trying to navigate difficult conversations with professors. For students who need more intensive support, SAS offers access to a learning specialist. For students who would benefit from some support, the ARC offers regular meetings with their trained time-management and study-strategy consultants. Often SAS students begin with the first resource and move to the latter for long-term support. In addition, we work collaboratively to offer larger campus-wide workshops and develop anytime use of online materials focused on:
  - reading and understanding the syllabus;
  - time-management strategies;
  - finding strategies to reduce text anxiety;
  - helping manage heavy workloads;
  - cultivating self-advocacy skills;
  - navigating difficult conversations with classmates or professors;
  - making appropriate referrals to other offices on campus based on the students' individual needs;
  - providing other supports as needed by students; and
  - access to study materials. (https://students.tufts.edu/sites/default/files/Finals%20Strategies%20Fall%202017.pdf)
- *Writing support:* The ARC offers a variety of writing support to our students, depending on their individual needs and what they are working on. We have a centrally located writing center that allows for drop-in appointments and collaboration with others working on written assignments. The ARC also offers graduate writing retreats and weekly writing drop-in sessions for those students navigating writer's block. The program is designed to be flexible and to fit the needs of the students wherever they may be within their process.
- *Study groups and subject tutoring:* The ARC offers access to small-group study sessions in a variety of subject areas to any student on our campuses. These small study groups are designed to mimic professional conversations

and workplace groups that students may encounter in their future profession. The idea is to help students not only study for the class that they are enrolled in but also learn from each other by teaching and talking about the material as a group.

- *Assistive and emerging technologies:* Students also have the option to use assistive and emerging technologies such as alternative-format texts and audio books, software (Read&Write, SensusAccess, NVDA screen reader, Dragon Naturally Speaking, JAWS screen reader), equipment for loan (smart pens, audio recorders, Bluetooth microphones), and an app resource list that identifies apps that may be helpful for college students (https://students.tufts.edu/student-accessibility-services/how-we-help/assistive-technologies).

> The SAS office really advocated for me and provided me with support. It is comforting to know there are people willing to support me and I can seek out help. For example, a professor could not accommodate my exam and it was less stressful knowing that SAS could help and proctor.
>
> —Tufts student

- *Materials in multiple formats:* All materials produced by SAS or the ARC are available in multiple formats. All print materials passed out at orientation and admission fairs are also available online. We often use QR codes to direct students to a specific resource. Our services are advertised through flyers, emails, social media, and our student groups. Our goal is to always offer information in multiple ways to ensure that as many students as possible are being informed of our services.
- *English for academic purposes:* This program is designed for students who do not have a strong handle on the English language. This program is unique in that its focus is on the information students need to know in order to be successful in the classroom. Students can utilize this program through a semester-long course in which they engage in academic conversations with other students, or through one-on-one consultations with our professional staff.
- *Day by Day:* Student Accessibility Services and Tufts' Department of Film and Media Studies recently partnered with two student filmmakers, Ben Hoskings and Ray Bernoff, to produce *Day by Day*, a short documentary about six Tufts students' experiences as artists living with disabilities. *Day by Day* is one of two efforts from SAS where current students can tell their

stories and offer advice to incoming students. The second resource is *Tufts Testimonials*, a booklet containing words of advice for incoming students that is available at all Tufts open house events (https://students.tufts.edu/student-accessibility-services/faculty-and-staff-resources).

- *Faculty Resource Center:* Both the SAS and ARC value the partnership we have with faculty immensely. We offer a number of opportunities for faculty to engage with us, including joining our Faculty Advisory Board, partnering on a workshop, refining our study groups, or consulting on a specific student. We also recognize the value of sharing information with our faculty and dedicate time each semester to attend academic department meetings to provide updates about our services and to answer any questions that they may have. Finally, Tufts believes strongly in the power of UDL and works with faculty to enhance their teaching strategies with UDL guiding the way (http://students.tufts.edu/faculty-resource-center).

- *Campus community:* SAS and the ARC are consistently working with the larger Tufts community to better understand the needs of our students and to create programs that are responsive to those needs. Each staff member sits on a number of committees that allow us to proactively design workshops and resources, offering them at a time and in a location convenient for the student, often in partnership with other campus offices.

Chapter Thirteen

Epilogue

Elizabeth M. H. Coghill

This book was written with one overarching purpose: to positively impact higher education institutions by inspiring the establishment of welcoming campus environments in which neurodiverse students can learn and thrive. The academy need not be only for a privileged elite, but rather can be inclusive of students whose collegiate experiences are marginalized and whose voices for support and worth go unheard. As neurodivergent student enrollment numbers increase in post-secondary campuses, it is imperative to their success that higher education leadership, faculty, and staff learn more about this rising identity of students, recognize their challenges and strengths, and work to implement the real-world solutions that are recommended in the chapters of this book.

Chapter authors come from all arenas of higher education and from campuses across the United States. They share best practices for their respective professions and seek to inform, educate, and promote change on behalf of neurodivergent students. Many of the book's authors are touched personally by neurodiverse family members and seek to be change agents on their behalf. Chapters are written intentionally for higher education practitioners in the hope that this book in its entirety becomes a handbook of ideas that inspires in us a vision for effective change on behalf of all learners, including neurodivergent students.

ESTABLISHING A CULTURE FOR SUCCESS

Many of the chapter authors discuss the importance of changing campus culture to embrace a wider diversity among students, faculty, and staff. Campuses that encourage collaboration and communication and foster opportunities for expression create environments that increase the effectiveness of support services and facilitate learning opportunities for diverse groups of students. Building on the foundation of belonging, a fundamental component for the establishment of welcoming learning environments is the belief that all students belong in the academy. Welcoming environments address the needs of all types of learners and benefit all students, not just neurotypical ones.

EFFECTING CHANGE IN THE CLASSROOM

It is imperative that faculty move to a larger vision for learning supports and go beyond an accommodations-only approach where students must disclose and be documented to receive additional methods of classroom support. Inclusive campuses base access to services with open availability versus only for properly documented conditions (Beardon et al., 2009). Faculty can use the Universal Design for Learning (UDL) practices presented in chapter 5 to ensure that all learners are supported in their classroom. Recognizing the relationship between learner diversity and beneficial practices, UDL strategies, classroom redesign, and assessment changes assist all students in the classroom, especially neurodiverse learners.

INTEGRATING SUPPORT SERVICES

Student support services are effective in helping neurodivergent students achieve campus success and degree achievement. There is no one method, service, or office that formulates the key to successfully meeting the varied learning needs and challenges experienced by neurodiverse students on the post-secondary campus. Disability Support or Accessibility Support Services offices do assist in meaningful ways, but the mission of support cannot stop or be delegated only to those offices. The chapter topics in this book were purposely selected so that all higher education leaders will take responsibility for the diversity of learners we encounter. A holistic perspective regarding student supports is needed to change the mindset of campus leaders to a neurodiversity mindset. A neurodiversity mindset works to ensure equal access to support services (Shmulsky & Gobbo, 2019). Uniting the work of campus offices, student support programs, and networks of services can make a significant impact on the success of diverse learners. Leveraging our efforts to increase awareness and promote understanding about learner variability widens inclusivity in learning environments. Together we can provide multi-tiered support services and work to ensure that students who have traditionally struggled are able to fulfill their potential.

CREATING SPACES THAT WELCOME NEURODIVERSITY

Setting a vision for space design efforts to better meet the needs of diverse learners on campus, higher education leaders should incorporate as many supportive design elements as possible into the space planning and redesign process. Regarding space as an influential element of the learning process, the integration of theoretical frameworks like UDL, the ASPECTSS model, and Universal Design can transform post-secondary learning spaces and environments for the benefit of all students, especially those identifying as neurodiverse. Looking at our spaces through a more inclusive lens, campus stakeholders can make simple changes that will improve the learning environment in their area of influence on campus. Consideration given to lighting, sensory spaces, and providing options for students in learning areas, residence halls, and support offices can make a meaningful impact on our campus.

CAMPUS TRAINING PROGRAMS

One of the common suggestions provided in the *Campus Essentials for High Impact* sections of this book has been the need for awareness training for all campus stakeholders. There is a significant gap in understanding neurodiverse learners among campus leadership, faculty, and staff. Many studies note the gap in neurodiversity awareness. Effective training programs should increase awareness of neurodiversity and be offered to a wide array of campus stakeholders. Disability/Accessibility Support Services staff should join with other campus professionals to develop programs that increase awareness, challenge stereotypes, heighten opportunities for neurodiverse student engagement, and support student advocacy and empowerment (Simonds & Hooker, 2018; Vaccaro et al., 2015). College stakeholders ought to examine their own misconceptions of disabilities and seek to implement processes that decrease the stigma that surrounds neurodiversity. Awareness training must address the opinions on campus that many neurodiverse students do not belong in higher education.

EMPOWERING NEURODIVERSE STUDENTS

Each student possesses their own unique combination of strengths and challenges that they bring to the college campus. One facet of student empowerment is fostering a student's advocacy skills. The ability to advocate for services and supports is essential for the success of neurodivergent students.

For some, lacking much-needed advocacy skills results in not using the available supports and campus accommodations that are key to their academic achievement.

Self-advocacy and neurodiversity identity empower students to view their learning differences from a strengths perspective rather than a medical or deficit viewpoint (Connor et al., 2011). When compared to other cultural groups on campus, students identifying with neurodiversity culture can be considered among student groups who are marginalized in higher education.

Students are empowered when their relationships with faculty move beyond an accommodations-only mindset to a greater understanding by faculty of neurodiverse culture and faculty can assimilate changes in pedagogical approaches to positively alter the classroom learning environment.

ENCOURAGING PEER ENGAGEMENT AND BELONGING

Establishing peer engagement is challenging for many neurodiverse students, as is noted by many studies. Accommodations do not address the needs for peer engagement and leave neurodiverse students with gaps in social skill-building. Lacking in opportunities for social interaction, students experience feelings of loneliness and isolation. Social relationships can be supported, however, when students become involved in neurodiverse student groups (Vaccaro et al., 2015). The formulation of neurodiversity student groups is a positive step toward reducing social-emotional challenges experienced by neurodivergent students.

Peer engagement and social relationships play a significant role in establishing feelings of campus belonging. Belonging is a fundamental psychological necessity for students to be successful on campus (Strayhorn, 2018). When students feel like they belong on campus, they gain confidence about their ability to succeed in college (Coghill, 2017). Belonging becomes an essential motivator toward achieving success.

BECOMING NEURODIVERSITY CHAMPIONS

This book is designed to provide readers with a stronger awareness and knowledge of the challenges faced by neurodivergent students on our campuses. Faculty and staff play a meaningful role in advancing awareness of and providing services for neurodivergent learners in higher education. Identifying ways you can better your campus on behalf of diverse learners is key for the advancement of all students.

Many of the chapter authors can be characterized as *neurodiversity champions* on their respective campuses. Touched by students they have served, these professionals are passionate about incorporating initiatives and infusing new approaches for the betterment of all students. They have joined together in this endeavor to advance our knowledge and abilities so that you, the reader, will be inspired to act on behalf of neurodivergent students.

According to bestselling author and neurodiversity advocate John Elder Robinson, it is time for neurodiverse faculty and staff to "speak their truth" regarding neurodiversity on their campus and become a champion or role model for students:

> It's time for neurodiverse faculty to come out and stand as role models for students and staff. Everyone knows how autism, ADHD, dyslexia and other neurodiverse conditions disable us as children. What we need to balance that are successful adults who attribute their achievements in part to neurodiversity.
>
> In doing so, we demonstrate that there is a spectrum for all the neurodiverse conditions. Some of us are more gifted; others are more disabled. In particular, many of us follow a pattern where we are less disabled the older we get as we learn to adapt to society and use our strengths to offset our weaknesses.
>
> Neurodiverse folks who are enrolled or employed in colleges may be the least disabled of our community, or we may just be the most determined. Or maybe we're just lucky or privileged. Either way, we should be standing as role models– particularly for younger people and parents–to show what's possible. That's the best antidote to talk like "He's autistic; he'll never go to college." While it's true that profound disability will leave some of us requiring substantial supports and residential care even as adults, most of us can grow up to live independently and we have great contributions to make. (Robinson, 2015)

From the academic advisor to the tutor serving in a learning center, each of us is presented with the opportunity to be a champion for the students we encounter. As a campus champion, whether with others or individually, you possess the power to positively impact your place of influence at your institution. Identify ways you can further the understanding of neurodiversity on your campus. Increase your awareness of others on campus working to advance services and supports for neurodiverse learners.

Are you the one who starts a neurodiverse student group or working group on campus like the College of William and Mary or Duke University? *Are you the one* tasked with raising student awareness of disabilities and learning challenges like the Boxes and Walls program at the University Wisconsin– Whitewater campus? *Are you the one* who integrates changes in academic coaching and tutoring support services similar to East Carolina University or redesigns spaces with neurodiversity in mind?

As an individual and as a collective, we can make a difference on our campuses for the students we encounter, seeking to unite our efforts by providing support and assistance in their academic journeys. Neurodiverse students add value to higher education. Their contributions to education and research are worthy of their inclusion. We invite you to unite with us and make room in the academy for all learners.

REFERENCES

Beardon, L., Martin, N., & Woolsey, I. (2009). What do students with Asperger syndrome or high functioning autism want at college and university? (in their own words). *Good Autism Practice (GAP)*, *10*(2), 35–43.

Coghill, E. M. H. (2017). *The impact of academic employment on the sense of belonging and engagement of military learners on the college campus* [Doctoral dissertation, East Carolina University]. The Scholarship. https://thescholarship.ecu.edu/handle/10342/6494

Connor, D. J., Gallagher, D., & Ferri, B. A. (2011). Broadening our horizons: Toward a plurality of methodologies in learning disability research. *Learning Disability Quarterly*, *34*(2), 107–121.

Robinson, J. (2015). *The challenges of neurodiversity in colleges.* https://jerobison.blogspot.com/2015/10/the-challenges-of-neurodiversity-in.html

Shmulsky, S., & Gobbo, K. (2019). Autism support in a community college setting: Ideas from intersectionality. *Community College Journal of Research and Practice*, *43*(9), 648–652.

Simonds, C. J., & Hooker, J. F. (2018). Creating a culture of accommodation in the public-speaking course. *Communication Education*, *67*(3), 393–399.

Strayhorn, T. L. (2018). *College students' sense of belonging: A key to educational success for all students*. Routledge.

Vaccaro, A., Daly-Cano, M., & Newman, B. M. (2015). A sense of belonging among college students with disabilities: An emergent theoretical model. *Journal of College Student Development*, *56*(7), 670–686.

Index

About the Editors and Contributors

Dr. Elizabeth M. H. Coghill has served as the inaugural director of the Pirate Academic Success Center at East Carolina University for the past 12 years. An experienced administrator in higher education, her research and practice interests focus on the academic and social success of marginalized student populations: neurodiverse learners, students of color, first-generation students, economically disadvantaged students, and military-affiliated students. She is an early adopter of Universal Design for Learning (UDL) techniques imbedded within a campus learning center. Dr. Coghill is an invited speaker for Academic Impressions on neurodiversity and recent podcast speaker on neurodiverse students and UDL for the *ThinkUDL* podcast series. Dr. Coghill's professional experiences are in learner support services, academic advising, registrar, systems training, career development, and admissions.

Jeffrey G. Coghill has been at Laupus Library, East Carolina University, for 19 years serving first as the collection development librarian and later becoming the outreach librarian and director of Eastern AHEC (Area Health Education Center) library services for 23 counties of eastern North Carolina. He has a BA in English from Methodist University, an MA in English from Western Carolina University, an MLIS from the University of Alabama, and a certificate of advanced study in health science libraries (CAS-HSL) from the University of Pittsburgh. His research interests include collection development, electronic resources, outreach services, technology trends, cool gadgets, aviation, and just about anything music related.

* * *

Clarissa Barnes, PhD, BCBA-D, COBA
Associate Professor of Special Education
Director, Hench Autism Studies Program
Defiance University
cbarnes@defiance.edu

Kirsten Behling
Associate Dean of Student Accessibility and Academic Resources
Tufts University
Kirsten.Behling@tufts.edu

Abby Benzinger, MS
Assistant Director of Tutoring Services, Pirate Academic Success Center
East Carolina University
benzingera18@ecu.edu

Kimberly Blackshear
Dissemination and Outreach Coordinator, Duke Center for Child and Family
    Policy
Duke University
kimberly.blackshear@duke.edu

Stacey Blackwell, MA
Senior Director, Learning Centers
Rutgers, The State University of New Jersey
stacey.blackwell@rutgers.edu

Jamie E. Bloss, MLIS
Liaison Librarian, Allied Health Sciences and Dental Medicine
Laupus Health Sciences Library
East Carolina University
blossj19@ecu.edu

Claytonia Boular-Woods
Student Success Coach—PT
TRIO Student Support Services
Central Piedmont Community College
Clay.Boular-Woods@cpcc.edu

Ellen Bunn, MA
As-U-R Director and Adjunct Instructor, Department of Reading Education
    and Special Education

As-U-R Program
Appalachian State University
bunnek@appstate.edu

Joshua A. Burk, PhD
Professor and Chair, Department of Psychological Sciences
The College of William and Mary
jabur2@wm.edu

John B. Caldora II, MEd
Case Manager, Community of Concern, Dean of Students
University of Kentucky
john.caldora@uky.edu

Tara Chandrasekhar, MD
Child and Adolescent Psychiatrist, Duke Center for Autism and Brain Development
Duke University
tara.chandrasekhar@dm.duke.edu

Elizabeth M. H. Coghill, EdD
Director of Early Warning and Academic Support, Pirate Academic Success Center
East Carolina University
coghille@ecu.edu

Jeffrey G. Coghill, MA, MLIS, CAS-HSL
Outreach Librarian and Director, Eastern AHEC Library Services
Laupus Health Sciences Library
East Carolina University
coghillj@ecu.edu

Robert Detwiler, PhD
Registrar
Defiance College
rdetwiler@defiance.edu

Cheryl L. Dickter, PhD
Associate Professor, Department of Psychological Sciences
The College of William and Mary
cldickter@wm.edu

Shawnté Elbert, EdD, MCHES, CHWC
Associate Dean of Health and Wellness
Division of Student Success
Central Washington University
Shawnte.Elbert@cwu.edu

Sara Gardner
Neurodiversity Navigators Program Director
Adjunct Faculty
Bellevue College
sara.gardner@bellevuecollege.edu

Alysha Gray, MA/CAS, NCSP
Instructional Specialist, Walter and Marie Williams STEPP Program
East Carolina University
grayal18@ecu.edu

Amanda Haberstroh, PhD, MLIS
Information and Research Services Librarian, Laupus Health Sciences Library
East Carolina University
haberstroha17@ecu.edu

G. J. Corey Harmon, MA, MSLS
Head of Access Services, Laupus Health Sciences Library
East Carolina University
harmong18@ecu.edu

Angela Holleman, MS, LMFT
Lead Service Coordinator, Disability Resource Center
University of California, Santa Cruz
adhollem@ucsc.edu

Jeanne Hoover, MLIS
Head, Scholarly Communication, J.Y. Joyner Library
East Carolina University
hooverj@ecu.edu

James W. H. Howard, PhD
Assistant Director of Tutoring Services
University of North Georgia
james.wh.howard@ung.edu

Morgan James, EdD
Director, Walter & Marie Williams STEPP Program
East Carolina University
jamesmo@ecu.edu

Emily Johnson
Associate Director for Transition Support, Walter & Marie Williams STEPP
  Program
East Carolina University
johnsonem@ecu.edu

Ta-Kisha Jones, MBA, CHES, CHWC
Assistant Director of Health and Wellness Initiatives
Indiana University–Purdue University Indianapolis
takldard@iupui.edu

Tamara Mancini, MEd
Director, Student Disability Services
Texas Tech University Health Sciences Center
tamara.mancini@ttuhsc.edu

Clark Nall, MA, MLIS
Business Reference Librarian, Joyner Library
East Carolina University
nallh@ecu.edu

Anna Sandberg, EdM
Administrative Coordinator, Cook/Douglass Learning Center
Rutgers, The State University of New Jersey
anna.sandberg@rutgers.edu

Jana Schellinger, MLIS, AHIP
Librarian Liaison, Brody School of Medicine, Laupus Health Sciences Library
East Carolina University
schellingerj18@ecu.edu

Terry Tumbarello
Director, Residence Life
University of Wisconsin–Whitewater
tumbaret@uww.edu

Jennifer Williams, PhD
College STAR Network Director, Department of Special Education, Foundations, and Research
College of Education
East Carolina University
williamsj@ecu.edu

Sarah Williams, PhD
Executive Director, STEPP Program and Office for Faculty Excellence
East Carolina University
williamssar@ecu.edu

Carolyn Willis, MLS
Outreach Coordinator, Research and Instructional Services, Joyner Library
East Carolina University
willisc@ecu.edu

Made in United States
Orlando, FL
01 June 2023

33706007R00188